About the Author

SOPHIE BESSIS was born and brought up in Tunisia and has subsequently spent most of her adult life living and working in France. A writer and journalist, she has held a number of important editorial and other posts, including head of research and subsequently editor-in-chief of *Jeune Afrique*; director of the Panos Institute in Paris; and editor of *Vivre Autrement*, which was published by ENDA at the major UN world summits since 1992.

She is the author of a number of books over the past twenty years, including, *inter alia*:

L'Arme alimentaire, Maspero, 1979; revised edition 1983.
La Dernière Frontière. Les tiers mondes et la tentation de l'Occident, J.-C. Lattès, 1983.
La Faim dans le monde, La Découverte, 1991.
Femmes du Maghreb. L'enjeu (with Souhayr Belhassen), J.-C. Lattès, 1992.
Femmes de Méditerranée, Karthala, 1995.
La Fin du tiers monde?, coauthored, La Découverte, 1996.
L'Occident et les autres. Histoire d'une suprématie, La Découverte, 2001.

Western Supremacy

Triumph of an Idea?

London & New York

Western Supremacy: Triumph of an Idea?
was first published in English in 2003 by
Zed Books Ltd, 7 Cynthia Street, London N1 9JF, UK,
and Room 400, 175 Fifth Avenue, New York, NY 10010, USA

www.zedbooks.demon.co.uk

This book was first published in French, under the title
L'Occident et les autres: Histoire d'une suprématie, by Editions La Découverte,
9 bis rue Abel-Hovelacque, Paris 75013, France, in 2001.

This work has been published with the support of the National Centre for the
Promotion of the Book at the French Ministry of Culture.

Designed and typeset in Monotype Ehrhardt by Illuminati, Grosmont
Cover designed by Andrew Corbett
Printed and bound in the EU by Biddles Ltd

Distributed in the USA exclusively by Palgrave, a division of
St Martin's Press, LLC, 175 Fifth Avenue, New York, NY 10010

A catalogue record for this book is available from the British Library
Library of Congress Cataloging-in-Publication Data available

ISBN 1 84277 218 X (Hb)
ISBN 1 84277 219 8 (Pb)

Contents

Foreword to the English Edition

Early in 2001, when I was putting the finishing touches to this book, I hardly suspected that events in the latter part of the year would give its hypotheses such topicality. The attacks of 11 September, then the US-led war in Afghanistan to punish their instigators, spectacularly illustrate the kind of extreme situation that can result from a set of global relations marked by the hegemonic obsession of a ruling hyperpower and the violence of those who claim to be its emblematic adversaries.

It is still too soon to know whether these developments – which some see as marking our entry into the twenty-first century – amount to a fundamental break in the fragile world order built upon the ruins of bipolarity. The 11th of September certainly marks a turning point, since the American empire was struck at its heart by a new-style terrorism detached from particular demands, one that draws more upon the heritage of nihilism than upon the legacy of any civilization. For the moment, however, that paroxysm and its sequel appear not so much to herald a breakdown of order unparalleled in world history as to highlight certain dysfunctions due to an imperial logic weighing with all its force on the planet. What we are witnessing, then, is not something completely new. As soon as empire seeks to extend itself without limits, crises begin to mount up both on the periphery and in the centre.

Let us first clear away any possible ambiguity. The question is not whether the attack on the Twin Towers and the Pentagon is explicable in terms of American arrogance, or whether Osama bin Laden should be seen as a righter of wrongs driven by the exasperation of the wretched of the earth. The complexity of North–South relations cannot be reduced to such a clash. It is true that the Saudi billionaire's network, using means made available to him through globalization and economic deregulation, has a potential for harm that must certainly be neutralized. But neutralized in the name of what?

For a short while after 11 September, it seemed that the scale of the trauma might possibly lead the Americans, and the West in general, to ask some serious questions about their relationship to the rest of the world, and to give their foreign intervention a new legitimacy by grounding it upon the universality of principle that they espouse. It did not take long to realize, however, that right was once again covering for might – and for the consolidation of American interests in a strategically important region of the world. The needs of the war against the Taliban and for the triumph of Good meant that Washington's new Afghan debtors were held up as democrats, while the most basic human rights could continue to be violated because the allies guilty of such acts were too precious to be called to account. The global hyperpower, which defines itself as the only possible horizon for the democratic ideal, sets little store by that ideal when it proclaims the rules for punishing its enemies or justifies acts of war scarcely compatible with the model it claims to embody. It cannot be said too often that such a manipulation of principles, such a discrepancy between the West's rhetoric and the reality of its politics, explains why those left out of account in the prevailing system of legality can applaud the bloody deception perpetrated by a bin Laden, and why the three thousand victims at the World Trade Center did not really cause such an outcry in the South.

The violent tremor of 11 September did not therefore shake the founding paradox of Western supremacy, the split between ostensibly universal principles and the actual reality of their application. Nor did it dissuade Western leaders from seeking to be the only ones to lay down the law – indeed, their claim to monopoly in this respect has assumed proportions not seen for quite some years. Since his country's drama transformed him from an insignificant leader into a global crusader, George W. Bush has been able to define exactly as he pleases, without facing the slightest challenge, the archetypes that are supposed to mark the frontier between the upholders of Good and the servants of Evil. Never in the recent past have the founding principles of universal rights been so instrumentalized in the service of power, to such an extent that now, in the opening years of the twenty-first century, we can speak of a veritable apogee of hegemony and an unprecedented crystallization of the hatreds that it arouses. Of course, the gradual erection of the United States as an unrivalled global empire has made it easier for this drift to occur, but it is not the only factor in play. In trying to understand the certainties that strike America with blindness, and the supremacy that nothing for the moment seems able to disturb, we need to trace the path that has led to the present state of things. What is the history from which the West draws its strength and its assurance that it has a right to rule the planet? But what are the recompositions heralded by the ever sharper jolts shaking the world?

Beyond the unforeseen twists and turns of an accelerating crisis, these are the questions that this book has tried to answer.

Sophie Bessis

Introduction

This book comes from afar. Perhaps one of its roots may be sought in the mid-1950s, in the yard of the Jules Ferry lycée in Tunis. In that old covered playground, national or communal divides did not lower their guard before the apparent ecumenism of childhood camaraderie. The Tunisian girls, Arab or Jewish, were almost as one in relation to 'the French', a general category whose homogeneity transcended particular friendships that might be forged with one of its parts. For the French girls overwhelmed us with their disdain. And although we never adjusted to their arrogance, we were not in any doubt about their superiority. First, they were fair-haired, with long 'straight' locks that they could toss back with an elegant movement of the head. Beside that truly angelic vision, it was for us an endless source of masochistic suffering to contemplate the dark curly tufts covering our own skulls.

Next, they made their first communion. Dressed as little brides with train and tulle veil, clutching a missal and handing holy images to all around, they walked in great pomp into the classroom to greet the teacher with triumphant modesty – and to receive from her a round of congratulations that used to break our hearts. Which of us Muslims or Jews, again sharing the same shadows, did not dream at least once in her childhood of being a Catholic admitted to this wonderland?

Finally, the French girls went 'to France' for their holidays. Each October, before the start of the new school year, we prepared for the terrible duty of confessing that we had spent the summer in Carthage, or south of Tunis, or even, for the humblest of us, in the city itself. To our timid question: 'And you?', the pitiless answer was always: 'In France.' An abyss then opened before us, and we felt that the most

1

brilliant exam results would never be able to fill it. For what lay behind the word 'France' was an intimate knowledge of snow, chimneys and pitched roofs covered with moss, of green grass and the unknown fruits that appeared in our reading books. Quite simply, the fact that they belonged to that world made their pre-eminence legitimate. Much later, when I began to discover the country whose minor reliefs and little rivers I had learned by name as a child, I sometimes thought – with a certain pleasure, I admit – of my former classmates spending the summer in nondescript market towns or joyless villages, in places devoid of the magic with which I had once adorned them.

The schoolteachers of the French Republic were scrupulously egalitarian in the ferocity with which they attended to the education of their wards; they terrorized each for her own good, with no ethnic or religious discrimination. One of these teachers, moreover, loved me so much that for a time I was plunged into depths of confusion. My last year at primary school coincided with the first stages of independence, as we had to choose the main language apart from French that we wanted to learn in the sixth grade. For my parents the question did not even arise: we were Jewish but first of all Tunisian, and so it would be Arabic. After the teacher had read my completed form, she sent for me and said: 'What a pity you didn't choose English!' I long kept the memory of her sad tone of voice as she deplored the cultural regression to which her good pupil was being condemned. It seemed all the more incomprehensible in that, not being an Arab myself, I was under no genetic compulsion to choose Arabic.

During our childhood years, then, we learned that we could hardly take pride in what we were. And yet, I did not really understand what my French schoolmates had that was so superior; nor did I ever see solid grounds for a belief in my inescapable inferiority. This was brought home to me again thirty years later, in almost the same terms, when I left Tunis after a long period of immersion in the Maghreb for the writing of a book and headed for Ireland in search of a little exoticism. 'So, after Tunis you're going among the civilized nations', joked a Parisian friend with an impeccably left-wing background. Then a dim memory suddenly welled up inside me, like an access of fever. I flung back at her the names of Carthage, Istanbul and Granada, indicating that from where I had come it felt more as if I was going among the barbarians – may the Irish please forgive me.

I have never ceased to be struck by the calm assurance with which most Westerners (a term to which I shall return) assert the legitimacy of their supremacy. This assurance is visible in their most trivial actions, their most banal attitudes. It structures public speech, intellectual authority and media messages. It establishes itself deep down in the consciousness of individuals and groups. It seems to be so constitutive of collective identity that we may speak of a veritable culture of supremacy as the foundation of the entity today called the West – a foundation upon which its relations with others continue to be built.

For a long time, none of these points was enough to give me the idea of devoting a book to this strange phenomenon. My youthful hopes, inscribed as they were within the utopias of a bygone age, led me to think that humanity was moving surely if chaotically towards a better world, which would be expressed in, among other things, the recognition of a kind of universal equality. Subsequently I studied particular trends in the relationship between the two great areas of the world, known for the sake of simplicity as the North and the South, and this was already a way of dealing with the question that concerns me here. If I now intend to tackle it head on, this is because the scale and rapidity of contemporary changes, completing a globalization process opened up (if a symbolic date is required) by the stemposts of Vasco da Gama's and Christopher Columbus's caravels, should be reason to pose anew the question of the West's place in the world and its relations with others.

As things stand, this question is not being posed. For a couple of decades there have certainly been plenty of books and articles which spin out zoological metaphors to express contentment or unease at the emergence of certain regions of the globe. But until now no economic projection has really dented the belief that Western nations have legitimate grounds for their continuing supremacy. Other texts dwell upon the prospect that one hegemony might be replaced with another, and remind us that civilizations too are mortal. But with their characteristic tone of warning, which makes them sound like exorcisms, they hardly seem to imply that an end to Westernization of the world has been accepted as a genuine possibility. On the contrary, the new vulnerability of Western societies, the resistance in their midst to the upheavals caused by a return to free-market capitalism after a half-century of social democracy, the loss of bearings due to a perception of new archipelagos of poverty as an encroachment of the South within the North itself: all this makes a stubborn affirmation of superiority seem more imperative than ever. I am thinking here not only of the far right in Europe and North America – which is always quick to match its discourse to the frustrations of people hit by convulsive change – but of a more wide-spread feeling in the West.

Now that the shock wave from colonial wars has passed, now that the third-worldist messianism of revolution by proxy has played itself out, it is exactly as if Westerners in general – beyond all question-begging and all political divides – again find it impossible to conceive the absolute, indisputable equivalence of all human beings. Neither the moments of prosperity nor the tremors of the last few decades have lastingly shaken the firm conviction of their own superiority, so firm that any question-ing of it belongs to the realm of the unthinkable. The mere possibility of losing their monopoly over the conduct of the world's affairs lies outside their comprehension.

We need to master the exasperation caused by this self-assurance if we are to take stock of what structures it, to examine the impulses behind it, to analyse the consequences that flow from it – for the cen-trality of the West, and therefore of what it does and what it thinks, organizes the world. This book will seek to explore the origins of the culture of Occidentalism and its persistence only marginally changed up to the present day; we shall follow its most recent shifts, weigh the reasons for believing in the solidity of Western power, and consider ways in which this might be called into question.

I thought long and hard about the risks of the venture before decid-ing to take it on. I feared that I would merely be adding one more facile critique of the West that would allow the horrors committed by others to be passed over in silence. For the area known by that name does not have a monopoly of violence, any more than in earlier times it had a monopoly of conquest and domination. Without going far back into the past, we can draw up a long list of massacres, atrocities, acts of injustice and displays of cynicism that have had little to do with the control of Europe and the United States over the rest of the world. We know how easy it was for the oppressed to mutate into oppressors, and many of the wretched of the earth have no need to look across the oceans to find those responsible for their plight. Far be it for me to absolve those in the South who refuse to take their share of responsibility for past failures and for the false tracks onto which they have strayed.

These qualifications do not, however, reduce the singularity of the West's position. Although the nations of the West are far from alone in having historically misused the principle of 'might is right', they are the only ones to have produced a theoretical (philosophical, moral and scientific) apparatus to legitimate it. With the exception of so-called wars of religion, officially waged in the name of different variants of monotheist revelation, conquering nations have generally felt little need to come up with reasons for their actions other than their will to power and the pursuit of their interests. The West, however, as it enters the sixth century of a hegemony whose limits it has ceaselessly expanded, continues to elaborate the theoretical foundations of its supremacy by adapting them to present trends.

The West is still grappling with a contradiction that has structured it ever since the onset of modernity. For although it did not have exclusive rights over the idea of universality, the West alone shifted the debate outside the field of religion to construct a secular universal from which it drew the principle of equality. Having thereby created the possibility of converting universal principles into rights in the real world, the West has subsequently never ceased to limit their field of application.

The paradox of the West lies in its ability to produce universals, to raise them to the level of absolutes, and to violate in an extraordinarily systematic way the principles that it derives from them, while still feeling the need to develop theoretical justifications for those violations. The planetary reach of its hegemony, together with the dogged attempt to justify itself over the centuries by means of a sophisticated cultural apparatus in which universality is constantly evoked, constitute a two-fold specificity that clearly deserves to be examined at length.

This is not my only concern, however. It is certainly worthwhile for its own sake to analyse the Western culture of supremacy – but not only for its own sake. I would probably never have begun this difficult exercise if it had not also led to a set of questions that I consider of capital importance. What shadows does that culture cast over the rest of the world? How should we understand the events taking place in what is known as the South: the ideologies developed, the discourses heard, the passions unleashed? Are they so many responses to a domination today less widely accepted than ever before? Or, in other words, what place should be accorded to reactive phenomena and autonomous constructs in analysing evolution and involution in the continents of the South? What should we make of the intensity with which the unequal protagonists of present-day global relations engage in mutual expulsion? Can we see anything new in the West's relations with the rest of the world, or do they merely repeat older patterns? I do not claim to have answers to all these questions. But, more simply, it does seem to me useful to pose them.

I shall do this by choosing a few areas for exploration in a field that is too wide to be grasped in its totality. First I shall take the story back in historical time; then I shall consider today's global relationships of force in order to determine whether current trends are renewing and consolidating the bases of Western supremacy, or rendering them more fragile and heralding their demise; next I shall examine certain forms of contemporary Western behaviour in relation to the culture of supremacy; and finally I shall try to weigh the role of endogenous factors in the convulsions now shaking the markets of the Western world. I know that, just as the eye cannot take in the whole of reality, the gaze that this book directs at the world is inevitably partial. It leaves in shadow whole patches that persons other than myself would have placed in bright sunlight. Some aspects are singled out for special treatment that may be thought unwarranted. My only hope in this respect is that I have managed to avoid being biased.

One last point. What does the West mean for me who am writing this book about it? Despite my place of birth, am I not a pure product of that West whose schools and thinkers shaped my consciousness? Indeed, did not the West's irruption into the world of my ancestors liberate me, like so many others, from the protective tyranny of the group and give me the attributes of the more or less free individual that I am? Has not Western modernity carried humanity from an iron destiny into an epoch where various freedoms are possible? As we are scarcely in a position to say whether there could have been other paths to modernity, let us grant the West those revolutions. But they do not fully compensate for the character of the people who stood behind them, nor for the acts of violence which accompanied them, and which some have sought to present as exemplifying the role of force as midwife of history. I would argue, rather, that the West's inexhaustible capacity to dissociate what it says from what it does has long made its modernity both unintelligible and illegitimate for those it designates as others, even if it is true that they have benefited from it by default. Today, as the West forges the tools and deploys the violence to reassert its supremacy, and as it continues to produce new discourses of self-justification, these all appear as so many obstacles to a new pattern of global relations less fraught with tragedy.

Such, in any event, is the way I see things from my position within and outside the West – in orbit around it, as it were, refusing to subject to the seductive simplicity of its abstractions my thinking that also carries other memories and experiences. Perhaps the tribe of those who span several different places – the tribe to which I happen to belong – knows better than others how to assess the true complexity of things.

And perhaps the fact of belonging to it impels us to explore the multiple senses of that complexity.

It is not that I really believe in the power of words to cure the autism of those whom Aimé Césaire called 'our naive and omniscient vanquishers', or to extricate the vanquished from their same old dreams of paradise lost. But perhaps I do believe in it enough to think that spelling things out can sometimes help us avoid despair.

PART ONE

The Formation of a Culture

ONE

The West Is Born

Why did my French classmates at the Lycée Jules Ferry in Tunis have such a natural sense of superiority, thereby showing an unwitting loyalty to the political figure who gave his name to our school? For it is well known that Ferry, the founder of the education system in the Third Republic, was also a passionate supporter of the imperial enterprise, believed in the duty of 'superior races to civilize inferior races', and helped to convince his contemporaries that, if France was to remain a great country, it had to carry 'wherever it could, its language, its customs, its flag, its arms and its genius'.[1] How far should we go back in European history to find the roots of such convictions and to trace their development? How is it to be explained that they survived all the twists and turns of European thought, and seem to have been only marginally challenged since the downfall of the colonial empires?

Since human memory needs dates, the founding year is usually taken to be 1492; certainly its quincentenary was celebrated in 1992 on both sides of the Atlantic with great pomp and a few questions. The discovery of America and the expulsion of the Jews and Muslims from Spain – even if the final departure of the latter occurred only in 1609 – defined the frontiers of the modern West, whose birth can be seen to have occurred at the turn of the sixteenth century beneath the twin sign of appropriation and exclusion.

It is not that the West had no existence before the modern age. On the contrary, throughout antiquity and what are called the Middle Ages, the Euro-Mediterranean world continued to be organized around an East and a West, although their precise contours were very different from those of today. Greece, while never ceasing to drink from its Eastern

11

sources, set off in conquest of the West and by the seventh century BC had established itself on the coasts of Sicily and Calabria. And some centuries later, no one in the Roman world would have dreamt of placing in the East the province of North Africa, one of the bastions of the Roman West that was split from the East in the division of 395 AD. The former spoke Latin and embraced the Catholic Church; the latter spoke Greek and was the province of Orthodoxy and various dissident forms of Christianity. In a world where it was never the Mediterranean that marked the frontier and where the demarcation between Europe, Asia and Africa did not mean much, these were the cleavages that instituted difference and outlined the corresponding areas of influence.

The birth in the seventh century of the third and last Abrahamic religion, followed by the Muslim conquest of most of the Mediterranean basin, certainly changed the shape of things. But it was not these upheavals which gave to East and West the face they would have from the sixteenth century onward. For the Byzantine Empire, resolutely Eastern, kept closer links with its Omayyad and Abbassid neighbours – in other words, with the Muslim East – than with Western Christendom. As to the Western dimension of medieval Islam, no one ever thinks of questioning its historical reality. From Sicily (Arab until the fall of Palermo in 1072) to Andalusia (which took nearly three centuries to die after a long and full life), Islam – or, to be more precise, a cultural alchemy resting upon Arab, Jewish and Muslim pillars – sank lasting roots in the far West of Europe.[2] Moreover, if we consider that in the Euro-Mediterranean Middle Ages the schism within Christianity was almost equal in importance to the rift between Islam and Christendom, we will grasp more clearly that the West then existed within shifting frontiers very different from those which later became so authoritative in Western minds.

The birth of a myth

The West that was born around the year 1492 involved a radical break in medieval cartography, at once ousting it and taking possession of it to impose a new geography that placed its own legitimacy upon a new foundation. In terms of the actual events, it may have been fortuitous that a victorious political-religious eviction so closely coincided with a process of discovery heralded by the whole European dynamic of the fifteenth century. But they formed a unity heavy with long-term significance that also founded a new ideology. While the conquistadors cleared everything in their path in what they called the 'New World', the Renaissance intelligentsia – if we may venture the anachronism – forged a total discourse that gave meaning both to the expulsion and to the taking of possession. In this way, it constructed a history that is still the basis of Western thought.

Modern Europe, which really began to see itself as such only in the course of the sixteenth century, first invented itself around a series of myths, each based upon a rejection. Of course, all civilizations have been built upon founding myths. But, unlike in the great systemic cosmogonies, it was at the moment when Europe lay claim to Reason that it developed its own founding myths. It was then that a selective reading of their history began for people in the West, and that the East began to change and to disappear from the modes of European thought that became dominant over the succeeding centuries.

In fact, since Petrarch and others gave it an initial form in the fourteenth century, the founding myth of an exclusive Greco-Roman source has functioned as an implacable machine for the expulsion of oriental or non-Christian sources from European civilization. Erased: the Babylonian, Chaldean, Egyptian and Indian influences on Greece, from the pre-Socratics to the late descendants of Alexander. Disregarded: the huge prestige that Egypt always enjoyed within the Greek world, whose literary figures happily recognized what they owed to its sciences and its religion. Obscured: the crucial dimension of the Hellenistic era, that hybrid of Hellenism and the East. Passed over in silence: the cultural pluralism of a Roman Empire for which the barbarians were men from the North, not the familiar peoples along the southern shores of the Mediterranean. In the end, the obstinate determination of Renaissance thinkers to concoct a direct line of descent from Athens even enabled them to forget how they themselves had picked up the thread. The expulsion of Islam from the political territory of Western Europe was matched by the expulsion of Jewish–Muslim thought from European intellectual territory.

Yet the role of Jewish–Arab Spain in not only the transmission but the new reading of Greek philosophy is hardly a secret. We know that, in just a few decades after the capture of Toledo in 1085, Christian Europe discovered a large part of the philosophical culture that had been accumulating for centuries in the lands of Islam. We should reread the medieval philosophers to remind ourselves that, for at least two centuries, Christian thought then identified the Arabs with men of reason. Indeed, if the Renaissance could so swiftly re-establish the greatly slackened ties that it claimed with antiquity, this was because Western Islam had in a way prepared the ground through its immense labour of adapting Greek philosophy to monotheism.[3] We cannot here go into the history of medieval Muslim rationalism (which reached its apogee in Ibn Rushd, known to Latin speakers as Averroës, the 'Great Commentator' of Dante's *Inferno*[4]) and its separation between theology and philosophy that was at the roots of modernity, but we must at least recall that it paved the way for the secularism of the Renaissance. From the sixteenth century this role virtually dropped out of sight. Thanks to its humanists, who manufactured a largely imaginary past and decided the stuff of its legacy, the new Europe invented frontiers beyond which everything supposedly non-Greco-Roman or non-Christian was summarily assigned.

This Europe of rejection was born in the extraordinary scientific, technological and cultural ferment of the last few centuries of the Middle Ages, but it cannot be reduced to an intellectual construct. Politically, it may be dated to the Reconquest and the eastward crossing of a continent under Ottoman domination with the aim of mastering new lands. Within a few years of expelling the Jews from Al-Andaluz,[5] Spain moved from religious closure to racial exclusion with its new concept of 'purity of blood'. After 1535, anyone seeking public employment had to prove that for at least four generations his family had had no Jewish or Muslim member.[6] For those who wished to remain in the peninsula, conversion to Catholicism was no longer enough to qualify as Christian: the criterion of religious affiliation gave way to a new obsession with race, so tenacious that the legal obligation to demonstrate freedom from contamination came to an end only in 1865, two and a half centuries after Spain had been cleansed of any crypto-Muslim presence.

The horsemen of the Apocalypse

Christianity, race: this was the dual membership which served to legitimize the conquest of America. My aim here is not to retell the story but simply to recall that Europeans, in the act of appropriating a continent, carried out the first genocide in history. It is a terrible word – but its use to describe the fate of the Amerindian peoples is hardly in question. For the last couple of centuries, the debate has centred more on whether the genocide was intentional or in some way accidental. Numerous accounts describe the resolve to exercise sole domination over the subject peoples, as well as the various acts of barbaric violence linked to the raging thirst for gain. Most also record the crusading spirit that drove the conquerors forward, as they showed greater inclination to impose the cross by fire than by persuasion.

These are the sources for the argument that genocide was perhaps not planned in advance, but was at least consciously accepted. Others argue that it was mainly due to the high post-conquest rates of Amerindian mortality resulting from the ravages of disease, population movement and forced labour. No one, however, denies the scale of the demographic cataclysm: over a period of barely thirty years 80 to 90 per cent of the indigenous population of the Greater Antilles were wiped out, while on the mainland the Indian population of Mexico plummeted from 25 million in 1519 to 1.9 million in 1580, and that of Peru from 10 million in 1530 to 1.5 million in 1590. Less than half a century was all it took to exterminate between half and three-quarters of a native population that is estimated to have stood at 60 to 80 million on the eve of the conquest.[7]

Whatever the motives, then, the European irruption led in a remarkably short time to the depopulation of America. This was what made the enterprise so distinctive in comparison with the conquests that had been the ordinary run of history down the ages. For although many earlier conquerors had enjoyed razing whole cities and decimating their populations, and although such episodes had often caused the downfall of a kingdom or ruined a whole region or helped to slow population growth in various parts of the globe, they had never before occurred on such a devastating scale. The only analogous events in previous history had been catastrophes due to so-called natural causes – from climatic disasters such as droughts to protracted epidemics. An awareness of this novelty developed very soon among those living at the time of the conquest, and the memory of Europe still resounds with the polemic between those who advocated a less crude colonization of America (to save what was left of its indigenous population) and conquerors who cared little about the cost in human lives and anyway justified themselves by pointing to the subhuman character of the Indians.

Now we are getting there. The fact that the Indians did not belong to Christendom was not really sufficient to justify either their extinction (since they could be converted) or the occupiers' brutality (once the conversion had taken place) – and so thinkers and scholars set about developing a basis for the power of life and death that the new masters had given themselves over the inhabitants they found in place. Most peoples, to be sure, have tended to make their gods declare them more human than their neighbours, as a way of justifying their own acts of plunder. Can the European attitude therefore not be seen as a variant of a quite ordinary belief?

The point is, however, that it was precisely at this time that European discourse began to take the peculiar path of grounding an ideology of domination upon the products of Reason. The banal religious justification had been abundantly employed by armies in parts of the world won over to monotheism – from the 'God wishes it' of the crusaders during the bloodbath in occupied Jerusalem, to the 'God is almighty' of Arab horsemen in their drive from the Gulf to the Atlantic – but that was no longer adequate to the scale of the dispossession or the brutality of the domination.[8] A new argument concerning the superiority of the conqueror was then added. Spain, having based its national existence upon the idea of pure blood, undertook to ground the legitimacy of its empire upon the idea of racial superiority. The rest of Europe fell in behind it.

Should this slippage from a religious to a racial register be seen as one effect of the gradual uncoupling of religious and temporal spheres from the sixteenth century on? Perhaps. But for Europeans it was now less a matter of propagating revealed truth than of advancing a rational basis for their right to domination. How generally this was the case may be gauged by the fact that the most famous churchmen of the age were among the propagandists of the nascent theory of racial superiority. Juan de Sepúlveda, famous for his role as bad guy against Bartolomé de Las Casas's defence of the Indians, became the apostle of a natural right to domination:

> And it shall always be right and in accordance with natural law that these people [the 'barbarous and inhuman nations'] should be subjected to the rule of more cultivated and humane princes and nations.... If they refuse this rule, it may be imposed upon them by means of arms – and this war will be just, as natural law declares it to be.... In conclusion: it is just, normal and in accordance with natural law that upright, intelligent, virtuous and humane people should have dominion over those who lack these virtues.[9]

The divine is not totally absent from Sepúlveda's reasoning, but it is there only in a supporting role: 'It is just and beneficial that they should be servile, and we see this sanctioned by divine law itself. For it is written in the Book of Proverbs: "The fool shall serve the wise man."'[10]

Defenders of the Indians emphasized their humanity, but without fully challenging the idea of a natural hierarchy. Bishop de Las Casas formulated the humanist version, in the sense that the twentieth century has given to this term:

> There are no nations in the world, however rude and uncultured, savage and barbarian, coarse or cruel and almost stupid they may be, which cannot be persuaded, led and transported towards order and civilization … if one acts with skill and competence…. Thus, the whole race of men is one … and no one is born educated; and so at first we all need to be guided and helped by others who were born before us. Hence, when such savage peoples are found in the world, they are like uncultivated land, which readily produces weeds and bramble, but which has in it so much natural virtue that, if it is worked and taken care of, it yields edible, healthy and useful fruits.[11]

What the good priest gives us here is the first version of the white man's burden. The idea of the Indian as a human being who has not yet outgrown the stage of childhood truly thrived among theologians in the sixteenth century. Both supporters and opponents of tough measures, in their different ways, raised Europeans to the highest level of human civilization – not as a result of divine election, but by virtue of a pre-eminence that gave them a natural right to rule others.

The bleeding of Africa

As we know, the sermons of Las Casas came too late to prevent the depopulation of America. Manpower began to run short in the colonies of the two Iberian monarchies and in the Caribbean islands where a plantation economy was spreading. And, as we also know, it was to Africa that the settlers turned in search of the labour they needed. A few cargoes of slaves had already wended their way to Europe in the mid-fourteenth century, but the first direct transport from Africa to the Antilles dates from 1518. It inaugurated a trade which, for nearly four centuries, would make the fortune of Europe and the Americas.

Again the estimates of the number of people deported from Africa vary quite considerably, but no one disputes that the slave trade was a key reason for the underpopulation of the African continent until the middle of the twentieth century. For 'although slavery has been the lot of all human societies at one time or another in their history, no continent has undergone over such a long period (7th to 19th centuries) such a constant and systematic bleeding.'[12]

It is true that Europe was not alone in organizing these massive population transfers. The Arab world started its own trade several centuries earlier, continued it until the end of the nineteenth century, and (if one includes the Arab–Bantu trade) was responsible over some twelve centuries for nearly 40 per cent of all the deportations.[13] The silence of Arabs today concerning this trade – which is almost systematically covered up or, at best, scandalously underestimated by Middle Eastern and North African historians – should not make us forget that it was a major and recurrent feature of their history. Nor should edifying stories about the prophet Muhammad's sympathy for blacks,[14] or the fascination of medieval Arab travellers for the splendour of the Sudanese and Sahel courts, conceal the contempt for blacks that is displayed in a whole area of Arab literature and popular speech. The constant discourse asserting the inferiority of blacks shows that, as in Europe, theological legitimations of the slave trade (Islam's authorization of the enslavement of pagans) soon became insufficient to justify such a massive enterprise. From the tenth century, various writers therefore began to draw upon themes concerning the alleged primitivism of the black race.[15]

Nevertheless, the European slave trade presents a number of distinctive characteristics. The long period during which the Arab trade was pursued is partly explicable by the fact that slavery remained a feature of Arab, Arab–Ottoman and Arab–Berber societies right down to the twentieth century, and indeed some forms persist to this day in certain countries. Within Western Europe, by contrast, slavery was already disappearing in the late Middle Ages, except in certain parts of the Mediterranean, before the Portuguese brought it back into favour around the middle of the fourteenth century, as they turned to African slave labour to promote the agrarian prosperity of Madeira, the Canaries and the Azores.

By massively exporting African 'black gold' to European outposts in the Americas, merchants and settlers were therefore breathing new life into a system that was in its death agony in Europe itself. A practice with a radiant future came into being, whereby the economics and legal systems governing life in the colonies were dissociated from those prevailing in the home country. At the same time that economic forms based on slave labour were disappearing in Europe, they were underpinning the prosperity of its overseas possessions and therefore of Europe itself. Between the sixteenth and eighteenth centuries, not one of its nations failed to venture into a three-cornered trade that would bring fortune to its factories and its Atlantic ports.

In fact, the second distinctive feature of the European slave trade was its massive scale, and its decisive role for the economies that practised it. Concentrated into a shorter period than its Arab counterpart (some four centuries instead of twelve), operated at a faster rhythm and on a larger scale than the trans-Saharan trade (nearly twice as many slaves in a third of the time), it took a more visible and more lasting toll of the affected areas of the continent.

As in America, the arrival of Europeans in Africa inaugurated a long period of demographic decline, so that, according to the most credible estimates, its population fell from 20 per cent of the world total around the year 1650 to 10 per cent a century and a half later. If we consider, with Aimé Césaire, that 'it is good for different civilizations to be brought into contact with one another, excellent for different worlds to be wedded together',[16] we must also agree with him that everything depends on the nature of the contact. And the reality is that, beginning in the fifteenth century, demographic catastrophes without known precedent (apart from those caused by natural disasters) struck peoples who became acquainted with European conquerors and traders. For America and Africa, contact with Renaissance Europe ushered in a deadly period whose consequences can still be felt today.

As to justifications for the enslavement of blacks, the main arguments had already been tested on the Indians, as it were, by the time that the slave trade got seriously under way. Many contemporary writers did consider inhumane the conditions under which it was conducted – but that was the only problem they found. Slavery itself was all the more readily accepted in that the Bible gave it explicit sanction: Paul's epistle to Philemon was one among several sources of legitimation, and a series of papal bulls had encouraged it since the mid-fifteenth century.

Yet, just as religion could not alone serve to justify the fate reserved for the American Indians, it was also insufficient to lay the ideological foundations for African enslavement. Theologians who defended the Indian population while denying a similar share in humanity to the blacks gave birth to a contradiction that they had to solve in one way or another.

The distinctively anti-black discourse that began to emerge in the sixteenth century drew both upon the biblical myth of the cursing of the sons of Ham, and upon ideas of Negro primitivism, to link up with the natural law theory of the ruler's right to rule. Constantly refined as the slave trade intensified over succeeding centuries, this discourse spawned an ever more sophisticated set of arguments concerning the inferiority of the black race, in which scientific rhetoric gradually displaced the religious argument and secured victory over it in the course of the eighteenth century.

This, too, was the European Renaissance, a new baptism that was supposed to have formally renounced the darkness of an earlier epoch. Perhaps it was this above all else. For although, in Europe itself, the Renaissance was celebrated as the century of poets, artists and scholars, a moment of civilization mingling new thinking and new art in a sweet alchemy, that same Europe was turning the world it discovered into a desert and providing new theories for the old conception of might as right. Let us try to summarize the main trends of this founding period.

First, it introduced the era of globalization: that is, the appropriation of the world by Western Europe, and the interdependence of all its parts for the needs of domination. Territorial and commercial expansion without precedent in human history meant that unexplored lands – unexplored by Europeans, that is – occupied less and less space on the more and more accurate maps of the time. 'Old Europe', so called because of a belief in its greater antiquity and its annexation of 'new' worlds, now looked well beyond the Mediterranean basin and surrounding areas that had long formed its only horizon. It discovered the existence of other peoples who had never previously heard of it, and in the process of discovery it subjugated and enslaved them.

As its horizon expanded to global dimensions and took in an amazing diversity of human life much greater than it had expected, Europe set about reducing the frontiers of the human race so that they eventually included it alone. Its identity was to be constructed upon rejection of anything that might spoil the image it wished to have of itself. After inventing a history that excluded what it thought of as the East, and after driving it out of its own geographical, historical and philosophical space, the brand-new Europe that emerged from the long medieval 'night' appointed itself the sole repository of the totality of human attributes. The other races – a word that acquired its present meaning in the seventeenth century – had at best only some of those attributes. Europeans held this privilege not only from God but from history and nature, which had made them more human than others.

One can hardly forget that the Europeans' self-election as full human beings gave them a free hand, as they saw it, to pillage everyone else – and to engage in the economic exploitation unparalleled in scale or form upon which Europe partly founded its modern wealth, and which made of it within a few centuries the richest area of the planet. Should the conclusion be that, in the end, Europe did no more than forge ideological tools for its domination? To use the terms of our contemporary questioning, without resorting to retrospective history, we can certainly ask why Europe seems to have been able to embark upon the globalization venture only by casting into outer darkness everything it could not identify with itself, thereby shutting out from its thinking any paths that could have given access to universality. Was it that dehumanization of the Other, together with the construction of a closed identity for itself, were the necessary ideological obverse of that venture? Or did they go beyond what was required for the purposes of domination? In any event, they very soon became a key mechanism of modern European identity and of the culture of supremacy upon which it rests.

TWO

Light and Shadow
of the Enlightenment

Then, happily, came the Enlightenment. By inventing a universal humanity and endowing this juridical abstraction with inalienable rights, it absolved Europe of crimes both past and future. I have no wish to simplify the thought of a period which, from the British Enlightenment of the seventeenth century to the French of the eighteenth, was so rich and innovative in the crucial questions it asked of humanity and itself. I still remember the admirable strictures of Montesquieu and Rousseau against the inanity of racism, or those of Voltaire against torture, even though for all his declarations he remained a convinced Judeophobe and was intermittently anti-Negro.

This Europe was the first to theorize the superiority of individual liberty over collective exigencies, and this sanctification of the individual as the horizon of all things enabled the secular ideology of human rights to make gradual headway.[1] Yet it was a contradictory century, and the tools it forged made it possible, both then and later, to justify the worst while ostensibly serving the best.

What we have to ask is whether the Enlightenment represented, or heralded, a radically new departure in the history of relations between the West and its others, or whether, on the contrary, it was the second founding moment of the culture of supremacy whose history I am seeking to trace. And if one tends to think it was the latter, should its crimes against other peoples in later centuries be considered its legitimate offspring? Does history since the nineteenth century come down to an ever renewed contest between defenders of the Enlightenment (who have drawn on it for arguments to support their freedom struggles) and opponents who have risen up against its declared principles?

22

Or did Enlightenment thought, like storm-bearing clouds, already carry future horrors within it, formulating the limits of universality in such a way as to make Europe its sole guardian? It was anyway with this new baggage that Europe continued in new forms the expansion it had begun over the previous few centuries. Much as the Renaissance created the West that Europeans subsequently made their mental habitat, the contemporary West has transformed the complexity of the Enlightenment into an edifying tale to preserve its clear conscience.

Right from the beginning, however, the Enlightenment bore the mark of ambivalence, reflecting its more sombre side. Of course, thinkers now had men born free and equal by virtue of a natural law that was the same for all – a law serving no longer to assert superiority but to ground equality. But as soon as it was a matter of political action, the declaration of this principle gave no guarantee that it would be respected. Indeed, over the next century, it was largely through its claim to the Enlightenment that the West set about violating it in a remarkably systematic manner.

America and slavery

Already in the eighteenth century, this paradox was illustrated in the lands supposed to witness the coming of the new man – that is, the American colonies of the British Crown. Those who liberated them wanted, as we know, to make them an advanced bastion of the Enlightenment and the rule of law. Thousands of miles from Europe and its archaic absolutisms, the American Declaration of Independence proclaimed in 1776: 'We hold these truths to be self-evident, that all men are created equal, that they are endowed by their Creator with certain unalienable Rights, that among these are Life, Liberty and the pursuit of Happiness.'

In the Constitution of the American Republic, the Founding Fathers reiterated this profession of faith yet hardly gave a moment's thought to the slave system that was developing in the territories freed from British rule. The clashes between delegates from Northern and Southern states to the Convention of 1787, which was called upon, in Thomas Jefferson's words, to draft a constitution for 'the last and finest hope of humanity', centred only upon continuation of the slave trade. The North finally obtained its prohibition in 1808. But the persistence of the slave labour already established on American soil was not a matter of debate in the country that the Founding Fathers wished to govern in accordance with

the moral law. After the abolition of slavery in the North in 1804, anti-slavery leagues became active in the South but had little resonance, and in 1819 Congress permanently legalized slavery in the States given over to a plantation economy.

While slavery flourished, the Indian question was coming onto the agenda. In the years following independence, the founders of the United States did not dare give free rein to their urge for conquest and recognized the property rights of Indians as 'original occupants' of the lands. In 1789 Congress gave a guarantee that 'their lands and goods shall never be taken from them without their consent'. Here we can see the influence of Diderot, who, less than a decade before in his *Histoire des deux Indes*, had recognized that Europeans had the right to settle peacefully in a country with the agreement of its inhabitants and to cultivate their own land there, but only on condition that this was duly awarded to them by its rightful owners. Still faithful to this legacy, Jefferson stressed a few years later that land could be acquired only 'by all honest and peaceful means'[2] – to which the Senate added, in 1817, 'with the consent of the tribes'. Such declarations did not, however, prevent the waging of large-scale military campaigns against the Indians from 1794 onward, nor their intensification after the turn of the century into a degree of violence that a few congressmen persisted in deploring.

Beset by the same contradictions as French Encyclopedists, these men entertained the dream that the Indians would acquiesce in their own despoilment and allow them to remain at peace with their principles. But this the Indians refused to do. Since there could be no question of giving up expansion, it was therefore the principles that had to evolve. All Indians, declared war minister John C. Calhoun in 1820, must 'be brought gradually under our authority and laws.... Our opinions, and not theirs, ought to prevail, in measures intended for their civilization and happiness.'[3] What makes these statements so remarkable is that their aim was not to challenge, in the interests of conquest, the moral basis of the new state, but rather to provide an interpretation of it that would actually legitimize further conquest. Henceforth, the Indians were held responsible for the consequences of their refusal to accept the particular kind of happiness offered them by the pioneers of free America.

As the settlers' land hunger sharpened, however, it became difficult to enlist Indian happiness on the side of conquest. By elevating Americans to the rank of God's chosen people, the 'manifest destiny' argument made it possible to launch the last phase of expansion, which then came to resemble a programmed genocide of the Indian population of North America.

We may suppose that the Iberian conquistadors of the sixteenth century did not plan the demographic consequences of their massacres and other acts of brutality, but there can scarcely be any doubt that an urge to empty the American West of its native inhabitants was the principal motive for the Indian wars of the nineteenth century. American democracy, that eldest child of the Enlightenment, was thus built in less than a century upon the deportation of African slaves and the elimination of an entire people – although it had no sense that it was betraying the ideal upon which it had been founded.

Limited universality

The discourse of 'manifest destiny' did, to be sure, draw upon a religious register that flourished better than elsewhere on American soil, and the argument from divine election seems a long way from that equality of rights which, ever since Locke, had been the creed of Enlightenment thinkers. Nevertheless, its secular equivalent very soon took up residence within the Enlightenment. Once again, my aim is not to obscure the debates that stirred this fertile period, nor to disregard the fact that colonization and slavery were outlawed by a number of its thinkers and politicians. The opening of citizenship to the Jews of France, as well as the early abolition of slavery that passed the Convention in 1794 against strong resistance, prove the existence of a will to anchor universal rights in reality. But it remains the case that this same universality was quickly confined within strict limits.

First of all, universality was from the outset limited to the male gender. Although the French Revolution granted women certain civil rights – rights withdrawn in 1804 by the Napoleonic Code, which generations of republican democrats left intact for more than a century – women were deprived of all political rights and excluded from the civil space within which modern France took shape. No one complained about this at the time. It is not the purpose of this book to take stock of that denial of universality which was for too long passed over in silence (so that even today the term 'universal suffrage' is used to describe an electoral system long monopolized by the male half of the population in Europe), especially as a start has been made on such an analysis in recent decades. But it should at least be recalled here, since it played a large part in the closure of universality that took place more or less simultaneously with its formulation.

What gradually emerged from the early decades of the Enlightenment, then, was a universal man who was neither female nor Indian nor Negro-slave (France, having set an example by abolishing slavery in 1794, went back on it in 1802). Soon he was firmly embodied in the figure of the 'white male',[4] as the sole holder of inalienable rights whose defence was declared a political and moral imperative. These exclusions thus transformed universality into a legal artefact which, by virtue of its very abstractness, could then be endowed with a gender and a geographical location.

But Reason needed arguments to make this mutation its own. Those who asserted the superiority of European civilization, then of the white race, set themselves the task of providing them. In fact, they did not find support only among people nostalgic for an order prior to the political upheavals that partly stemmed from the intellectual revolution of the Enlightenment, or among the ranks of entrepreneurs concerned for the development of their business. In France, as in the Southern States of America, the planters' lobbies certainly proved the fiercest defenders of the status quo in relation to slavery, appealing to the prosperity of their respective nation and, naturally enough, to their own. Again in France, parliamentary deputies representing ports connected with the slave trade enlisted further precious support for the cause. But even revolutionaries, though mostly against slavery, sometimes hesitated about the line they should take, as if they were not completely sure of the rightness of their principles when they threatened to become reality.

Although colonization did not yet seek its theoretical justification in racism, one already finds among people in the eighteenth century certain pointers towards the theories that would thrive in the following century.[5] Throughout the nineteenth century, those who claimed to be following Locke and Montesquieu made a decisive contribution that helped to root in Western minds a conviction of their superiority and of the legitimacy of their supremacy. The existence of intellectual minorities passionately defending a less restrictive conception of human rights did not prevent their discourse from remaining marginal in the course of this century of conquest.

'I repeat,' Jules Ferry retorted less than a century after the French Declaration of the Rights of Man and the Citizen, 'there is a law for the superior races because there is a duty for them. They have the duty of civilizing the inferior races.'[6] He was echoing Ernest Renan: 'There is nothing shocking about the conquest of a country with an inferior race by a superior race that settles there to govern it.... As much as con-

quest between races should be criticized, the regeneration of inferior or
degenerate races by superior races is in the providential order of humanity.'[7] The secular version of America's 'manifest destiny' is wholly
present in these phrases. Not such a long time would be necessary for
the sons of the Enlightenment to rally to it with enthusiasm.

A moment of hesitation

Thus, at the end of an intellectual revolution that theorized the idea of
equality and the principle of universality on which it rested, only Europe
and its children across the Atlantic were eligible for the rights that it
implied. This meant, in effect, that the rights had been transformed
into privileges. But it is difficult to end our discussion of the Enlightenment on this bald note. The depth of questioning, the new attention
to non-European peoples, the fact that many of its elite figures publicly
denounced the most abject forms of exploitation imposed on them: these
dimensions, not counting the new philosophical autonomy of the subject
from the sphere of religion, forbid us to reduce that period to the most
negative of its progeny, even if these did rapidly gain the upper hand
over others.

The Enlightenment should also, perhaps, be seen as one of those rare
moments in the last five centuries of the West when the ideology of
superiority and its accompanying culture lost their secure hold. However
obvious it may be, we should not overlook the fact that the Enlightenment was the intellectual and political expression of a shift affecting all
areas of the collective life of Europeans – from the technological revolutions that revolutionized production to the economic and political
developments that created new social classes, new forms of state organization and novel types of legitimacy. The old world of feudal orders and
ecclesiastical or royal absolutism fell apart, while the modern Europe of
nation-states and conquering bourgeoisies gradually emerged from its
ruins. Before asserting in new forms its will to unify the *oikumenē* under
its own hegemony, Europe looked questioningly at the postulates underlying its presence in the world and the legitimacy of its past enterprises.
Through the voice of its thinkers and moralists, it rejected the image of
itself that it had given to others and recognized, as a matter of right,
their share of humanity.

This idea was meant to involve a radical break with the past, so
radical that Saint-Just, for example, could propose in his *Essai de*

Constitution pour la France, without fear of being taken for a dreamer, that 'the French people shall vote for the liberty of the world'.[8] What an extraordinary aim to embody the universal of the *philosophes*; and what an extraordinary ambition to appoint oneself for the task! It is a phrase which sums up the ambivalence of that fertile period by making liberty the horizon of the world to be built and by assigning to France – it could have been Europe – the role of leading the change. Here is one reason among others why a Ferry or a Renan could feel they were not betraying the Enlightenment when they said that Europe had a vocation to lead the world, for its greater benefit and for the happiness of those it had a 'duty' to rule.

That brief period when the Other existed, not only as an object of compassion or curiosity but as a subject endowed with rights, seemed for a moment to shake a culture of supremacy already well entrenched in the Western unconscious. The European colonial appetite and economic interests bound up with overseas expansion, the land hunger of the new white North American nation, the dynamic of conquest (itself the child of Enlightenment inventions) that would mark the nineteenth century: these aspects soon swept away that moment of hesitation with its ambiguous discourse and practical drifting. Nearly two centuries later, in a quite different context, the West would revive its questioning about the nature of its relationship with others. After a Second World War that spelt the end for many a deeply rooted conviction, the decolonization of the late 1950s and early 1960s opened a new period in which the Other burst into Western consciousness, with the result that the West began to question itself about the crimes committed in its name and to seek a new relationship with those shaking off the yoke it had imposed. I shall consider below what became of this second moment when questions had the upper hand over certainties.

Those two epochs may perhaps share the characteristic of being a kind of interregnum between successive forms of Western domination over the rest of the world: both, we might say, proclaimed a break with the old colonial order but failed to block the emergence of new forms of subjection; both expounded egalitarian convictions that were quite unlikely to have a future. Was this because neither broke with a deep conviction that it was the West's natural prerogative to set forth the universal, whatever its content? Let us not jump too far ahead, but rather turn to that apogee of colonialism when the culture of supremacy acquired its well-known discourses and became, more than ever before, a popular culture.

THREE

The Roots of a Conviction

As the nineteenth century advanced, and with it the modern colonial enterprise, the whole of human knowledge was gradually summoned to make of that culture a coherent body of doctrine. Thanks to the growing secularization of thought, the Western thirst for conquest had long ceased to justify itself by religious argument alone, although this was still deployed whenever the need was felt. A bare asssertion of superiority, as the basis for a natural right to subjugation, had contours that were too fuzzy to meet the requirements of the age. A scientific register therefore took over from the old arguments, which had been seriously weakened by Enlightenment probing. The path opened by the eighteenth-century naturalists turned into a taxonomic obsession, involving racialization of even the slightest differences within the diversity of the human species.

The proof by race...

Nineteenth-century physical anthropology brought with it the birth of modern racism, that scientific theorization of 'white' (that is, European) supremacy,[1] since it placed 'light' peoples not originating from Europe on middle or lower rungs of a sophisticated hierarchy. Population groups in the Mediterranean were thus classified in accordance with their proximity to European characteristics: 'Semites' found themselves at the bottom of the ladder, while others, such as the North African Berbers, were wisely Celtized by colonial science for the needs of French strategists, allowing political variations to develop on the, as it were,

29

natural basis of antagonism between Arabs and Berbers.[2] Those who are
called Caucasians or Aryans (racially, and therefore culturally, superior)
must accordingly rule as masters over the myriad groups of humanity
hierarchically arranged by distance from the chosen race. Renan, as so
often, lucidly summarizes the scientific advances of his time: 'Nature
has made a race of workers (the Chinese race) with a marvellous manual
dexterity and virtually no sense of honour ...; a race of farm labourers,
the Negro race ...; a race of masters and soldiers, which is the European
race.'[3]

Even among blacks, considered the closest in general to the animal
realm, some groups were more human than others because less 'negroid'
in their features and colour. Here, too, science undertook to furnish
proof that brain size was directly proportional to fairness of complex-
ion. The 'Hamites' of the African Great Lakes area – a completely
fabricated racial category – thus found themselves designated the whit-
est of the Negroes, with the various privileges that this entailed. Superiority was now simple to define: it was physical factors which had
given rise to all the scientific, technological, cultural and political aspects of the distinctive genius of the white race.

Philosophy and then sociology also made their contributions to this
historic enterprise. Everyone knows what later became of Hegel's
hypothesis of peoples without a history. German philosophy, itself the
inheritor of Enlightenment hostility to Negroes exemplified by Hume
and Kant, denied Africa the historical depth that was the essence of a
civilization: it 'has remained shut up' in itself, 'the land of childhood,
which, lying beyond the day of self-conscious history, is enveloped in
the dark mantle of night';[4] it scarcely has any existence of its own except on world maps, where its location has hardly gone beyond the *hic
sunt leones* of antiquity. Western historiography, moreover, never ceased
to widen this gulf, so that by excluding Africa from history it could cast
it outside the civilized world.

In this connection, we should pause for a moment to consider how
historians viewed ancient Egypt as if it did not belong to any continent,
a kind of island anchored in the Mediterranean through which flowed
the longest river in the world (though no mention was made of the
source of the Egyptian Nile, beyond the fact that it watered Nubia to
the south). It was also said that caravans used to travel by land in search
of gum and ivory to the distant country of Punt. We know that many
dark-skinned men and women were painted on the tomb walls of the
pharaohs. And yet, the fact that Egypt was part of Africa was never

mentioned in any book; we had to wait until disputes in the 1960s around the blistering work of Senegalese historian Cheikh Anta Diop allowed some African origins to enter the picture. This geographical amnesia is easy enough to understand. One of the most ancient and brilliant of human civilizations – which had left behind such spectacular remains, and whose influence on the Greek world could not be totally disregarded, even if the most eminent historians constantly tried to demonstrate the latter's superiority[5] – could not decently be thought of as located on a primitive and barbaric continent lacking in history.

By 'relocating' ancient Egypt, Western historiography achieved two aims: it permanently deprived sub-Saharan Africa of the possibility of being in the world as part of its recognized history; and it appropriated Egyptian civilization (too close and too significant to be wholly alien to the European spirit), by making it a civilization of the Mediterranean *mare nostrum* of the Greeks and Romans. Still today, most European or American schoolchildren would be hard pressed to identify in which continent lay the pharaonic Egypt whose splendour is revealed in their lessons.

The same lust for dispossession, based on a belief that racially inferior peoples could not build anything of importance, drove colonial historians of southern Africa to invent Asian or even Portuguese origins for the famous ruins of Mwene Matapa Zimbabwe. And in the field of sociology, Lévy-Bruhl's distinction between logical and prelogical mentalities had so much success that it survived a challenge by its own author.

By the end of the nineteenth century, the journey begun by the Renaissance seemed to have come to an end. The cumulative effect of four centuries of arguments to legitimate Europe's attempts at exclusion and domination had finally produced a 'fully fledged' racism and a theoretical system that seemed impervious to challenge. 'Purity of blood', divine and natural selection of the white Christian male, the old need to justify enslavement of dark-skinned peoples, laborious efforts to legitimate exploitation, segregation and elimination: all this was somehow sublimated in the dogma of biological determinism. With this new charge, racist discourse found increased resonance amid the colonial adventures and xenophobic nationalism that began to flourish in this period.[6]

The speed at which racist discourse became a popular culture may be attributed both to the depth of its historical roots and to its capacity to transcend political and ideological divides. Since there was a consensus among the political and intellectual elites of Europe and America about their absolute right to supremacy,[7] nothing prevented this conviction from spreading among the population at large. This proceeded all the more smoothly when the turn of the century inaugurated in Europe the massive entry of the popular classes into the educational system. In France, it was the republican school which firmly anchored a popular belief in racial superiority and democratized the culture of supremacy.

However different were the legacies constructed by the right and the left in Europe, what separated Gobineau (emblematic of the former) and Ernest Renan (long praised to the skies by the latter) was less important than what brought them together. In the nineteenth century and the first few decades of the twentieth, left and right shared the same conviction that the human species was arranged along a ladder with the Europeans at the top; their disputes centred on whether this hierarchy was immutable or susceptible to change. A kind of left Darwinism, following the paternalist humanism of the early inheritors of the Enlightenment, tended towards the second view: that is, they held that, through the colonial self-sacrifice of Europeans, primitive races or those having some but not all the elements of civilization might one day, in the distant future, become part of developed humanity – so long as they meanwhile accepted Western domination. This, we know, was the difficult civilizing mission which white men gave themselves, and which could then serve as cover for all their undertakings.

On the right, the gulf was considered too wide ever to be bridged. After 1865, the Englishman Francis Galton and his successors presented as science a major boost to the theory of racial inequality and the impossibility of improving inferior races. 'Educate and nurture them, I do not believe that you will succeed in modifying the stock', the main disciple of the founder of eugenics wrote in 1905.[8]

These differences over the nature of what everyone saw as evident inequality would have enormous consequences. Galton's emulators on the Continent shared his belief that it was unreasonable to oppose 'the gradual extinction of an inferior race'[9] – a belief whose sequel is well known to us all. Once again, however, the distance between the two sides was not as great as we are led to suppose, especially as crossovers from one to the other were not all that exceptional. The left – from Blanqui to Proudhon – contributed to a racialization of the traditional hostility to Jews, and distinguished itself in this respect by the most despicable calls for murder. If Léon Daudet described Captain Dreyfus as having 'a muddy, flat and common face lacking any indication of remorse, most assuredly an alien face, a piece of wreckage from the ghetto', Proudhon could proclaim that 'the Jew is the enemy of the human race' and that 'this race should be either swiftly sent back to Asia or exterminated'.[10]

The fact that attempts to justify the massacres accompanying colonial conquest did not all draw upon the same ideological registers does not mean that they were all that different. Tocqueville, who did not favour extermination of the Arabs, nevertheless confided to Colonel La Morcière that 'once we have accepted the grand violence of conquest, I do not believe we should shrink from the smaller acts of violence that are absolutely necessary to maintain it'.[11] Karl Pearson, who saw nothing scandalous in the extermination of the Indians of North America, noted that although the Europeans had certainly had to wipe out whole tribes the final outcome 'has given us a good far outbalancing its immediate evil'.[12] Scruples or no scruples, the justification for widespread massacres was forthcoming. And those charged with carrying them out were unanimously hailed as national heroes – even if some dared to speak out against the worst horrors they were committing.

...and its applications

The first phase of European expansion in the Caribbean and now-Iberian America was accompanied with a genocide which, despite its excellent results, might be described as homespun. The second phase of expansion displayed its roots in the industrial age by consciously planning massacres and, when the need arose, actual genocide. The bloodiest deeds were not, with a few exceptions, committed by army hotheads or civilian mavericks operating on their own account; they were the result of decisions at army headquarters responsible for the implementation of government strategy.

Elsewhere, some massacres were so extensive that their effect on population levels was felt for many long years. At the end of a 'pacification campaign' lasting half a century, the population of Algeria had decreased by nearly one million.[13] In Central Africa population figures plummeted during the first phase of occupation, between 1890 and 1920; this was due partly to the spread of contagious diseases by European troops and population movement following the invasions, but even more to the massive use of indigenous labour for jungle penetration and porterage, the systematic levying of food, the extraction methods of the mining concessions, and recruitment for the 1914–18 war. In some parts of the Congo basin, the population fell by a third in the space of thirty years – or even a half in the worst affected areas. There is also abundant evidence that widespread use of forced labour and unprecedentedly brutal methods of exploitation caused a terrible loss of life in the Congo of Leopold II, Roi des Belges.[14]

More generally, European occupation of the African interior, which was stepped up after the share-out at the Berlin conference of 1884, went together with a major population decline throughout sub-Saharan Africa. Once again European conquest, like no other before it, caused a sometimes massive depopulation of newly occupied regions. These particularly deadly episodes in the history of European penetration and exploitation cannot be classed as genocide, however, because they did not endanger the collective existence of the peoples in question. Let me repeat: there is no question here of confusing genocide and massacres, or of using the former term to denote the latter reality, as some of the anti-colonial literature has too often done.

All the same, genocide too was available for consideration as a means of European penetration. It was an invaluable card to play when a certain area had to be cleared for the purposes of settlement, or when it had not been possible to break the resistance of the local population. As we have seen, the Europeans of North America especially favoured it as a way of expanding their territory, and no one upset themselves about it in the Old Continent. Their example was followed by Germany, which in 1904–07 carried out a true and proper genocide of the Herero people of South West Africa. The operation was relatively successful, because it is estimated that the size of the Herero population passed from some 80,000 at the beginning of the century to 15,000 after the campaign waged by Governor von Trotha.[15] Admittedly the German general considered that 'the Herero nation as such should be annihilated or, if that is not possible, driven out of the country'. 'I find it perfectly justified', he went on, 'that this nation should perish rather than infect our soldiers and diminish our supplies of water and food.'[16] Nor did the British think twice about using this tried and tested method to crush the resistance of the aboriginal population of Tasmania in the first few decades of the nineteenth century. Between 1831 and 1835, two hundred survivors were deported to neighbouring islands, where the last of them expired in 1876.

The point is not to recite a litany of the tragedies bound up with European expansion, but to recall that massacres and 'final solutions' were the ordinary stuff of conquest. Mostly, those who perpetrated or ordered such actions justified them by referring to the necessity and legitimacy of despoliation, or sometimes even to a strange kind of 'humanism'. Bugeaud, for example, advocated the systematic use of terror in Algeria, to put a swift end to resistance so that the suffering of indigenous people should not go on for ever. In black Africa, many campaigns were justified in the name of a moral duty to free local populations from the despotism and slavery inflicted on them by traditional chiefs. Until the First World War at least, reactions were few and far between in the metropolitan countries – and, in some of these rare cases, were quite remote from any humanitarian concerns. Although the 'smoking-out operations' in Algeria were criticized by a few deputies,[17] this was mainly because such practices were liable to harm the soldiers' morale and to give other countries an unfortunate image of French grandeur. Those who spoke in the debate did recognize the cruelty, but in response to some overheated interventions the defence minister pointed out: 'In Europe such a deed would be terrible, loathsome. In Africa it is the reality of war. How else would you like it to be waged?'[18]

In the name of civilization

In the eyes of nearly everyone it considered an intellectual, Western Europe's colonial vocation therefore soon became and long remained perfectly legitimate. The doubts came much later. If criticisms were made, it was not to challenge the natural right of Westerners to rule, but to argue that the conquest was pointless and costly or – in the case of liberals – liable to damage freedom of trade, since colonial preferences gave the metropolitan country a monopoly on trade with its possessions. In France, the right and some of the Radicals were for a while hostile to an adventure that they considered to be, among other things, a diversion from the Alsace-Lorraine question; the great majority of Republicans, on the other hand, were all in favour of expansion, seeing it not only as good business for French industries but as a glorious epic worthy of the European spirit. The lone diatribes of Paul Lafargue, or even Jean Jaurès, remained almost inaudible in an atmosphere which, at least until the First World War, involved an ever wider consensus.

The only major European protest – and even that challenged the forms of colonization but not the principle – was prompted by the cruel methods of exploitation in the Belgian Congo. From 1890 some travellers returning to the United States or Europe began to report atrocities that they had personally witnessed or of which they had seen the traces.

The Congo scandal erupted in Belgium in 1908 as a result of these denunciations, becoming the first vast campaign for human rights to be respected in Europe's colonial possessions.

But, just as the victorious mobilization of sections of the French public and intelligentsia for the rehabilitation of Captain Dreyfus did not stem the tide of anti-Semitism, condemnation of atrocities in the Belgian Congo did not prevent their repetition elsewhere – in the French Congo, for example, where in 1898 Paris introduced a Leopold-style leasing system for those companies awarded concessions. In 1905, the so-called Grand-Toqué trial ended with token sentences on two colonial administrators in Africa found guilty of murders and numerous acts of physical abuse. The following year, a commission of enquiry headed by Savorgnan de Brazza delivered its report, only to see it hushed up. And fifteen years later the building of the Congo–Ocean railway, locally known as the 'death works', piled up 20,000 corpses in a decade among riverside peoples driven into forced labour.[19]

From the mid-nineteenth century, then, the most intolerable mani-festations of colonial barbarism were known in Europe and gave rise to a few parliamentary debates and sporadic denunciations. I do not lightly use the somewhat overworked term 'barbarism', which Westerners so easily applied to those they were seeking to conquer. In relation to Africa, however, we are talking of barbaric acts in the sense nowadays given to the term – a few accounts of punitive expeditions or forced recruitment would be enough to convince anyone of this. And all these acts were ultimately committed in the name of the values of Western civilization, the only one worthy of the name. The General Act of the Berlin Conference of 1885, which divided Africa among the European powers, stipulated in Article Six:

> All powers exercising sovereign rights or influence in the said territories undertake to preserve the native peoples and to improve their moral and material conditions of existence.... They shall protect and promote all institutions and enterprises ... tending to educate the natives and to make them understand and appreciate the advantages of civilization.[20]

'Our rule', stated Joseph Chamberlain, Britain's colonial minister, a few years later, 'does, and has, brought security and peace and compara-tive prosperity to countries that never knew these blessings. In carrying out this work of civilization we are fulfilling what I believe to be our national mission, and we are finding scope for the exercise of those faculties and qualities which have made us a great governing race. [Indeed,] the British race is the greatest of governing races that the world has ever seen.'[21] We shall see below the effects which this constant and tragic dissociation between speech and practice had upon recent history and the behaviour and political practices of the formerly dominated peoples.

In the 'civilized' countries,[22] a few voices did attempt – sometimes with success – to battle against the xenophobic hatreds flourishing at home and the bloody imposition overseas of arbitrary rule with civilizing pretensions. Placing themselves on the other side of the Enlightenment heritage, they wanted to convince people that the principles were worth something only if they were turned into reality. We should, however, be careful to distinguish between two positions regarding colonization.

The first, which challenged the very principle of colonization, remained totally marginal until the 1920s when communism redrew the ideological and political map in Europe. The second, which pleaded for colonization with a human face, was more widespread but still limited to a minority with little influence on public opinion. Those who took this latter position might well express shock at hideous crimes committed in the name of national aggrandizement, or at the pursuit of interests that were far from always the same as their own. They might express concern over the fate of soldiers in campaigns that cost too many lives, or criticize high levels of spending if there was no visible pay-off. Often they were simply indifferent to what was happening outside the home country. At the end of the day, however, they did not raise any fundamental doubts: the colonial adventure may not have been a priority for them, but only their race had a vocation to embark upon it, only their race had the right – and hence the duty – to project itself outward to the four corners of the world.

It is true that all the writings, and later all the films, dealing with relations between the West and non-European peoples were remarkably homogeneous in their espousal of a culture of contempt. From scientific and academic literature to the popular novel, the discordant notes were rare. Textbooks for generations of European schoolchildren exalted first the acts of conquest, then the civilizing work of colonization and the progress due to Western expansion around the globe. In the United States, the pioneer myth and the glorification of white territorial advances against Indian barbarism soon crystallized into a national ideology and a popular culture. In this field the nineteenth century did represent an innovation. Unlike in previous eras, not a single sector of

European opinion remained ignorant of its country's overseas adventures; not a single American failed to keep up with every advance of the
Frontier against Indian resistance. The channels of information and
propaganda became ever more numerous – from schools to mass media,
from civil associations to the serial accounts for which newspapers desperately vied. The public trembled at the perils facing discoverers or
pioneers, and thrilled at each of their exploits.

Dozens of authors, mainly British and French, related glorious and
tragic tales of their countrymen in far and distant lands: heroic soldiers
who had returned home after confronting the cruel deceit of Annamite
rebels or the savagery of African hordes; brave wandering families who
had migrated across the world and been eaten or scalped by a local
tribe. Without speaking of the greatest, from Mérimée to Hugo, Loti or
Kipling, we can see in the nineteenth century and the first part of the
twentieth the blossoming of a whole literature that would today be
regarded as definitely second-rate, drawing its inspiration from the
colonial enterprise and describing in luxuriant detail the barbarism of
regions opened up by Westerners to the benefits of civilization. I still
remember with some alarm an English novel that related how Maori
cannibals put to death gentle white maidens, or those countless tales in
which the Countess of Ségur told of young heroes returning from an
adventure in the antipodes.

Europeanizing the world

What had they gone out to do, the characters of those novels published
in tens of thousands of copies? The fact is that, from the late nineteenth
century on, Europe was at home everywhere. For its vocation was not
only to conquer and civilize, but also to populate continents which,
being seen as empty or barely inhabited by savages, offered their spaces
to emigrants from the old continent. With the exception of Asia, already
densely populated and largely outside the scope of direct colonization,
the whole planet became settlement land for a population characterized
throughout the nineteenth and early twentieth centuries by fast growth
and an unprecedented flight from the countryside. Rapidly though European industry developed, it was never able to absorb the whole population shaken out in this way, and for a century or so the new worlds
received millions of surplus Europeans.

Particularly North America, but also the Southern Cone of Latin
America, Oceania and humbler settlement areas such as North Africa

for the French, Italians and Spanish, or eastern and southern Africa for the Germans and British, served the purpose. From 1830 to 1920 more than 35 million Europeans set sail for the United States, including 4.5 million British, 4.6 million Irish, 2.5 million Scandinavians, 6.5 million Germans, nearly 1 million Poles, some 4 million subjects of the Russian empire, and 5 million Italians. Nearly half the survivors of the great famine that decimated Ireland in 1848 left their land of birth in the second half of the century, and nearly half the population of Sweden (then an extremely poor country) embarked for America around the turn of the twentieth century. As to the other major destinations of the exodus, 8 million people arrived in Canada in the course of the nineteenth century, and between 1820 and 1940 a little over 2 million Europeans chose to settle in Australia, while some 12 million Italians, Spanish, Portuguese and Germans set off for South America and hundreds of thousands for the African colonies. All together, more than 60 million Europeans left their native continent in little more than a century – the equivalent of 14 per cent of the population of Europe in 1914.[23]

None of these lands that they made their own was completely un-inhabited. Some were almost empty, others had a very sparse population which, as in South America, had already shrunk away in the first period of European colonization, while others still had quite a large population for the time. But the indigenous peoples hardly figured at all except in adventure stories and academic theses, or in the military planning designed to crush their revolts or simply to wipe them out. In any event, their presence was never thought of as a factor limiting the scope for European settlement.

In one of the guides that France regularly published from the mid-nineteenth century for aspiring settlers in Algeria, and later in Tunisia and Morocco, we can read the following description:

> Tunisia offers ... a vast field for the activity of our fellow-countrymen. A farmer now vegetating on a little property without any hope of expanding it ... will find across the Mediterranean the means of giving his life a broader horizon. A large property-owner will find in colonization the means of lessening the impact of inheritance legislation, for he will be able to keep his whole estate in the hands of one of his children if, during his lifetime, he makes the moderate sacrifice of giving the others the means later to become landowners in Tunisia. It is impossible ... to list all the advantageous combinations that ... a colony whose good repute becomes daily more apparent can offer to well-advised individuals.[24]

And in the chapter on labour: 'There is little reason for building labourers or manual workers to come to Tunisia, because of the cheap
supply of manpower and the Arab, Italian, Maltese or Jewish competition.' The indigenous population appears in the rest of the document
only as part of the local scenery.

Still in 1953, the inhabitants of the colonies merited a little less than
one line in a French history textbook for schoolchildren in their final
year; it appears in a chapter on the forms of imperialism that included
'the invasion and conquest of regions inhabited by backward peoples'.
Those in the so-called 'new lands' are not even mentioned for the record:
'The main effects [of European emigration] have been the settlement of
the new lands ..., and their promotion, in varying degrees and at varying paces, to the rank of civilized countries and economic powers.'[25]

North Africa, moreover, was more densely inhabited, closer and more
familiar than other regions that became objects of occupation. Perhaps
this is why, to justify their settlement, French historians developed a
range of arguments beyond the mere necessity of satisfying a European
population in quest of living space – although Bugeaud, for one, preferred to keep it simple by arguing that 'Algeria needs a great invasion
like that of the Franks or the Goths'.[26]

But if others shared this kind of view,[27] closer to the brutal frankness
of conquerors from any past time or place than to the sophisticated
Western apparatus of justification, they were by no means a majority.
The West seems to have too lofty an idea of itself to make brute force
and self-interest the only reasons for its endeavours. Thus, in establishing
itself in North Africa, France was supposed to be carrying forward the
ancient torch of Latin civilization. It was probably the historian E.F.
Gautier who most clearly theorized this kind of right of return *avant la
lettre*, when he explained in the 1920s that North Africa experienced its
most brilliant period of civilization in Roman and Christian antiquity,
that it then became trapped in a historical oscillation between West and
East and underwent a millennium of stagnation amid 'Islamic slumber',
and that the European return in the form of colonization had again made
possible its regeneration. The Roman-Christian antecedent thus justified
French occupation against the illegitimate Arab-Muslim presence.

The limits of progress

In this kind of view, two types of population apart from the European
shared this planet. The first were mere savages still caught up in the

dross of animality; only colonization, by putting them in contact with higher forms of human life, could speed up their evolution. Other peoples, however, did not seem to qualify for the term 'primitive'. Since the Chinese, Indian, Arab or Persian worlds had created civilizations that were recognized as such by the West, they at least had some of the attributes of civilization, or had been plunged for centuries in an obscurantism from which only Western tutelage could raise them clear. Against empires deemed to have been worn out by their archaic features and frozen into immobility, European discourse opposed the dynamic character of its own modernity. It offered itself as a model to societies that a (perhaps genetic) incapacity held back from further evolution.

Once again, we need to remind ourselves that the European powers ceaselessly blocked any attempt at modernization in parts of the world they wished to dominate; the Egypt of Muhammad Ali and the Ottoman Empire offer well-known examples of this. We cannot know, of course, whether a hypothetical modernization of Egypt in the 1930s under a pasha of Albanian origin or the Ottoman Tanzimat reform movement could have resulted in changes that ushered in a modern society – and, if so, how much time would have been needed. What we do know is that the imperialist powers put an end as quickly as possible to any such attempt, most often through the use of force. In the 1830s, the state created by Muhammad Ali became an annoying rival to British interests in a crucial area of the Mediterranean. In 1840 Britain, carrying with it Prussia, Austria and Russia, used military means to terminate the Egyptian experiment and restore the authority of the Ottoman Empire over what had by then become a virtually independent province. The Porte then had the task of fully opening up the region to trade with Europe.[28]

Thus, in the first part of the nineteenth century two states – one east, one south of the Mediterranean – reacted to the advances of European imperialism by launching a modernization drive and attempting to join a process of globalization with a view to some profit for themselves. In addition to military force, the weapon of free trade was then deployed against their fledgling industries. It would prove useful in later times too.

We also know that, beginning around that time, Egypt and the Ottoman Empire became the theatre of a vast debate on modernity, and that a number of new ideas were introduced from Europe and discussed out. Here we must again underline the discrepancy between the West's words and deeds in all the episodes of its relationship with its others. In proclaiming itself the secular arm of progress, it exhorted the world to accept its inevitability and to comply with the prescriptions of modernity – but only on the (unstated) condition that the modernization of peripheral countries in accordance with its own model did not interfere with its interests.

Saturated with universality, Western discourse was also the bearer of a modernity which, to a greater degree than one usually thinks, captivated intellectuals in the less remote societies. Yet, for most of the colonial era, the European powers never ceased to favour archaic structures, to encourage immobilism and to base themselves upon the most conservative segments of societies that came within their sphere of influence. Once 'pacification' had been achieved, the conquerors everywhere forged alliances with local notables and repeatedly urged that nothing should be done that might undermine traditional hierarchies. On the contrary, they more than once relied on such hierarchies to organize the forms of colonial exploitation, and in many regions left chieftains and monarchs in control of their subjects.

If the West's discourse had limited itself to a mere defence of its interests, such practices might with good reason be considered commonplace. For it seems part of the logic of imperialist expansion and colonial occupation that the emergence of other nations should be held back, or that new forms of domination should be securely rooted in local powers enjoying greater authority than the new masters in return for the retention of their privileges. The problem is that, while the West endlessly trumpeted itself as the bearer of a modernity that would be of benefit to all, it shrank in horror from sharing those very benefits.

This contradiction goes a long way to explain some of the incoherent features of colonial policy in the twentieth century, as well as of subsequent Western strategies in the contemporary world. It also points forward to twentieth-century debates on the wisdom of the whole imperial enterprise. Nevertheless, these debates did not call into doubt the West's vocation to serve as the model for worldwide modernization; they bore, rather, upon the legitimacy of the means employed to globalize modernity, without shaking the culture of supremacy which reached its peak in the first few decades of the twentieth century. That culture has developed, of course, in response to each shock inflicted upon it by events in the world. But its roots are so deep, and its arguments draw upon such varied sources, that it is able to change its discourse at the margins while preserving the real essence of its structure.

FOUR

Continuity beneath Wrenching Changes

The early history of the East ... was marked by frequent migrations and resultant mingling of peoples, among which we may distinguish a number of important groups: the primitive peoples who had been in the East since the dawn of history (mainly the Hamites of Egypt and the Sumerians of Lower Mesopotamia); the Aegeans, whose origin is obscure; the Semites, who gave birth to Phoenicians and Hebrews, as well as Akkadians and Assyrians....

All these peoples were rather short in stature, had white or sometimes brownish skin, a rounded head and dark hair, although the Semites were taller than the others and their typical profile had quite a sharply hooked nose.

The Indo-Europeans or Aryans. While often powerful states were taking shape in the East, the plains of central and eastern Europe were inhabited by other people with a very white skin, blue eyes and especially fair and fine hair.... They worked iron ore ..., whereas the East knew only copper and bronze.

This long quotation, which revives all the themes of nineteenth-century physical anthropology, actually comes from a much later date. It appeared in a 1950 French textbook for use in the sixth grade, in line with a syllabus drawn up in 1947.[1] Thus in France, just a couple of years after the Second World War and the discovery of the first genocide at the very heart of European civilization, schoolchildren were still learning that Semites had a hooked nose and that fair-skinned Aryans were superior to their neighbours. They were also learning that 'by virtue of its civilization, which started to develop in contact with those of the East but outstripped them by far, Greece has played a role right at the forefront of history.'[2]

43

The textbook world

Post-war Western children learned many things. Their sisters and brothers in the United States were brought up on the pioneer epic, played at good cowboys and bad Indians, and knew little else about slavery than the events surrounding its abolition. They were not informed that much of their country was still living under a strict apartheid regime. Meanwhile children in Spain, raised in the cult of the Catholic Monarchs, heard about the Andalusian past only when their textbooks went over the glorious episodes of the *reconquista*; they had no idea that Ibn Rushd and Moses Ben Maimon were their distant compatriots.

Future citizens of the great European powers learned that colonial imperialism had meant 'the invasion and conquest of regions inhabited by backward peoples'.[3] They learned that Bugeaud, Faidherbe, Lyautey, Lord Cromer, Cecil Rhodes and Lord Kitchener were great men on whom they should model themselves. They were told nothing about Bugeaud's 'infernal columns', or about the methods used by Kitchener in the conquest of Sudan. The colonial empires were experiencing their first cracks, but the textbooks did not record the massacre at Sétif on 8 May 1945 or in Madagascar two years later. Admittedly, at that time the European powers were trying to save the key components of their overseas possessions.

Some ten years later, when decolonization was being completed, the language of French schoolbooks had not changed. The civilizing work of the conquerors was still acclaimed, and there was still the same silence about the horrendous crimes that had accompanied it. A first-grade manual published in 1961 is a model in this regard, not so much because it describes the Senegalese as 'little evolved' – which was then a pretty banal judgement – as because its language scarcely differs from that of the great age of conquest. Faidherbe, the top colonial cadre and governor of Senegal, appears as 'a friend of the natives who wanted to educate them'. And further on: 'At a moral level, European expansion was often beneficial.... Peace and order replaced constant guerrilla warfare.' But, alas, all this 'involved some unforeseen setbacks. There were feelings of disappointment at the natives' reaction to the expansion.... Instead of gratitude, the colonizers often encountered resentment or even rebellion. Why?'

In a chapter on decolonization, another textbook teaches that Indian independence in 1947 was due to a 'misunderstanding' between British and Indians, that a 'rush of nationalism' in 1951 drove Mussadeq in Iran to take over the Anglo-Iranian Oil Company, and that the decolonization of French Indo-China and the Dutch East Indies took place 'at the price of long and terrible ordeals' – for whom? being a question for which the young reader would be hard put to find an answer. She or he certainly learned that, before 'decolonization' (always written between inverted commas), 'troubles, sometimes very grave, occurred in several parts of Africa', but had no way of discovering the nature of their gravity.

Such was the knowledge that schoolchildren acquired in the 1960s to understand their epoch. As to their heritage, the textbook taught that the West was the single child of Greece (which first invented Reason), Rome and Christianity, and that 'the value which the European West most prizes is probably *respect for human beings*'. What was never spelt out were the humiliations endured by the Asian and African embodiments of 'human being'. In a pure Enlightenment tradition, abstract humanism made it possible to cover up the actual violations of human rights that the West continued to perpetrate.

In a different register, the school manuals of post-Franco Spain have not changed the way in which the past is regarded, despite a clear evolution in official and academic discourse to integrate the Andalusian period into the sweep of national history. Younger generations are still taught that the only 'real' Spaniards in the age of Al-Andaluz were Christians, and that the eight centuries of Arab presence were not really part of the country's history. In a book dating from 1992, for example, we read that 'some of the Christian population, the Mozarabs [living under Islamic rule], remained faithful to their religion and preserved their language and national awareness, even though they were unable to avoid gradual cultural contamination.' A secondary-school manual of history and geography published in 1989 taught that 'in 1525 Carlos I granted the Moors forty years to abandon their practices, but at the end of that period they had remained an inassimilable cyst'. The same attempt to preserve a minority culture in the face of majority domination was thus considered, in the Mozarab case, a claim to glory, and, in the Moors' case, proof that they were congenitally alien. With this to support them, schoolchildren could easily justify the expulsion of the last Muslims from the country in 1609. A manual published in 1992 stated that 'the Arab invasion altered Spanish history in all its aspects'.[4]

In the United States, the wave of 'political correctness' that began to sweep the country in the 1980s did not render obsolete a belief in the 'manifest destiny' of the race of pioneers. The occupation of frontier lands was still presented in most history textbooks as a legitimate enterprise corresponding to historical necessity, even if it should have been carried out with less inhumanity. The tone usually evolved, but without calling into question the foundations of official history. The manuals began to give at least a partial account of the crimes and systematic treaty violations committed against Indians during the conquest of the West, and to recognize that 'the solution to the Indian question' most often took the form of organized massacres.[5] Similarly, they now dwell more than they used to on a possible conflict between glorification of liberty as the basis of the American republic and the preservation of black slavery. But American history remains the history of the great white epic, whose deviations are redeemed by the efforts of 'good' whites to calm the deadly passions of overhasty pioneers or to end the old-fashioned slave system of the Southern planters.[6] Although the cruelty of Indians and the savagery of blacks no longer dominate the accounts, it cannot be said that either Indians or blacks appear as actors in their own right.

Did nothing happen in the twentieth century, then, for the dogmas invented in previous centuries to lose their self-evident quality, or for young Westerners to stop learning that they came from a higher form of humanity? How can we explain that the certainties of the nineteenth century were able to survive the seismic shifts of the twentieth? Three key elements mark out the evolution of the culture of supremacy which, though sometimes flagging, also picked up new strength by changing its language. These elements are: communism and the way it saw relations with the non-European Other; shock waves from the genocide committed by Nazi Germany; and decolonization.

Communist contradictions

It is a truism that communism marked a radical break. From its birth amid the mass graves of the First World War, the communist movement was the only political current of its time to challenge the very principle, not just the forms, of colonization. It alone applied to the colonial context the phrase that Marx, the founder of the First International, had used of the Irish question: 'A nation that oppresses another cannot itself be free.' It alone, at the end of the war, called for the independence of countries that were part of colonial empires.

The eighth of the twenty-one conditions for admission to the Communist International, adopted at its second congress in 1920, stipulated:

> A particularly marked and clear attitude on the question of the colonies and the oppressed nations is necessary on the part of the communist parties of those countries whose bourgeoisies are in possession of colonies and oppress other nations. Every party that wishes to belong to the Communist International has the obligation of exposing the dodges of its 'own' imperialists in the colonies, of supporting every liberation movement in the colonies not only in words but in deeds, of demanding that their imperialist compatriots should be thrown out of the colonies, of cultivating in the hearts of the workers in their own country a truly fraternal relationship to the working population in the colonies and to the oppressed nations, and of carrying out systematic propaganda among their own country's troops against any oppression of colonial peoples.[7]

In the actual colonies, any existing communist parties long remained the only formations spanning communities and nations. In the Arab world, for example, they contained the whole national–religious mosaic of Syria, Egypt, Palestine or Tunisia, even if they did not exactly reflect its proportions.[8]

At no point, however, either during their successive peaks before and after the Second World War[9] or during the anti-colonial upsurges that they supported – one thinks of the campaign in favour of Abd El-Krim and the Rif liberation war in Morocco, or the independence struggle in Indo-China, led, it is true, by a sister party – at no point did the communists impel a real challenge to the conceptual foundations of Western supremacy that matched their weight in society. This strange fact may be due to the way in which the colonial question was constantly manipulated by the Western epigones of the CPSU, in line with Moscow's shifting political alliances in Europe. Despite the early principled actions, the emancipation of the colonies was not a priority for Comintern or Cominform strategists; it served as a useful irritant when the task was to make life difficult for a bourgeois government not allied to the Soviet Union.

In any event, for the theorists of the communist movement, colonial emancipation would arrive in the wake of revolutions in the imperialist heartlands. Just as supporters of colonization exalted the civilizing mission of the West, the model of emancipation – for the professors of the International – could come only from the European proletariat. A resolution passed in 1922 by the Sidi-Bel-Abbès branch of the Algerian

Communist Party, even if it was criticized at the time, expressed the feelings of a not insignificant section of communist cadres: 'A victorious uprising of the Muslim masses of Algeria which did not come after a victorious uprising of the proletarian masses in the metropolis would inevitably lead in Algeria to a return to a regime close to feudalism, and that cannot be the aim of any communist action.'[10] Moreover, when a national liberation movement inverted the order of priorities laid down by the European revolutionary vanguard, it found itself being combated by the communists. In the end, the latter would rally to nationalist formations only when they were in a weak position in relation to them – that is, when such a formation was proving its capacity to carry with it a colonial people more concerned about its own liberation than about the world revolution.

However far 'international solidarity' may sometimes have gone, for the USSR and the communist movement as a whole the colonial question remained subordinate to the struggles of the proletariat in the imperialist centres – and to the interests of the Soviet Union. If the communists thought the oppressed peoples were right in their drive for emancipation, they were prepared to help them achieve it so long as this did not upset the political agenda of the International; what they never really questioned, however, was the 'natural' right of the West to hold a monopoly of thinking and to present itself as the only true subject of history.

Was this an original sin? Enough has been written about the extent to which the founding fathers Marx and Engels were moulded by their time. And, despite Marx's brief flashes of insight into certain non-European modes of production, his Eurocentric inheritance – as a legitimate offspring of the narcissistic universalism of the Enlightenment and German philosophy – could lead him to write: 'Indian society has no history at all, at least no known history. What we call its history is but the history of the successive intruders who founded their empires on the passive basis of that unresisting and unchanging society.'[11] As to Engels's often brilliant work *Origins of the Family, Private Property and the State*, which takes the unity of the human spirit as beyond dispute, one can nevertheless clearly see the influence of the anthropology of his time and the ersatz culturalism of post-Darwinian evolutionism.

Finally, we know that Marx himself and a number of later Marxist thinkers subscribed to the colonial enterprise, on the grounds that it was hastening the entry of precapitalist societies into the sphere of capitalism and thereby (certainly without wishing it) the advent of world communism. Thus Marx believed that 'England has a double mission to fulfil in India: one destructive, the other regenerating – the annihilation of old Asiatic society, and the laying of the material foundations of Western society in Asia.'[12] In his late writings, it is true, Marx partly recognized the possibilities of progress contained within precapitalist structures, but he continued to think that the only signal for progress could come from the West.

Although twentieth-century communists were steeped in an egalitarian political tradition going far back into the history of Europe and finding global expression in internationalism, they inherited nothing that might have allowed them to make a clean sweep of the hierarchical constructions of the world that formed the basis of their culture. Indeed, their leaders and members were children of that same self-assured Europe which thought it was accelerating progress wherever it deployed its weapons, its industries or its working-class vanguard.

Thus, while their discourse (with all its ambiguities and contradictions) extended the universalism of the Enlightenment, communists reproduced the models stemming from the culture of supremacy with which they were imbued, and of which paternalism represented the politically acceptable version. A report on communism and the colonies presented at the first congress of the PCF in Marseilles, in December 1921, emphasized: 'Another difficulty lies in the almost general inability of the indigenous peoples to emancipate themselves. They have no revolutionary past.... Our efforts to emancipate them, and to gain their assistance thereby for our revolutionary action, will not be seriously supported by them, at least not at first.'[13] A document from around the same date alludes to the difficulties of mixing in a colonial situation: 'Efforts must be made to ensure that each branch has indigenous components. On this, it must be said that there are many indigenous people in branches in France, but very few in Algeria. No doubt this has to do with their prejudice and fear about how they will be received by European comrades in Algeria.'[14]

Such efforts were undoubtedly made, and they helped to give non-European communist parties the appearance of counter-societies operating within strongly communalist environments. Yet the Eurocentric hegemonism of comrades from the metropolitan country put off a good number of 'indigenous elements', after their initial attraction to the first Western discourse that accepted the legitimacy of their aspirations. Aimé Césaire gave voice to these disappointments in his letter of resignation to the PCF in 1956, by listing the evident faults we notice among all members of the French Communist Party: their inveterate assimilationism; their unconscious chauvinism; their pretty simplistic faith – which they share with European bourgeois – in the all-round superiority of the West; their belief that evolution as it has occurred in Europe is the only possible and the only desirable form ...; and, to sum it all up, their rarely admitted but nevertheless real belief in civilization with a capital C. If the goal of all progressive politics is one day to give the colonial peoples back their freedom, then at least the day-to-day activity of progressive parties should not conflict with the desired end and should not every day destroy the very foundations ... of that future freedom.[15]

Communist contradictions, the timidity expressed in such positions as the PCF's membership of the Union française in the 1950s or its repeated references to 'French grandeur' and 'the interests of France' after it joined the government in 1945 and again at the start of the war in Algeria,[16] were not only in a line of descent coming from Marx and Lenin; nor were they only the result of Soviet calculations. They also reflected the ambivalence of Western working classes with regard to colonial enterprises from which they, not as much as others but they too, received the dividends. The anti-capitalist and messianic rhetoric of communism enabled it, with some rare and partial exceptions, to skimp on analysing the relationship of European working classes to the question of colonialism or later immigration, as well as the question of gender relations. Since racism, sexism, anti-Semitism and colonialism were all vices of capitalism destined to go under with it, the proletariat was, so to speak, naturally free from them.

The selective tracing of a philosophical and political line of descent, the obscuring of the cultural matrix of Marxism and Leninism, the identification of class division as the only meaningful one in history, enabled communists to exclude any other factor from their analysis of relations of domination. The Western working classes were exonerated from any responsibility in colonial exploitation or the eruption of nationalism in Europe.

And yet, when imperialist exploitation reached its climax in the first half of the twentieth century, it helped to tighten the grip of poverty in which the Western working classes were held. It is not a question of downplaying the decisive role of the workers' struggles that punctuated the history of industrialization and wrested concessions from the employers. But the successive social advances in the West since the beginning of the twentieth century have in part been paid for by crumbs from the increased exploitation of colonial peoples and non-indigenous immigrant subproletariats.[17]

As they rose to the level of a wage-earning aristocracy, the indigenous working classes changed their strategy. Western Europe did not witness any major working-class revolts after the First World War. The crushing of the Spartacist movement in defeated post-imperial Germany marked the end of the violent phase of class struggles, which were henceforth expressed within a framework of bourgeois legality. As the century wore on, the gradual conversion of the workers' parties to reformism went together with a more ambivalent attitude to the nationalist movements that were beginning to shake the colonial empires. Exploited but also indirectly exploiting, the Western proletariat expressed its contradictions through the discourse of its political leaderships.

This combination of factors explains why, despite its egalitarian principles, communism was unable to build a coherent alternative to the culture of supremacy. In fact, it offered a new variant of that culture, by attributing to the proletariat of the capitalist countries the messianic task of freeing the world from oppression. In this respect, communism did not carry within it a cultural revolution.

Around Nazism

If the (at least partial) failure of communism to bring the West's colonial periphery into the sphere of egalitarian relations confirmed that the culture of supremacy had taken root, National Socialism posed questions of a different order. In what sense can the genocide committed under its banner be described as unique, and why did people in the West assign it that quality? Why, at the end of the war, did they show such stupefaction at the 'discovery' of Nazi crimes? Does Nazism appear as inventor or inheritor in the history of the West? Should it be considered an accident, or a monstrous but logical consummation of a possibility already present for centuries, since the *reconquista* and Spain's campaign for 'purity of blood'? Let us take this a little further. Was the Europe of the Third Reich unique in seeking to exterminate Jews, Gypsies and assorted 'degenerates', or only in giving particular forms to that goal?

Enough has been written about the unprecedented industrialization of genocide and the criminal bureaucracy in charge of the whole chain leading to the death camps, and enough emphasis has been placed on

the extraordinary sadism of Hitler's butchers, for me not to have to
dwell here on the originality of the Nazi killing machine. But can the
act of genocide itself be characterized as novel in the history of the
West? We have seen that, from the plains of the American Midwest to
the bush of the African South West, sons of Europe quite ruthlessly
employed the weapon of extermination to clear a way for their own
settlement. We know that over a long period of time honourable thinkers
produced theories *ad nauseam* to justify such actions, deploying arguments that evoked the superiority of conquering races and the need to
open new spaces for their expansion. The Nazi theorists, then, could
scarcely have felt that they were innovating. It is true that they turned
for inspiration to the extreme champions of eugenics, but we have
already seen that these did not have a monopoly on racial discourse; the
leaders of the democracies also made ample use of it. In 1924 the United
States introduced measures to restrict the entry of 'racially inferior'
persons, and in Britain and France the glorification of the virtues of the
white race, in Gallic or Anglo-Saxon garb, was continually used during
the pre-war period to justify imperial domination.

Thus, neither the obsession with purity, nor the certainty of belonging to a higher form of humanity, nor the will to carve out 'living space'
should be credited to Hitler and his associates as their own invention,
just as neither their genocidal aim nor their arguments in support of it
were peculiar to Nazi barbarism. I do not want to be misunderstood: it
is not my intention here to 'banalize evil', in Hannah Arendt's words,
but to recall that evil had already been banalized for a long time.

Apart from the practicalities of extermination, the uniqueness of
Nazism comes down to the fact that it brought genocide into Europe
itself and that this operation 'had no point'. In setting itself up as the
shrine of civilization, the West became convinced that, even if it was
sometimes forced to use methods incredibly like those of 'barbarians',
barbarism was alien to its very essence. Remember how the French
government defended its smoking-out operations in Algeria in 1845: 'In
Europe such a deed would be terrible, loathsome. In Africa it is the
reality of war. How else would you like it to be waged?' Besides, the
genocide in America or Africa was always 'utilitarian': it was necessary
to clear spaces, or to crush local resistance. One did not exterminate for
the fun of it; one's hand was forced by the lack of space or the reluctance of indigenous peoples to knuckle under. The Nazis, in a way,
carried their obsession with purity to an irrational level, believing in the
superiority of their race as the ground for utterly pointless genocide.

Should we conclude with Césaire that, in the eyes of Westerners, the only sin of Nazism was to have committed the crime of genocide at the heart of Europe, and that Hitler's Germany was held accountable for that transgression alone?[18]

Although it is difficult to accept this as the only reason (weighty though it certainly was) for the intolerable quality of Nazism for the Western mind, Césaire's point should prompt us to look into the way in which Europeans tried to explain that 'accursed share' of their history. During the first few decades after the war, they obscured the fact that Hitler's sinister enterprise might have had something to do with that history. The Frankfurt School of Adorno and Horkheimer was then alone in pressing further and questioning Enlightenment thought itself; they even went back to Renaissance humanism and found the opposite of what it proclaimed – the signs of a totalitarianism of intolerance. They were for long the only theoreticians to see in Hitlerism a direct descendance, not a sharp break.[19]

More generally, Europeans took time to recognize – some never did – that the genocide of Jews was an action that had been prepared by ages of religious and racial hatred, a long century of theorized secular anti-Semitism to which all the ideological families made their contribution, decades of hysterical calls for murder of 'the enemies of the human race'. They gradually accepted that this long past had made it possible for a majority of the population of Europe not to see the horror under its very eyes, not to want to know that it was happening, and for the leaders of the major democracies fighting Germany not to do anything to prevent an extermination whose scale they very soon had the means to detect.

Yet, if most Europeans now seem willing to accept this responsibility, many still do not admit that the (widely supported) massacres and the genocide[20] in parts of the world under Western domination might have played some role in the spread of Nazi theories and made it easier for Nazi crimes to be accepted in Europe itself. They suggest that indifference to horror is the reason why some peoples who suffered the worst of colonial cruelty find it difficult to understand what is so unique about Nazism. Worse, apart from some tiny minorities, Europeans have generally pushed those massacres out of their memory, as if following Renan's injunction: 'Forgetting history, and, I would even say, mistakes about history, are a key factor in nation-building.'[21] Not long ago, a French historian commenting on a work of history could describe the nineteenth century (1814–1914) as 'relatively lacking in violence, if one thinks of the carnage that preceded and followed it' – a phrase that manages to obscure the bloody adventures that accompanied European expansion.[22]

The trauma that the Nazis' vast charnel house represented for Europeans led to some acceptance of collective responsibility in the genocide of the Jews, but it did not lead to a broader focus on the deadly consequences of Western racial discourse. This incomplete awareness had two contradictory dimensions: it delegitimized the whole range of racial-eugenic arguments and made it impossible for this version of racism to become publicly respectable; but it did not radically alter the gaze that the West had previously cast upon its non-European Other.

Colonial upheavals

From 1945 onward, Europeans could no longer legitimate their supremacy in terms of genetic superiority. The Nazis had given proof that certain kinds of discourse had the capacity to kill, and resistance to their barbarism in the occupied countries had risen up in the name of universalist principles (alongside appeals to patriotism) that postulated the absolute equality of all human beings. It was also in the name of these principles – and to defend freedom – that the English-speaking democracies waged war against Germany, while for their part the Soviet Union and the communist parties laid claim to the emancipatory content of proletarian universality. The victors of a war in which millions died because they were racially 'other' therefore saw it as their duty to reject out of hand any discourse of racial inequality. The adoption of the Universal Declaration of Human Rights in 1948 was intended to give solemn expression to this rejection, and it is true that racist discourse was in retreat in the years following the end of the war.

This shift was not without consequence for relations between the metropolitan countries and their colonies, since physical inferiority of the colonial subjects could no longer be used to justify occupation. Nevertheless, the new Western awareness was never complete. Most people in Europe and North America continued to scorn 'non-whites', and various powerful interests campaigned for the maintenance of empire, even if it required modernizing the forms of exploitation. This led not to the death agony of the culture of supremacy but to its reformulation in more acceptable terms; the collective consciousness was more convinced than ever, after victory over the Beast, that it was the repository of humanist universality, while at the same time retaining its certainty of superiority.

The evolution of discourse, still with its sharp contrasts, took place against a backdrop of violence. The West, which, in order to forget its share of darkness, wanted more than ever to think of itself as the inheritor of the Enlightenment, once more displayed that fascinating schizophrenia which had marked its whole history. It expelled from its repertoire anything that might recall the anthropological racism of the pre-war years, leaving the far right in exclusive possession of that embarrassing legacy, and it condemned the aberrant ideas that led to Nazi mass murder and built itself up as the worldwide champion of freedom. Yet Europe also proceeded to stage an impressive series of colonial massacres, while in the south of the United States a legal regime of apartheid continued to classify Negroes as subhuman and ruthlessly punished any threat to the purity of the master race.

Less pragmatic than Britain, which soon came to see that the time had come for decolonization, France distinguished itself after 1945 by the brutality of its attempts to reassert authority in its empire, notwithstanding some cosmetic measures to calm the colonial peoples. A long list of bloody acts of repression testifies to France's obstinate refusal to give up its possessions – from the Sétif massacres in 1945 to those in Madagascar in 1947, not to speak of the hundreds of thousands killed during the wars in Indo-China and Algeria.[23] Now, these massacres and the dreadful crimes that accompanied them, such as the general use of torture against nationalist prisoners, took place in the fifteen years following the Second World War, when French men and women still had a keen memory of German atrocities during the occupation and when official France celebrated the heroes of the Resistance. From de Gaulle to the Socialists who led a number of governments in the Fourth Republic, the same people who prided themselves on having liberated their country from foreign oppression ordered the colonial massacres of the post-war period. The main factors in this strange splitting – apart from the alignment of most of the French political class with the ultras of the colonial lobby and the extension of a cold war logic to the treatment of nationalist movements – were the continued perception of non-Europeans as inferior and the notion that they were blind to the progress brought by the tutelage of civilized nations.

Although the grading of nations by their proximity to civilization no longer rested upon physical characteristics, it continued to impose itself with the force of a certainty. The centre of civilization had not moved:

it was still the West which was spreading its benefits. During those years, the discourse of supremacy adapted to the new requirements, as the field of Western superiority was reorganized around the dimensions of technology, science, economics and culture.

There were no longer 'primitive peoples', although the term did not yet disappear entirely from the vocabulary of the West. Now they were 'backward nations', whose elites had to understand that they had nothing to gain from breaking the link with their guardians. The fact that they did not understand the nature of this link and insisted on an independence for which they were not yet 'ripe' proved their lack of discernment and the incompleteness of their conversion to progress. Together with the theme of ingratitude, the immaturity of the colonial peoples crops up like a refrain in most of the speeches delivered by apologists for the colonial order. In an interview on 26 June 1947 with Ferhat Abbas, who had come to submit a proposal for an Algerian republic federated with France, the French president Vincent Auriol replied:

> You have never been a state, and you were delivered from servitude.... Besides, you yourself are the living symbol of what France has done. You were nurtured on our own milk and our own culture, as were all those now wishing to break French unity. But what will you do without France? What is it you want?[24]

A few months later, de Gaulle said his piece during a visit to Algiers: 'The well-meaning French intend that France shall continue its work in the interest of all Algerians.'[25]

As if the stock of justifications for supremacy was running low, an argument as old as the earliest conquests gained a new lease of life on the threshold of the great movement of decolonization: namely, the duty to stay with peoples from childhood to adulthood before releasing them from guardianship. A number of supporters of decolonization, though favouring the emancipation of oppressed peoples on grounds of justice, were also not convinced that they had reached a sufficient degree of 'maturity' to take control of their fate. Paul Ricoeur, for instance, one of the first French intellectuals to come out in support of independence for the colonies, and one of the first to say that 'the original fault of colonization preceded any one-sided aggression on the part of the indigenous population', defended the thirst for freedom among the colonized peoples – but he did so in a phrase that was not lacking in ambiguity: 'The demand for liberty, even if premature, carries greater moral weight than all the civilizing work of the colonizers.'[26]

Primitives no longer existed, or did so only as vestiges of another age, yet fear of the savage had not disappeared. The violence of Algerian nationalist reactions to the brutal repression was commonly explained by the savagery of peoples among whom civilization was still only a thin veneer. Most of the French press and public opinion considered that the real massacres of Europeans at Sétif on 8 May 1945 or in Saigon in September of the same year were proof that those who had committed them were still incapable of mastering their true nature. Only a minority of intellectuals suggested some relationship between the violence of the occupied and the violence of the occupier. And subsequently, in the 1950s, the ever more numerous presence of people from the remaining empires or post-colonial countries – Indians, Pakistanis and West Indians in Britain, Algerians and West Indians in France – gave new vigour to racist arguments that had been knocked off balance by the post-war recompositions. We shall return to this below.

The period of doubts

During the post-war years, then, the culture of supremacy underwent change but did not disappear, continuing to benefit from all the channels that maintained its place in popular culture. Are we right, then, to speak of a change in the relationship of Westerners to the rest of world during those years of global change? The fact is that it never evolved so much as it did in the third quarter of the twentieth century. For, although Westerners kept an acute sense of their own superiority, although their schools continued to diffuse certainties as if they were eternal, and although the world was still seen as inhabited by peoples at a lower level of evolution, the Other now burst through into the very core of the West. Unlike in previous centuries, it existed not by unsuccessfully trying to resist the terrible strike force of the conquerors, but by reviving a long-lost historical initiative and using for that purpose a language intelligible to the masters.

Now the Other existed by virtue of speaking the same language. Of course, India was still characterized by its starving masses, but Gandhi and Nehru addressed Mountbatten as equals. The exotic China of mandarins and warlords was vanishing beneath portraits of Marx and Lenin. Africa and the Maghreb remained 'deep' and inscrutable, but Nkrumah quoted Locke, and Bourguiba Auguste Comte. Aimé Césaire called upon black poets to 'brown' (*marronner*) the French language,[27] while Kateb

Yacine appropriated it as 'war booty' to write his *Nedjma*. In the United States, blacks wielded the Constitution to demand their rights, forced open the doors of buses and universities, shouted that they were equal, and said they dreamed of an America that would welcome them as citizens. Poets, novelists, polemicists, philosophers and politicians, born under colonial rule in the vast band of the tropics, began to demand explanations and to call for freedom in the name of the rights that the West said it was proud to have invented. Intellectuals of what would later become the third world had already demonstrated on occasions before the Second World War. But it was after 1945 that they really came out into the open.

We shall analyse below the huge misunderstanding caused by the West's illusion that it had produced exact replicas of itself. But for the moment let us just note that the intellectuals of Europe and North America, or at least a large number of them, found that they had gained a following and began to listen as others spoke like themselves to say different things and to announce the end of submission. In a mixture of pride (since those new men were their pupils) and remorse that they had so long undervalued the histories and cultures now being revealed to them, these intellectuals took up the cause of the often armed revolts of the 1950s and the new states that emerged out of the death agony of empire. Once again the misunderstandings were legion, although they were not yet noticed.

For the first time in centuries, the certainties began to totter. A huge wave of doubt engulfed a not insignificant section of the Western intelligentsia as the ground shook beneath their feet. Now it was a question not just of criticizing the forms of worldwide expansion that were part of their history, but of arguing that the very principle of domination could never claim legitimacy and of accepting the humanity they recognized in others. For the first time since it was invented, the concept of universal Man ceased to be a convenient abstraction fitted to the interests of real Western men and took on the multiple features of the human race.

The times were certainly changing. Great writers were discovered in different, unsuspected places. Sartre wrote for Fanon's emblematic *Wretched of the Earth* a preface that placed Europe's 'old, oft-repeated crimes' in the dock,[28] while historians like Basil Davidson discovered Africa 'before the whites'.[29] Spurred on by a sense of internationalism (of which the communists made themselves the ambivalent champions), many Western activists would place themselves at the service of nations which seemed to be awakening to liberty and to have 'everything to learn' from them.

The decolonization period marked a break in the history of the West, even if the West still weighed down the world with its power and was far from vacating the top of a pyramid of its own design. For the first time since the Renaissance, it was forced into retreat and watched as the world map was redrawn for it. For the first time, a 'non-traditional' intellectual and political elite was emerging in what people started to call the 'third world', and was proclaiming its determination to organize it outside Western control. For the first time, too, the words that the West had used for centuries to conceal its global grip beneath a cloak of virtue began to turn against it. Its subjects learned how to use those words, believed in them and manipulated them in their turn, and in doing so they made them weapons for their own liberation.

It is quite understandable that such wrenching changes led a section of Westerners to revise their firmly held convictions, to admit the obvious fact that others also had rights and legitimate grounds to demand that they be exercised. Along the way, some were no longer content to recognize humanity in others, but gradually saw them as equals. This differentiated them from their predecessors between the two world wars – from the surrealists to André Gide or Albert Londres – who had reached only a limited public with their violent denunciations or their stark descriptions of the effects of Western hegemony. Now the challenging of old dogmas became the open activity of whole groups, who, if not a majority, were large enough to be heard.

We need to assess the scale of what then appeared, rightly, to be a revolution. Some wondered why it had taken so long to recognize equality in others and – especially as they had not really got over Europe's totalitarian lurches – sharply raised the question of Europe's collective responsibility for denial of that equality. Never had doubts run so deep. Never since the Enlightenment had the West so intensely questioned its relationship to the world or, rather, its inability to maintain with the rest of the world relations that were not based on subjugation. Unlike in the Enlightenment, however, the doubt at the core of the Western intellectual machine was now the result of a direct encounter with the Other.

Thinkers in the seventeenth and eighteenth centuries had mainly been concerned to challenge the divine legitimacy of royal power and, with this in mind, to create a man who was human before he was a believer or a ruler's subject. The birth of 'free men equal before the law', essential to the new world for which they sought to lay the foundations, led them to consider the fate of those left out of such freedom and equality and, in some cases, to contest the reasons for it. But the Other did not really wear different clothes from those of the 'Negro from Surinam',[30] and neither Louis Delgrès nor Toussaint L'Ouverture managed to alter the images that Europeans or their worthy sons in America had of that Other. Nearly two centuries later, the opposite approach was taken and the trauma was greater. The men of the Enlightenment voted on their own initiative for the liberty of a world that was theirs. Westerners in the 1950s and 1960s had to accept that others were snatching it away from them.

In much the same way that the turmoil of the Enlightenment opened a new chapter in Western history, the recomposition of the world that began in the third quarter of the twentieth century inaugurated a period that we still do not really know how to read. Did it herald the end of a hegemony that the West had difficulty registering, and whose effects it tried relatively successfully to prolong? Or, in altering the shape of world geopolitics, did it merely usher in a new era in the long history of Western supremacy? Did that supremacy simply change its forms to keep up with the requirements of a changing world, or did it weaken before the many unconcerted efforts to bring it to an end? In other words, were the two decades of redrawing the world map a kind of interregnum during which the West was forced to yield ground before recovering it in different forms? Or did they mark the chaotic dawning of an epoch when the West would gradually lose control? The rest of this book will try to provide some answers to these questions. The moment of transition – whether between two forms of the same hegemony or two different epochs of human history – was in any case a moment of doubt.

Alternative messiahs?

Post-war Europe and America asked themselves questions; the next generation went a stage further. In the 1970s a section of Western youth, no longer just averse to fighting for the imperialism that it considered the most implacable enemy, looked around for new idols among the once inferior peoples of the world. Waving portraits of Uncle Ho on demonstrations, its more radical fringe went to learn what they thought was revolution in the Palestinian camps, and its mentors had such names as Mao Tse-tung or Angela Davis. German–Palestinian commandos hijacked aircraft, and their Japanese counterparts, in the name of a better future, machine-gunned tourists at Lod airport in Israel.[31] What was called 'third worldism' was then at its height.

But what was the meaning of this paroxysmal challenge? What was the context in which it arose? Once again, the paradoxes were legion during those decades when sons worshipped what their fathers had burned, but also when both fathers and sons sought to recreate alterity in their own image and seemed to accept the emancipation of others only on condition that they aspire to become like themselves in every respect.

This wish took two forms, contemporary with each other. Thirdworldist messianism and the theory of stages of development seemed at first sight antinomic, but were in fact two variations of the same tendency to appropriate the Other more than expressions of a new contradiction of the West. As always, reality partly eluded the categories intended to grasp its meaning. Third-worldism was not devised by some Machiavellian figure to impose on the peoples of the South his own interpretation of the meaning of history. The young rebels amid Western affluence – who had broken with communist parties more concerned to bury their own past mistakes by praising third-world regimes 'with a socialist orientation' – supported and sometimes joined guerrilla forces in the tropics, in the belief that they were participating in the advent of global happiness. The dominant theories of development, for their part, had also involved much trial and error and a conviction that no one should be condemned to remain underdeveloped. But a moment's reflection on these two chapters in North–South relations should allow us to see that, beyond the profusion of ideas and the dreams incorporated within them, they expressed the certainty of a Western intelligentsia that it 'naturally' held a monopoly on thought. Revolution, like development, could therefore be to them only a copy of the history of the West.

The Western proletariat had been growing more bourgeois. During the thirty-year 'golden age' that followed the Second World War, dreams of justice partly became reality through the welfare policies introduced in Western Europe and North America. The spread of mass consumption standardized lifestyles, making desires more attainable and inequalities less bearable. Now the proletariat had something to lose, and it preferred to extend its material gains rather than risk everything in perilous adventures. The international order resulting from the East–

West divide was anyway there to discourage them. In the eastern part of Europe, where a Soviet freeze prevented any challenge, the imposition of 'actually existing socialism' was supposed to correspond to their aspirations. Nowhere was revolution part of the agenda. Only women, who waged decisive struggles and occupied public space as never before, could use that word to describe the changes they led.

Since the masses of the rich countries seemed to want no more than reforms to their lot, and since the only revolutionary changes since 1945 had occurred in the South, a younger generation began in the 1960s to reverse the communist theses of the inter-war period by appointing the 'wretched of the earth' as the new bearers of a revolutionary impetus absent in the old working-class heartlands. The only revolution to occur at that time in the West – the 'carnation revolution' in Portugal in 1974 that overthrew the last descendant of European fascism – seemed to confirm the correctness of their vision. For the Portuguese army captains had learned their political lessons while fighting the maquis in Guinea-Bissau and the other African colonies; there they had read Amilcar Cabral and even approached the leaders of the liberation struggles in Cape Verde, Angola and Mozambique. The main protagonists of the Portuguese revolution stressed that it had begun in Africa, through real ties with a new generation of African ideologists.

Yet this changed perspective did not, as one might think, entail recognition that the peoples of the South were capable of again weaving the cloth of their own history. These were invested with a messianic mission, but only on condition that their vanguards did not stray from the reading lists and organizational principles laid down by the founding fathers. The facts were certainly imposing some adjustment. Chinese reality, and its theorization by leaders of the Communist Party, had raised the peasantry to the status of principal actor in the revolutionary epic. Similarly, whereas a few decades earlier the Communist International had viewed national liberation struggles with the deepest suspicion, Marxist theorists of the 1960s and 1970s legitimated them as a 'national stage' in the revolutionary process and, in the absence of authentic revolutions to get their teeth into, sowed constant confusion between two different types and logics of struggle. Attachment of the revolutionary label to the Algerian war of liberation and then the Palestinian struggle for national existence was the clearest example of this conflation.

We shall return to the way in which certain local elites instrumentalized this mimetic obsession for their own benefit. For the moment let us just note the wish of the Western left to uncover on all sides vanguard parties in which it could place its revolutionary hopes. Its mania for describing hegemonic liberation movements as the 'only legitimate representative' of the peoples in question helped to smooth the way for the post-colonial single parties.

We are touching here on one of the dramas of the decolonized South: the fact that, whereas Euro-American social democrats discredited themselves by conducting colonial or imperialist wars (from Algeria to Vietnam), the liberation movements that became state-builders after independence found their most solid external support in a section of the Western elites then breaking with the 'formal liberties' of a 'bourgeois democracy' that they held guilty of too many crimes, including the crime of colonization. In the name of what they saw as the priorities, this radical European left closed its eyes to the political hijacking operated by those they considered their protégés, and to the violations of rights from which they themselves benefited. In their communist, Trotskyist or Maoist guises,[32] they attempted for two decades to make the revolution vicariously.

The failure, as one might have expected, was all too evident. Yet the end of revolutionary dreams, rapidly become nightmares in many countries of the South, did not lead to the self-questioning that one might have expected about the redemptive role of the peoples of the third world. Once the hopes placed in them were disappointed, the dreams shifted from the realm of politics to the spheres of development and charity.

The particular case of Latin America confirms the truth of this observation. So far, I have deliberately not mentioned Fidel Castro and Che Guevara among the exotic idols of Western youth. For Iberian America, at once familiar and remote, has a special status in the Western consciousness. The forms in which it achieved sovereignty in the early decades of the nineteenth century, under the banner of the Enlightenment, were closer to the secession of the United States from the mother country than to the independence victories of the second half of the twentieth century, and they permanently established in power elites whose origins went back to the European metropolis. 'A hybrid, polycultural and multiracial area, Iberian America seized the opportunity of the French Revolution to become in one leap modern, progressive and Western, leaving behind Spanish, Indian and black "barbarism".'[33] These white elites, which constituted an ever smaller minority of the population as one moved out from the Southern Cone, were everywhere politically and economically hegemonic, and before turning to the United States they continued to regard Europe as their spiritual home. 'Indigenist' movements among a section of intellectuals did not prevent transatlantic exchanges from enjoying a virtual monopoly over the formation of thought. The Western intelligentsia has always been grateful to Latin Americans for evidence of their loyalty as the 'interchangeable face of the West',[34] and has rewarded them for this by taking them under its wing.

This long history of closeness meant that in the 1960s Western revolutionaries were on familiar intellectual ground in Latin America as they indulged their dreams of exoticism, and that Latin American revolutionaries were often closer to their European cousins than to compatriots who were 'Indian, black, creole, mestizo, mulatto or one of a thousand other intermediate shades'.[35] Some – but that is another story – saw in this gap one of the reasons for the failure of the guerrilla movements of the 1960s. Latin America's 'Westernness' has certainly forged across the Atlantic ties of shared identity much stronger than those it has with other continents of the South. Thus, the 1973 coup in Chile that brought down the government of Salvador Allende was perceived almost as an internal affair of the West, as was the struggle of the Brazilian left against the dictatorship. And intellectuals fleeing military repression were welcomed with open arms by their Western colleagues.

For these Western colleagues, in fact, the North–South divide was never geographic but cut whole societies in two. Without clearly formulating or even perceiving the tendency, they integrated the Latin American elites into their own political reading of history and sent the coloured masses off into the fields of development and charity, as they had done with Africans and then Asians once the illusion of redemptive messianism had passed. The infatuation of Western youth with the revolutionary romanticism embodied by Che represented a kind of acme of this illusion: it cherished its own double in the *barbudos* of guerrilla warfare, while believing that it was opening out towards the Other.

An economic model

The economic side of this wish to reduce the Other to oneself, through which the culture of supremacy was expressed in the period under consideration, seems at first sight easier to analyse. Although the liberal and Marxist schools differ profoundly in their reading of underdevelopment, the solutions they offer to so-called underdeveloped countries resemble each other in that they draw exclusively upon the Western experience. Their economic tropism pulls them together more strongly than their divergences pull them apart: both see development as basically consisting in economic growth; both have had a purely quantitative view of growth and have taken a long time to measure its consequences.

The so-called Rostowian theory of stages of growth carries the mimetic obsession to the point of caricature.[36] As development is supposed to be an essentially linear historical process, each country will gradually pass through the same stages until it finally reaches the developed state. Underdeveloped countries, then, have only to retrace the steps of others that have preceded them on this single path and to follow them on every point. The time scale is not spelled out – or, rather, it is assumed that they will have the opportunity to proceed more quickly, since they can build on the gains of already industrialized countries to shorten the period of growth and accumulation prior to 'take-off'.

Other variants – such as Arthur Lewis's dualist theory that the traditional sector is bound to be eaten up by the modern sector existing alongside it in underdeveloped economies[37] – do not cut against the basic idea. There is only a single model, and the undeveloped world has no alternative but to line up behind it.

The stages theory, which has the huge advantage of clearing the industrial countries of any responsibility for underdevelopment and emptying history of any dialectic of conflict, won the support of an overwhelming majority within the huge machinery of development aid that came on line in the 1960s. It was the basis on which international agencies and Western governments built their aid policies, whose costly aberrations are only now apparent. In the end, the whole view of underdevelopment as merely involving a time lag in relation to development transposes nineteenth-century evolutionism, without changing very much, to the sphere of the economy.

Just as theorists made Western civilization the model for humanity and declared themselves to be enlightened guides for peoples at a lower stage of evolution, so did liberal economists of the 1960s see no other future for the underdeveloped countries than the one offered by the industrial world. They could not imagine that particular histories might follow other paths to modernity than the one taken by Western countries. Here, too, they showed themselves loyal to earlier theorists in other fields of thought: their inability to conceive a plurality of social and cultural formations, and therefore a diversity of ways into modernity, came in a straight line from the notion that peoples at a lower evolutionary level had no historical existence.

For Marxists and their more or less legitimate offspring, the dependency theorists, underdevelopment is a product of development, a historical moment in it own right rather than a stage through which every region of the globe must inevitably pass. Marxist economists and their epigones – most notably, Raúl Prebisch and Celso Furtado, the two most influential theorists of the United Nations Economic Commission for Latin America and the Caribbean (ECLAC) – positioned themselves outside the fashionable evolutionism of their liberal counterparts. In their view, the first requirement to escape from underdevelopment was a radical redefinition of world economic relations that put an end to the North–South structures of dependence and inequality. The idea of catching up, inherent in strategies formulated within a liberal framework, did not figure as such among the foremost concerns of dependency theorists. But it was not absent from their body of doctrine. Although they made struggle against the new versions of imperialism a sine qua non for entry into economic modernity, their reading of modernity itself scarcely differed from that of their ideological opponents.

Whether in its liberal or its socialist form, the model was presented as the only way forward: the future world would have the features of an industrial society, governed either by the market or by the state. The Soviet reference, which was fundamental in the Marxist school and permeated most of its developmentalist offshoots, accentuated the industrial bias of the theory by taking the USSR as the perfect example of a 'historical shortcut'. Against an earlier background of underdevelopment vis-à-vis capitalist Europe, it had experienced over barely one generation a process of accelerated industrialization and modern statebuilding within a context historically defined by peasant preponderance. An industrialization along similar lines, occurring later but more rapidly than in the European and American industrial heartlands, was the only alternative to the capitalist path. And, whatever the pertinence of certain aspects, the import-substitutionist strategies long dominant in the major third-world countries, as well as the variant based upon the creation of 'industrializing industries', testified to the strength of a model which marginalized any alternative way of thinking (from either the liberal or the socialist galaxy) as a quaint piece of folklore.

The fact that the idea behind development theories was scarcely questioned until the early 1980s further suggests a basic affinity between the two antagonistic rivals of Western economic theory, a common denial of the historical existence of peoples in the so-called underdeveloped countries. The contemporary challenges confronting matter in its raw third-world state had to be answered by following in the footsteps of the West, which was more than ever convinced that its own embodiment of progress was destined to become universal. By that yardstick, the most deserving countries of the South were always those which made the greatest effort to stick to the model. Advocates of a state-socialist short-cut to industrialization praised Algeria to the skies as the most disciplined copy – until its economy began to collapse. Successive versions of liberalism, for their part, celebrated the soon-to-fade Asian or Latin American miracles, seeing among the reasons for their success only the things they wanted to see. In neither case did obedient disciples see the broader historical picture, or the underlying dynamic that was transforming the model from within.

But then reality made it blindingly obvious that the third world was incapable of picking up the flame of revolution or exactly copying, in less than a generation, an evolutionary path that had taken centuries in the original model. Now was the hour of disappointment in the West. In the 1980s, as its theorists, economists and developers became aware that their stubborn pupil was applying the recipes much less smoothly than they had expected, they began to think that development could not be kept within the constraints they had set for it, that endogenous factors could not be simply left out of account, and that development was more akin to a makeshift operation whose results could not be mastered.

As in the time of decolonization, the autonomous propensity of non-Western areas compelled a section of intellectuals to reconsider the nature and possible consequences of some of their axiomatic beliefs. But this was far from a majority trend – on the contrary, the general change of scenery in the 1980s put an end to the earlier questioning and restored the comfort of certainty to those whom a world in recomposition had thrown off balance.

FIVE

The Backlash

Both in America and in Europe, those strange years witnessed the re-emergence of the most thoroughly outmoded forms of the culture of supremacy which, though known not to have succumbed to the challenges of the century, were for a while thought to have lost some of their force. In a still changing world, historians, journalists, anthropologists and economists – whether their roots were in the radical left or the liberal right – set about reconstructing a discourse that legitimated the pre-eminence of the West.

A new discourse

This endeavour took a number of forms, each adapted to its context. In the United States, a new anthropological–sociological literature addressed the marginalization of a section of blacks by bringing back into fashion arguments that ascribed to them lesser intellectual faculties,[1] while in Europe it was rehabilitation of the colonial enterprise that attracted the greatest effort. On both sides of the Atlantic, moreover, attempts were made to breathe fresh life into rhetorical defence of the Western spirit and its aptness for supremacy. Thus, in a *Histoire générale de l'Europe* published in France in 1980, we read that 'Europe has always tended to consider the human person as the primary value, the one which is sacred above all others', and that its inhabitants have 'an irresistible tendency to carry to all parts of the world that which [they] consider to be best for themselves'. Being overmodest, however, 'Europeans refuse to examine, weigh up and use the best they have which is superior to what exists elsewhere.'[2] The West seemed to have accepted that it was not alone in the world and that it had not alone made history. The restoration, initiated at the beginning of the 1980s, applied itself to sweeping away doubts and giving back to the West (or its collective consciousness) a place that it had briefly seemed to be losing.

From that time, what was called third worldism fell into disgrace, and those who still upheld it were severely taken to task. The economic and political failure of progressive regimes in the tropics had, it is true, seriously discredited them. Neither Cuba nor Vietnam could any longer serve as a countermodel, and the Cambodian horror forced those who preached the redemptive virtues of revolutionary war to fall silent. Voices were raised to condemn the blindness that could follow from a stubborn wish to find alternative messiahs to the Western proletariat. But if the totalitarian aberrations of comrades in the South and the economic disorders that occurred instead of development gave rise to a degree of salutary questioning, most scourges of third-worldism soon rejoined the ranks of those who denied the reality of inequalities between nations or found justifications for the hierarchies underpinning them. The crimes in the tropics, the bloody acts of madness of a few puffed-up dictators, the kleptocracy of certain post-colonial state personnel: these phenomena created an unhoped-for opportunity to dispense with analysis of world relations and to blame stagnation or regression in the South purely on local causes. To those who had for too long made post-colonial imperialism alone responsible for the dire poverty of 'proletarian nations',[3] the simple answer now was to absolve it of all responsibility for the persistence of their plight.

In both cases, the third world had the peculiarity of both being the main theme in debates among the Western intelligentsia and having no tangible reality for it. Just as utopian leftists had not concerned themselves with the reality of the third world, those who thought of themselves as the realists of the 1980s scarcely paid any attention to what was bubbling up in the alchemists' cauldrons of more and more countries in the South. The third world over which the defenders and prosecutors of third-worldism clashed was most often only stage scenery; what could be seen on it mattered less than their contending views about the mission of the West. The subtitle of Pascal Bruckner's book that gave the signal for battle in France – 'the third world, guilt, self-hate'[4] – testified to the domestic character of the settling of accounts. For the real issue in the dispute was the expulsion of the most recent incarnation of nineteenth-century revolutionary utopianism from the horizon of the West – that utopianism which saw the oppressed masses of the South, and the minorities originating from it in North America, as the force with a mission to occupy the ground deserted by the bourgeoisified proletariat of the North.

A number of intellectuals, moreover, having worked off their disappointment by burning their former idols, manufactured new certainties that helped to construct an apologetic discourse for the West. In this, they were comforted by a few tired prophets who laid down their arms and found their way back to a system whose downfall they had sworn to bring about. In the United States, legendary Black Panther leaders such as Eldridge Cleaver – who, unlike most of his comrades, had eluded every American police force and gone to live in Algeria and Cuba – rejoined the ranks of *bien pensant* America. In an interview he gave to me at the time, Cleaver cast a disenchanted look over his past commitments and said that he no longer found it unbearable to live in the United States, a relative democracy which in the end he accepted as his country.[5]

It now became easy to argue that, if some of its most striking victims ceased to hold it up to contempt, the system must have some virtues after all. And as the list of these was drawn up once more, the questions that others had posed a decade and a half before were deleted from the memory. So it was that the crimes committed by dictatorships in the South made it possible to forget the crimes of colonization, to glorify the era of colonial peace,[6] and to pick up the thread of a briefly discredited epic. The violence of precolonial times also began to serve as cover for that which accompanied European expansion: the bloody military-religious nature of Aztec or Inca power put the appalling crimes of a Cortés or Pizarro into perspective,[7] and the existence of African kingdoms touting black slaves to European merchants allowed some to place on their shoulders the principal responsibility for the trade.

The French geographer Yves Lacoste, for instance, who rightly recalled the importance of the Arab slave trade in nineteenth-century tropical Africa, went on to rehabilitate Europeans by placing the main blame for African tragedies on local and intra-African slave traders. 'It is possible', he wrote in 1987, 'that the intra-African trade of the nineteenth century weighed less heavily in terms of the number of victims.... Be this as it may, it is the nineteenth-century slave trade which today has the most serious geopolitical consequences, because it is the most recent in date.'[8]

Such reviews enabled two types of justification to be used. The first located Western violence in a long and banal history of human cruelty and found that it was no worse than anything which had preceded it – a thesis that would have been defensible if its supporters had not also insisted that the humanism of Western civilization was its distinctive feature and the reason for its superiority. The second placed the emphasis on the 'humanitarian' concerns – the term was already spreading – of European expansion, which distinguished itself by the progress it brought to newly subject peoples. Of course, these new discourses covered over much less glorious aspects of colonial domination, but they also claimed a new legitimacy for it without ever noticing the contradiction with the supposed universality of human rights. The history rewritten since the 1980s thus presents the colonial period as a fine adventure, whose occasional regrettable errors take nothing away from the generally positive balance sheet that it would be right to claim for itself.[9]

As history has always been one of the pillars of the Western myth, it was indeed natural that historians should have played a major role in the work of restoring the image of the West.

From the restoration of myths...

Nostalgia usually suffuses these discourses which have had such resonance and found such powerful support in the press. The historian-turned-journalist Alexandre Adler is among the most representative of this restoration, and we must quote him at some length to understand the strength of imperial nostalgia combined with a reassuring fantasy of French generosity that we find among many of his peers.

It is a matter of simple justice also to recall the grandeur of the enterprise.... The Republic ... took from late Latin civilization this capacity to mix blood, to consider the African subject to the laws of France as a potential Frenchman, ... all of which the Anglo-Saxon world finds hard to understand. As to Africa, people in France loved what was best about it: the white fathers and pastors who spread the gospel to the Mossi of the distant Sahel and the Kasrès of Togo; the officers of the colonial army who spent their lives among their infantrymen; the doctors who a century ago invented humanitarian action; the freemasons who initiated the sons of African witch doctors into customs that seemed to have been invented for them; and the parliamentarians of the Republic who made a place beneath the village tree of the Bourbon Palace for the future heads of state of independent Africa.... Of course France loves its Africa and feels poignant nostalgia for a Republic that we are losing drop by drop. Of

course France has not been discredited in Dakar, Abidjan or even Libre-
ville, in Yaoundé and Tananarive.[10]

We are not dreaming. It is a left-wing intellectual, a former communist,
who is indulging in this hallucinatory hagiography.

In his defence it must be said that he is not alone. Jean-Pierre Cot,
briefly minister for cooperation in 1981 in the first Socialist government
of the Mitterrand period, a man who for a moment embodied the vague
desires among sections of the left to decolonize French development
aid, drew the following balance sheet in 1984 of his activity: 'I do not
believe that colonization has been discredited; I know it has had its day.
Now the consequences must be drawn.'[11] Among the numerous variations on the theme, we might also mention Claude Imbert's 1997
editorial in the weekly *Le Point*: France, he writes, 'has fallen asleep
with the idea that the indisputable successes of its colonization, and still
more of its decolonization, will bring it enduring attachments.'[12]

This return to the certainties of old suddenly sends the former
possessions back into the unfathomable otherness that they had at the
moment of conquest. And, in descriptions of that otherness, a simplicity
of imagination again conceals the complexity of truths which, one has to
say, never really gained universal recognition. Fantasies once more gain
ground. Images of chaos sum up the whole of Africa, which thus re-
covers its old aspect as a mysterious, dangerous, savage land evidently
incapable of governing itself.[13] This recently led another journalist to
describe the Sierra Leone tragedy as 'the graveyard of some generous
ideas which Africa, if left to Africans alone, is not capable of defending'.[14]

I do not mean this anthology to imply that the dangerous evolution
of certain regions in the South does not raise questions, or that the
bloodbaths being committed there should not cause us serious concern.
Nor do I wish to deny that the changes brought about by colonization,
when taken together, amounted to a revolution. Present horrors should
not be downplayed on the grounds that Westerners committed worse.
There are some crimes which do not owe much to the colonial heritage
or to Western control over the rest of the world, and the disasters
affecting some countries today are not all orchestrated by some Olym-
pian deity whose only aim is to bring them to ruin. I shall attempt
below to take due account of non-indigenous legacies and indigenous
memories, as well as of certain new features, in the present drift of so
many regions of the world.

But what is distinctive about the backlash I have just described is
precisely that it does not pose questions, does not seek to understand

the multiple reasons for these regressive phenomena.[15] Arguing from current disorders to a glorification of colonial peace, it claimed a right to nostalgia for the imperial epoch. In reference to France's present-day overseas territories, the DOM-TOMs, one historian wrote: 'These scattered remnants of a defunct empire are still precious. They give France an opportunity to remain a great maritime power.'[16] History here weighs heavily on France – although the United States and Britain are similarly unable to think of themselves as anything but world powers. It is exactly as if the 'manifest destiny' underlying their mission were, in the eyes of their thinkers and politicians, a condition for the very existence of the major Western countries.

The myth has it that this calling derives from a native genius: the West remains persuaded that it built itself and owes its greatness to itself alone. The Western press has often echoed this conviction, being for a long time the preferred vehicle – and an invaluable barometer – for that culture of supremacy which stretches back unbroken into the distant past.[17]

In 1998 a short-lived weekly, *L'Européen*, devoted its triple summer issue to the history of Europe.[18] 'This epic story,' explained Christine Ockrent in an editorial, 'which still dazzles us today, carried a culture, values and customs to the far corners of the earth. We do not praise it enough; we can be proud of it.' The issue here is not the admiration for a (in many ways admirable) civilization, but the manner in which it is described. Europe made itself and, so that readers should be convinced of this, writers take whatever liberties they wish with the actual history – not to speak of the countless factual errors littering the dossier. Thus we learn that, under the Antonine empire, 'peace stretched from the mouth of the Rhine to the Danube Delta, excluding the lesser "barbarian" tribes. In Africa and the Middle East, the Empire was reduced a narrow fringe.' This is a fine example of a recurrent theme whereby Africa and the Middle East are expelled from Rome to give a non-existent historical depth to their present-day exclusion. Peripheral regions of northern and eastern Europe, on the other hand, are fully integrated so that the Empire can be made to coincide with contemporary Europe. As for the Eastern Roman Empire, it 'is a synthesis of Roman political conceptions, Christianity and the legacy of Hellenism'. Apart from these three components, Byzantium supposedly owed nothing to anyone: no mention is made of its relations with the Arab or Persian empires that were contemporaneous with it. If the Eastern capital 'played a fundamental role in the transmission of ancient texts

[and] the Renaissance owes it a great deal', nothing is said of the way in which that legacy arrived in the West. Nor would the reader find out that a Muslim Western Europe existed in the Middle Ages, as there is not a word about Andalusia or medieval Sicily. This omission also makes it possible to keep silent about the expulsion of the Jews and Muslims from Spain.

The Europe of *L'Européen*, a heritage from Greece and Rome, is exclusively Christian; no other influence is supposed to have polluted it. It knew only pages of glory, and its genius created the humanism that was the main force driving its actions. It did, to its great misfortune, suffer the assaults of the Turkish barbarians – and the description of the Ottoman Empire is meant to fill us with horror. In the fifteenth century, we learn, 'darkness fell for nearly five centuries over the Balkans, ... where the subject population ... was grouped into a captive religious minority administering itself under the leadership of a chief.... This permitted certain specialists in the Ottoman world to speak of toleration. But it was highly precarious.' Here the Ottomans are not credited with any contribution to civilization. At the same time, there is nowhere any reference to anti-Semitic violence in Christian Europe, to the Inquisition or the black slave trade. But I will stop here, for the dossier breathes hatred and contempt from one end to the other. It is an instructive example of what happens when one obstinately refuses to move away from the myths.

Official voices in the Western countries also made crucial contributions to the embellishment of history, often transforming it into a legend for the edification of their citizens. Thus, the almost century-long abolition of slavery[19] has been presented on both sides of the Atlantic as a 'white affair' in which humanists descended from the Enlightenment waged a fierce battle against economic interests for the liberty of blacks. Recognition of the major role played by abolitionists need not have precluded mention of the black insurrections, as a factor often hastening the move to abolition. But the official histories have passed over those revolts, which punctuated the history of the United States from the 1830s and wove the fabric of the Caribbean in the eighteenth and nineteenth centuries. It is as if Lincoln's proclamation of 1863 owed nothing to the revolts of 1831 and 1858, or to the 'underground railway' that organized the escape of hundreds of slaves from the South to the northern States and Canada. In France, the commemoration in 1998 of the hundred-and-fiftieth anniversary of the abolition of slavery took the form of a consensual celebration of republican humanism, which those taking part managed to smother with their self-satisfaction. The official speeches insisted that abolition was the work of the Republic whereas slavery had been a vice of the monarchy. The decree of 27 April 1848 was presented as 'an exemplary episode in the struggle for human rights, when the fight for the abolition of slavery [was identified with] the fight for the Republic',[20] no one seeing fit to mention the original act of abolition in 1794 or the restoration of slavery in 1802.

While historians in recent decades have stepped up their work on the black uprisings and recognized their importance,[21] Western politicians seem to be filled with a desire to keep the legend intact. Their silence and their general approach maintain the fiction that their only legacy is that of the Enlightenment, a largely mythical Enlightenment, moreover, wholly on the side of Good and without any complicating shadows. In suggesting that the subject peoples took no part in their own emancipation, that it was purely a result of the philanthropy of Western governments, they show their inability to imagine that the West might not have a monopoly on historical initiative. In this conception, even if the role of material interests is sometimes recognized, the main driving forces of imperial expansion have been humanism and a mystique of progress as something invariably positive. The West remains alone in having made world history, for the greater good of the world.

With such lessons, it is understandable that Western citizens should remain cautious when their leaders take it into their head to inflect the dominant discourse. Thus, in 1997 when Congress apologized to American blacks for the period of slavery, one Democrat was surprised to receive a mailbag full of protests. One man even thought that the government should apologize to him for robbing his grandfather of his slaves, while others considered that American blacks should be grateful to the slave traders for bringing them over from Africa. According to two opinion polls on the issue, two out of three blacks supported what Congress had done and two out of three whites were against it.[22]

...to the rewriting of histories

However loud the voices opposing them, such discourses have again become dominant. Colonial humanism is once more presented as evident, even if the facts plainly contradict the dogma. One of the favourite examples, 'native' schooling, may help us gauge the distortions upon which the dogma is based. For the truth is that it nowhere acquired mass proportions during the colonial period. In this regard, the colonized countries may be divided into three groups. Those which, before coloniz-ation, had had their own tradition and infrastructure of education (India, Ceylon or Madagascar), and those which had already embarked upon administrative modernization (as in Egypt or Tunisia), saw these structures strengthened during the colonial period and recorded quite high rates of primary-school attendance. In some other countries, a major missionary presence or state delegation of educational tasks to the churches could also achieve fairly high rates: this was the case of Belgium's African colonies – Congo, Rwanda and Burundi – where on the eve of independence roughly a third of the relevant age group attended primary school.

Elsewhere, however, where there was hardly any prior experience of schools or where knowledge had been passed on by oral tradition, the colonizers did not bring about any major changes. In West Africa barely three hundred Africans had a school-leaving certificate in 1940, and the rate of primary-school attendance was no more than 5 per cent in 1945.[23] By 1960 this rate averaged just 10 per cent for all Sahel countries under French control. In Morocco, in 1956, fewer than 12 per cent of school-age children attended an educational establishment in the modern sector.[24] In Algeria, that inseparable part of France, 20 per cent of primary-age children attended school in 1961.[25] As to secondary and higher educa-tion, it was a marginal phenomenon until the 1950s in Asia and until the 1960s in North and sub-Saharan Africa; in South Africa, by contrast, all the children of the white population were covered. In general, then, school attendance rates only began their rapid increase after independ-ence; the previous failure of colonial administrators to democratize edu-cation should certainly dampen some of the enthusiasm for colonialism as a civilizing force.

The same observations may be made in respect of public health, where it was only in the 1950s that the ruling powers agreed to serious efforts. In 1950 life expectancy was no more than 40 years in the lands of the former Indian Empire, and in sub-Saharan Africa it was higher at independence only in countries with a sizeable white population. Every-where else it was well below 40. In Algeria it stood at 46 by 1960 (an average including the population of European origin), whereas it had already reached 70 in the 'metropolis'.[26] Nevertheless, the timid advances had a huge impact: the introduction of modernity-bearing educational systems, if only for an elite, were among the changes revolutionizing colonial societies, just as the improvement of public health from the

1950s gave the signal for the fastest population growth in human history. But that is another story. For the moment, let us keep in mind that civilization was measured out parsimoniously for those who are said to have swum in its benefits.

A new chapter of arguments for 'colonial humanism' has focused on the costs of colonization and the meagre profits that the mother countries derived from it. Those seeking to rehabilitate colonialism conclude from recent economic research that it was simply not 'good business', and even that the metropolitan countries lost out in the final balance sheet. It was a zero-sum game, and since the West gained nothing from exploitation of its colonies, the latter for their part could not have lost anything from it; their poverty cannot therefore be attributed to foreign exploitation, which was less predatory than the anti-colonial literature has claimed. Of course, such reasoning has the advantage of freeing the colonial enterprise of any responsibility for what is called underdevelopment, but this exoneration has first required a certain shift in meaning to take place.

The French historian Jacques Marseille attributes the archaic features of French and British capitalism until the 1950s, and their related difficulties 'in falling into step with industrial growth', to the fact that their trade was for too long geared to their empires, whose existence thus delayed necessary changes in the structure of production apparatuses.[27] In the case of France, Marseille wonders whether 'decolonization was a conquest of the colonial peoples supported by metropolitan forces hostile to capitalism, or whether, on the contrary and at the same time, a certain (modern) section of French employers saw it as a jettisoning of ballast to stimulate growth in their operations.'

The author of these stimulating remarks does not doubt that the metropolis extracted wealth from the subject countries, but he emphasizes the pernicious effects of the colonial arrangement for core capitalist economies. The questions raised were equivalent to an answer for a section of French intellectual opinion, which concluded that colonial occupation had been economically neutral. And it is true that, in other writings, Marseille lent himself to such a shift when he gave historical research the task of questioning the 'alleged burden of the colonial legacies'. In arguing that 'the colonial legacy was not as "destructuring" or as "traumatic" as people have said', he himself falsely jumped from the slow development of a French capitalism imprisoned by empire to the innocuousness of its intervention in the colonies. Later, the secondary-school history textbooks published under his direction made the argument still simpler by stating that empire had brought nothing to France.

The Swiss economist Paul Bairoch in his *Economics and World History: Myths and Paradoxes* (1993)[28] places among 'the myths of economic history' the notion that the West relied on its colonial empires for its own industrialization. But although his aim, rightly, is to stress the crucial weight of sociological shifts and endogenous technological advances in the process of industrialization, the arguments he uses are by no means all convincing. For example, he attaches greater importance to the role of colonies as suppliers of raw materials than to their much more crucial function as an outlet for metropolitan industrial production. Equally difficult to defend is his use of the fact that Britain's industrial revolution preceded its colonial expansion to explain why the latter had little influence on the former, for this overlooks a long previous history and the crucial phase of the accumulation of commercial capital.

Furthermore, Bairoch invalidates some of his own assertions by showing the extent to which the nineteenth-century imposition of free trade on soon-to-be-dominated countries hastened their deindustrialization and promoted industrial growth in the metropolis – the first relocation of industry in modern history. 'Economics', Bairoch explains, 'is actually not a "zero sum game". For example, although exports were not important for Western industries,[29] their low cost resulted in almost total deindustrialization of the future third world.' We may agree with his conclusion that the colonies did not directly play a decisive role in the industrialization of the metropolis, yet still insist that, through migration and other mechanisms, they did make a major contribution to metropolitan prosperity, and therefore to the creation of internal markets, that would be invaluable for the acceleration of industrial growth. In any event, we may well ask why Bairoch measured the role of the colonies only in relation to industrialization in the strict sense of the term, and why he wished to stress the exclusively endogenous character of the West's march to the industrial revolution.

Despite the cautionary note sounded by Bairoch and others, the conception of economics as a zero-sum game has become the majority view. Of course, it does have the advantage of lending some economic credibility to two recurrent themes of Western discourse: the absence of a link between the colonial system and the phenomena grouped under the term 'underdevelopment'; and the purely endogenous character of the accumulation that led to the industrial revolution.

The end of an era?

In recent accounts of colonization, then, its balance sheet has been generally positive: the Western powers fulfilled their civilizing mission by leading the continents of the South – by force, it is true, but they had no choice – along the road of prosperity and progress. The slow evolution of the South is due less to the consequences of the colonial period than to later regression, which is explicable by the inability of the newly independent nations to manage their legacy. The violence accompanying colonial domination was its least glorious aspect, but it did not affect the nature of its economy geared to the universalization of progress.

Now, the only way in which one might find this schema at all pertinent would be to share its accounting logic. Only then could the traumas resulting from the colonial system be largely offset by the modernization of production structures, the opening to the world of vast regions hitherto closed in on themselves, the clash between their often frozen traditions and a system of thought based upon individual autonomy and freedom of enterprise, and the education of elites capable of assimilating modernity.

No one will seriously think of denying that colonialism was the bearer of modernity, or that it gave the signal for certain trends and acceler-ated others in the areas under its influence (that is, everywhere in the world). But the adoption of an analytic approach like the one I have just sketched out makes it impossible to draw up a more exact balance sheet of the globalization of Western domination. No doubt it would be a pointless exercise to imagine how the non-European regions might have evolved if they had not gone under the flattening steamroller and if their relations with the West had taken a different tack. But nor can one grasp the scale of a seismic shift if one remains within the framework of cost–benefit calculation.

The great phases of European expansion – the push into the Ameri-cas and, three centuries later, its extension to the rest of the world – meant one of two things for civilizations that encountered this voracious appetite and the paradoxical ideology that bore it along: either death pure and simple, or a radical break that had scarcely any equivalent in the history of earlier times. Although much ink has been spilled over the centuries on the nature of that radical break, no one has ever weighed it up in its entirety, followed all its endless shock waves, recognized all its sequels through to the mysteries of the present day.

Of the intellectuals in the South who have tried to say what it was, only poets have perhaps had some success. Other surveyors of those earthquake-jolted sites have sometimes pretended to move forward into hesitant syntheses concerning what they were, what was imposed on them, and what they would like to become. Others have taken refuge – when illusion was not totally impossible – in the fiction of a colonial 'parenthesis', while still others have gone back in history to find new myths to tell themselves. All have sought consolation for the despair of no longer knowing who they are and not yet knowing who they will be. Whether one likes it or not in the West, the contemporary history of the continents of the South and of their various diasporas is still largely one of multiple confused reactions to the delayed effects of Western domination.

It would seem that, in attempting to settle the balance, the West has also wanted to close the 'parenthesis' – without recognizing that centuries of overseas adventures have shaped the West as much as they have its involuntary partners, that they have covered the way in which Westerners relate to others with a dross of supremacy. The stubborn manifestations of this culture of supremacy prove that it lies at the core of Western identity, and that decolonization and the granting of citizenship to minorities descended from formerly subject peoples have not radically shaken the perception of others by which the West also defines itself. The current wish to forget the questioning of thirty years ago and to restore the prestige of the Western adventure, combined with the refusal of most Europeans and North Americans to probe the impulses behind their relations with others, shows that they are incapable of imagining a world that is not built around themselves at its centre.

Yet the pugnacity of the present backlash, the way in which many intellectuals have regrouped around the old founding myths of the West and converted its real specificity into superiority, is probably not due only to the continuing strength of the culture of supremacy on which they were brought up. The revival of discourses that legitimate Western history, sometimes in the most grotesque forms, may draw as much upon future uncertainties as upon past certainties.

While people in the West and elsewhere have a strong sense that the world is changing faster than in the past, no one seems capable of predicting all the consequences of this change. And, though Westerners remain convinced that their hegemony is legitimate, they are much more questioning about its future. Will they continue for much longer to be the almost exclusive beneficiaries of a globalization that they initiated and whose successive forms they have so far controlled? Will the self-assertiveness of the most prosperous or populous countries of the South lead sooner or later to the ending of the West's monopoly hold over the fate of the planet? And are the technological transfers from which the South supposedly benefits likely to accelerate, at the expense of the present world powers, the progress of nations seeking a change in status?

In other words, are we witnessing the gradual but unstoppable closure of that long period in which the West could spread across the earth at a pace limited only by its means and its determination? And, if so, is the retreat of intellectuals and public opinion into certainties that once seemed eroded not the expression of a refusal to accept that closure? Does the new assertion of the West's superiority not serve to drive away the intolerable prospect of its shrinking influence?

Western public opinion, which for generations has been shaped in the belief that its race has a calling to rule the world, is no longer so sure that the future belongs to it. Demographic growth in the South has reduced the West to no more than 20 per cent of the world's population. The danger of a flood of migration – after a long period in which the influx has worked to its advantage – can be seen every day in the growth of non-indigenous populations at the heart of its big cities who gradually acquire the attributes of citizenship. The old spectre of a 'yellow peril' is also resurfacing, though now in relation to industrial relocation and VCR imports. Although extremist groups like the white supremacists in America or the xenophobic right in Europe or Australia remain a minority, the issue of identities under threat goes well beyond such limited circles (how far beyond, varies from country to country) and into mainstream opinion. The fear of being forced to give up the West's hegemonic position – a position that has shaped its way of relating to the world – tends to be synonymous in people's minds with the fear of seeing their identity crumble. This inability to conceive an identity without the posture of hegemony demonstrates the narrowness of the links established over the past five centuries between the West and its Others.

In point of fact, it is not clear that existing tendencies in the world are pushing so strongly in this direction, for the West's reassertion of the legitimacy of its superiority might also correspond to the current effort to renew the bases of its superiority. Is it fear of a future built without them, or against them, that impels people in the West to draw up one-sided nostalgic inventories of what they have contributed to the world? Or, on the contrary, is this to be explained by the fact that the

technologies they invent or disseminate, and the new webs of dependence in which they wrap their partners, guarantee that they will have
control of the future? No doubt both phenomena are present. And no
one would claim to be capable of precisely mapping out what the future
will be like.

Signals and tendencies in various parts of the world give rise to
contradictory readings, just as what is called globalization may be seen
either as the most recent variant of Western domination or, on the
contrary, as a factor redistributing the world economic cards. Since the
age of direct political control ended in the 1970s (with the exception of
a few specks of imperial confetti), it is in the field of economics that the
strong and mighty are today seeking to consolidate their positions and
to conquer new ones, and that global relations are today being redefined.

PART TWO

The Way of the World

The West does not exist for economists, or for those who have pledged to concern themselves with development. What has taken its place is the North, an entity with shifting contours that has no official existence and only distant connections with geography. No group of countries bears that name in the files of international agencies, which do not use the term 'South' either to describe the rest of the planet. Nevertheless, these are the two cardinal points for one of the most significant divisions of the world – there are others – which has been internalized by people living in the respective regions. To move from one world to the other is not impossible but is still rare, especially from South to North but recently less so in the other direction. Although the possibility of re-drawing frontiers keeps hopes alive in the 'emergent' countries, they are in fact more rigid than one thinks.

At first sight, West and North do not seem to be synonymous, since Japan is a major presence in the latter and South Korea was co-opted by the OECD in 1996 in recognition of its economic achievements. For a time, it was not even essential to belong to the capitalist world, since it was tacitly accepted that the Soviet Union and its European satellites were part of the North, even if they had strayed into socialism, that deviant offshoot of the Western spirit, and deserved to be combated for that reason. If it is possible to leave the South for the North, as Mexico too did after signing a free trade agreement with its North American neighbours, then it is also possible to pass from the North to the South. The collapse of the Soviet Union cast most of its republics into the darkness with it, and only a few European countries formerly under its control have escaped this degrading relegation.[1]

North or South, as we see, is more a status than a location on the
world map. Facing a relatively unified North that groups only countries
from which the label 'developed' is not withheld, the South or the
Souths or the third world – which for a while also took capital letters in
the anti-imperialist literature – or the underdeveloped, developing, poor
or less advanced countries share the rest of the planet among themselves.[2]

The conditions of belonging to these two entities are not all explicit.
The countries of the North are the wealthiest and the most industrialized in the world, even if they are not the only ones to be prosperous or
industrialized. It would never occur to anyone to place in the North the
ultra-rich monarchies of the Arabian–Persian Gulf, or various states in
the South whose GNP comes mainly from manufacturing production.
The World Bank, which classifies countries according to their GNP,
tries to avoid confusion by distinguishing between two groups of high-
income countries: those in the OECD, all of which (apart from Japan,
South Korea, Turkey and Mexico) are part of North America, Europe
or Australasia; and 'others with high incomes', a kind of ragbag in
which one finds the major tax havens, the most fortunate emirates, the
last specks of empire and a few unclassifiables such as Hong Kong and
Israel.[3] The United Nations Development Programme (UNDP), which
divides the world into developing countries and industrial countries to
establish comparative criteria of 'human development', places the industrialized developing countries in the former group.[4] To belong to the
North, then, is to have long-standing wealth and industry, even if the
doors are half-open to newcomers particularly deserving in economics
(the sphere that officially sets the norm).

This is not the whole picture, though. If it were, it would not be
possible to understand why countries long considered among the poorest and most rural in Europe – Greece and Ireland – sit in the North
with full rights,[5] whereas others seem to have broken and entered, as if
there were criteria defining an inner circle of the North that certain
countries are unable to join. One recalls the contempt in which the
West held Japan in the 1950s and 1960s, when it was looked upon as a
vulgar producer of bottom-of-the-range transistor radios whose sem-
blance of know-how came from its practice of industrial espionage. Although reality has since dissipated this image, an abundant literature in
North America and Europe continues to probe the Japanese enigma and
to reduce all its aspects to a single question.[6] How could a non-Western
country figure among the world's leading economies and even keep right
up with the old industrial nations in terms of innovation? The wording

of this question shows that, under Western eyes, Japan's development was not 'natural' but a mystery that needed unravelling if its potential danger was to be warded off. Similarly, the financial crisis that struck in the second half of the 1990s was an opportunity for many Western analysts to shut Japan back up in its *Asian otherness* (which explained, among other things, the persistence of clientelism), although the same people did not find any cultural specificity in the economic weakness that had afflicted the countries of Europe and North America since the late 1970s.

The reservations with which the USSR and its satellites were accepted into the North were due to almost opposite presuppositions. The fatherland of socialism and its East European acolytes had once put forward solid economic arguments for their claim to membership, and despite the vicissitudes of the cold war the Western powers had recognized the reality of their fast economic growth, its roots in industrialization, and an undeniable social modernity that could partly compensate for their political totalitarianism. This was the period when Nikita Khrushchev could argue, without provoking laughter, that the Soviet economy would soon overtake that of the United States;[7] the West did not believe him, but its scepticism referred more to Gosplan's time schedule than to the challenge as such. Eastern Europe too had been undergoing intense industrialization, in some cases for a very long time indeed. Yet so long as they did not repudiate their socialist economic system and their political regime, those countries could inhabit only the margins of the North, despite their ambition to be fully part of it.

In fact, the ideological gulf long masked geographical divisions within the huge area over which socialism then had control. Its western part, made up of European Russia, the European republics of the Soviet Union and the socialist countries of Central Europe, was always seen by the West as potentially part of the North. Its eastern part, on the other hand, made up of Soviet Asia and sometimes the unclassifiable Balkan periphery of Europe, was expected one day to return to an otherness only momentarily obscured by the banner of the Soviet Union. Awareness of this division was expressed during the cold war in General de Gaulle's wish to cancel it on the Old Continent by building Europe from the Atlantic to the Urals, an entity that would alone be capable of standing up to the United States. The Western reading of Russian history also bore the mark of this split: by opposing the 'Asian' Ivan the Terrible and the 'European' Peter the Great, Moscow and St Petersburg, and by making Stalin the last embodiment of oriental despotism, it

identified Russia's Asiatic dimension as the essential reason for its incapacity to achieve real modernization, and its European tropism as the
only source of hope in the vast and enigmatic empire. Today it is exactly as if the recompositions of the 1990s involved the return to a
'natural' order, as if the North–South divide within the Soviet empire
had re-emerged after a period when it was masked by the East–West
confrontation, as if the end of the cold war had brought the true cousins
back to the fold and sent south those who had only accidentally counted
as part of the family.[8]

If the 'North', economically speaking, is a kind of drawer containing
the major industrial countries, it cannot be reduced to that. This area,
notwithstanding the occasional new admission or forced entry, mainly
groups the inheritors of a single industrial civilization – a civilization
feeding on a dynamic cultural specificity ostensibly rooted in the constant tension of progress. To this economic modernity is supposed to
correspond a democratic political system. The old West, whose established powers in Europe and North America are long accustomed to
laying down the law and serving as a reference (positive or negative) for
the rest of the world, are clearly the centre of this geographically
untraceable North and alone define its membership conditions. If a
country is on its doorstep and has enough trump cards, it can sometimes move to the North. In today's world there are a few grey zones
which, no longer really part of the South and not yet in the North, are
waiting to be co-opted. But that does not mean they will enter its core.

The countries forming the core of the North certainly have divergences that should not be underestimated, but these do not detract from
the family ties. The anti-Americanism of a section of Europeans seems
more a question of spite at having their role as a first-rate power taken
away from them, or of fascination mingled with fear before the strangeness of Europe's own creature – did not Sartre call North America 'that
super-European monstrosity'?[9] – than of political indignation at the
flaunted or candid cynicism of a self-conscious superpower. No doubt
these quarrels may affect Euro-American relations, but the underlying
closeness can be gauged by the similar fears that the South arouses on
both sides of the Atlantic.

For the South, or rather the Souths, are there facing the North. In
the course of the 1990s, we saw a reversal of the elements that had
governed the organization of the world since the late 1950s. For a third
of a century, the third world had tried to set itself up as a nearly homo-
genous bloc vis-à-vis a North split along the line of the East–West

divide. But then the collapse of the Soviet empire unified the North. There has certainly been keen rivalry between its components, but today the North is welded together around similar economic logics and political practices, and presides with the same liberal conviction over the construction of a single world market. Conversely, as a result of differential evolution over the past few decades, the South is now composed of disparate elements that no one would dream of placing in a single group. Even if simplification is still a winning formula among the Western public, the Asian 'dragons' are never bracketed together with the countries of the African Sahel, which are seen as drifting aimlessly. They do not inspire fear for the same reasons.

The only thing that may still unite both groups is that they do inspire fear in the West. For, although the fracture lines have become so deep as to cause a veritable continental drift, the South continues to exist for the North, with dangers that may be different but are all threatening. The opportunities offered by the emerging economies are the stuff of dreams for Western companies. At the same time, however, there is concern about the competition they represent for the old industrial heartlands, and fear that their economic success will sharpen political ambitions which might one day challenge the hegemony of the West. At the other extreme, the North fears as it once did Barbarians the masses of the most impoverished countries, and seeks to protect itself from them. These images, which are communicated in various ways to the South, furnish it with a kind of negative counterpart of the unity that it is unable to achieve for itself.

The North and the South, taken separately, do not therefore have a precise existence. But the North–South opposition structures international relations and the mental habitat of nearly all the earth's inhabitants, whose identity includes the dimension of membership in one or the other of the two groups. For the North is the contemporary economic figure of the West, and the Souths comprise the regions where not so long ago it exercised either direct control or various other forms of domination. This is why the inhabitants of the respective Souths have so easily taken on board this new zonal division of the planet, which reminds them of all too familiar hierarchies.

But is this cleavage, which continues to polarize the world arena, still relevant to a time in which many states wish to force open the frontiers of the North and are challenging the Western monopoly on a power that they consider themselves justified to exercise? Does the world relationship of forces that is now taking shape herald an uncoupling of the West from a North with a new geography? And might this paradoxically force the West to kiss goodbye to its supremacy, or at least to take the edge off it by sharing with others the dividends of power? Is the writing on the wall for the centrality of the West, as countries emerge in the fragmented South which wish to have an influence on international relations commensurate with what they see as their true weight? Or is the West in the process of renewing its central role in different forms, as it has known how to do in the past? Did the post-colonial period, which ended with the twentieth century, start to deal a new hand of cards, or did it provide the West with the opportunity to make itself a new pack? In short, does globalization mean that the Westernization of the world is coming to an end? Does it mean that Western is finally becoming synonymous with universal, and that the dream which the West has pursued for such a long time is thereby becoming reality? Or does it set limits to a trajectory that began some five hundred years ago, by introducing other players and creating out of them new alchemies? Or could it be that globalization is covering over the old tracks and rendering obsolete a North–South divide inherited from history and geography, eventually to give birth to hierarchies ever more dissimilar from those of today?

SIX

The Great
Post-colonial Illusion

Times have certainly changed, and today it is hard to recollect the relative euphoria that prevailed throughout the 1960s and 1970s in what was already being called the third world.[1] The great majority of people living there were desperately poor, but their countries were not; and development in whichever form – one still had the illusion that there were several – would eventually make real use of their resources. The third world was defined by, among other things, its refusal to belong to either of the two blocs vying for power over the world, but the old colonial powers and, more broadly, the rich nations as a whole declared their readiness to come to the aid of the 'young' states. The enemy of the West was not in the South but in the East, and only countries that succumbed to the Soviet sirens deserved ostracization and punishment. In such cases, the big socialist brother gave them the benefit of its assistance, on condition that they showed unfailing allegiance towards it. There was no shortage of money, even if everyone agreed that more was always needed for development.

People in the West did, of course, baulk at what they saw as the excessive demands of the third world, but it seemed to have the wind in its sails. Its new leaders believed that independence would find its apotheosis in a 'new international economic order' that would finally make it possible to finance 'take-off'.[2] The United Nations, where countries belonging to this restive third world were in a majority, was given the task of establishing the new global architecture, while a plethora of other organizations created on a national basis during these years took up and gave resonance to the demands of the non-aligned Group of 77.

89

The 'development decades'

For a moment, it seemed that victory had been achieved by some and was within reach for the others. In 1973, the price of oil quadrupled following the October war in the Middle East and the OPEC embargo against Israel and its allies. The oil-producing countries – some, like Algeria and Venezuela, fully geared up for struggle to raise the value of third-world riches – were laying down the law. The Western economies seemed to hang on the least decision at OPEC meetings, and the European capitals began to tremble at the apparent reversal of the familiar world order. The prices of other minerals and agricultural raw materials skyrocketed in the wake of hydrocarbons.

The new international economic order, demanded in every organization where third-world countries formed a majority, seemed to be springing into place. Through the magic of price hikes for well-known basic products, the equally well-known deterioration of the terms of trade seemed to have been halted – and many countries in the South that had never expected so much so soon found themselves becoming rich. These glittering prospects boosted their growth potential to such a degree that their ambition to achieve as much as their models, only faster, no longer seemed so fanciful. Their leaders, seeing their old guardians treat them as important people, believed that the wealth would last for ever. If they did not pay cash for what they ordered, it was always a simple matter to raise a loan. We know what came of all this.

My purpose is not to tell an edifying tale in which the North calculated everything in such a way as to keep the levers of command, duping naive young states ill prepared to face its superior wiles. The West really believed, in the 1960s, that it had a duty to help the countries of the South attain material prosperity, which did then seem within reach.[3] Its leaders really thought that development aid was the updated version of the 'white man's burden' borne by their parents and grandparents, and that they should continue to shoulder it until the underdeveloped countries – a term that had replaced the outmoded 'non-evolved peoples' – had irreversibly taken the path of progress. Whenever the countries of the South grew uneasy at a possible exhaustion of their goodwill, they renewed their promises of assistance, not all of which were the product of outright duplicity.

A number of initiatives to cut corners were another feature of North–South relations, reflecting a real concern to kick-start the development of countries through aid. Until the 1990s, trade relations were based on the principle of non-reciprocal advantage, whereby rich countries showed a readiness to grant tariff concessions to partners in the South without demanding the same treatment for their own exports. Most of the bilateral trade agreements – a form then much more common than multilateral regulation – gave the countries of the South various specific exemptions.

This was the case of the Yaoundé accords of the 1960s, which linked the six-member European Common Market to eighteen (mainly African) former colonies. Then the Lomé Convention was signed in 1975 between the European Community and the new ACP group of ex-colonies in sub-Saharan Africa, the Caribbean and the Pacific, and regularly renewed in almost the same terms until the end of the century. The agreements reached in 1976 between the Maghreb states and the EC, which remained in force with a few minor changes until the mid-1990s, also guaranteed free access to the European market for a series of North African products, while European goods destined for the Maghreb were subject to high duties. In the early 1980s, developing countries were exporting to the United States some $10 billion worth of duty-exempt goods, within the framework of an American general preference system.[4]

Compensatory finance systems were also devised to soften the impact of price fluctuations for the basic commodities that made up the bulk of exports in many countries of the South. The European Community tried to show its good will by creating, under the Lomé Convention, the Stabex and Sysmin funds to compensate ACP countries for loss of export earnings due to a fall in world commodity prices. Similarly, beginning in the 1970s, the International Monetary Fund worked out a series of compensatory mechanisms to mitigate the effects of fortuitous declines in export revenue for the countries concerned.

But although the states of the North constantly proclaimed their willingness to get other countries started on the road to development, their main concern was to safeguard their own interests by keeping the South's demands within what they considered acceptable limits. The actual procedures for managing international economic relations and development aid had the effect, if not the explicit aim, of emptying the few concessions of their content. Products from the South that competed with those of the North were systematically excluded from special tariff status or exposed to non-tariff barriers upon entering the destination country.

In all the major industrial countries, the lowering of customs barriers went together with a strengthening of non-tariff barriers, such as the self-limiting export 'agreements' imposed on some particularly dynamic countries in the South, or the seasonal quotas for agricultural goods. The European Community wholly or partly excluded from its trade agreements with the South foodstuffs covered by its Common Agricultural Policy, and only the products of nascent industries (still not much of a threat to European competitors) were exempted from import duties. In the textile sector, the Multifibre Arrangement (MFA) signed in 1974 between the OECD and Asian exporters to limit the latter's market share illustrated this determination not to allow industrialization of the South to become a threat. Indeed, in the 1980s nearly all the OECD countries strengthened their import quota restrictions.[5]

Such apparently inconsistent behaviour should not be seen as one of those contradictions of which the West seems to know the secret. Rather, it expressed a hierarchy of concerns. Third-world development was certainly a duty, but it also had to remain good business, so that aid was most often tantamount, officially or implicitly, to an investment from which economic and political dividends were expected.[6] To be sponsored by its guardians in the North, the South must never strike out in a direction that could threaten their interests.

While the West accepted the wish for development as legitimate – because it amounted to a recognition, by the whole world or almost, that the Western model was universally valid – it remained convinced that nothing should challenge its vocation to control the world market. A brief look at some aspects of North–South relations may help us to understand why the economic tremors of the 1970s did not upset the traditional relationship of forces between the two parts of the world, why the post-colonial recompositions did not bring about (or only marginally brought about) a redistribution of global wealth, and why the North could so easily regain control from the early 1980s on.

Two variants of a single model

The dice were probably loaded from the start of the quest for mimetic development: that is, once the Western model was presented to other countries as the horizon for their aspirations. Without going back over the genesis of the concept and its place in Western thought,[7] we should recall what it may have meant at the time of its birth in the 1940s. Straightaway it set itself up as the semantic inheritor of the term 'civilization' (whose colonial connotations were now too strong) and the password permitting entry into modernity, that other contemporary synonym for civilization. Now known as the developed countries, those which used to describe themselves as civilized invited those which were not yet civilized to follow their example – if they wished to enter the universe of modernity.

But it was a question of modernity only in the material sense, since development was purely a matter of economics, growth was its only real measure, and the happiness of nations mainly concerned the rate of growth of their GNP. Political modernity, embodied in the democratic system, remained the exclusive preserve of a West that was then hardly concerned to globalize its benefits. This uncoupling of the two sides of modernity (which in the South was reduced to an economic caricature) scarcely helped to clarify its meaning. Throughout the East–West conflict, membership in the 'free world' was a certificate of democratic good conduct in the eyes of the United States and Western Europe, while anti-communism served as a vaccine against totalitarianism.[8] On the other side, it is easy to understand that the Soviet Union did not make political pluralism a criterion of development and reduced modernity to the number of factory chimneys a country could line up. Thus, beyond their differences, both West and East limited development to the sphere of the economy and measured in purely quantitative terms the common dream which they called progress.

Economic development – viewed by Marxists and *dependentistas* as a condition for political sovereignty and a change in the world relationship of forces, and by liberals as the only way of gaining access to modernity – became the only figure of progress available on the ideas market. It was also the only viable alternative to the political risks that the expansion of communism entailed for the West. In 1949, after the trauma of China's fall into the hands of the communists, the Truman Doctrine identified the poverty of the peoples of the South as the best ally of subversion, hence 'a threat to the most prosperous regions', and development as the best means of countering this and depriving revolutions of fertile soil. The United States, then, set out to make of economic growth (and the benefits that would supposedly ensue) the civilian counterpart of military containment.[9] In East Asia, the region of the world where the threat was greatest in the 1950s, South Korea and Taiwan served as laboratories for this dual system of military and economic containment. In the early 1960s, John F. Kennedy tried to apply the formula to Latin America by launching the 'Alliance for Progress' to stem any contagion from Cuba, but the results were much less convincing.

Development, then, was a one-way street that was supposed to offer various options, in so far as its forms were regularly and bitterly discussed. Economists, academics and activists in the different camps fought for decades over which were the shortest roads to development and the most effective methods to achieve it, but it was only at a very late date that the paradigm itself was called into question. However lively were the debates between champions of state-tempered liberalism and state control over all the mechanisms of the economy and society, between supporters of limits on private ownership and initiative and of the promotion of local capitalism, the goal to be achieved was always the same: the creation of an industrial, wage-based, urban society with accumulation regimes similar to those tried and tested during Europe's industrial revolution, whose successes could be measured by the single yardstick of growth.

However deep their differences, supporters of the two rival versions of the model reduced the ostensible beneficiaries of progress to the level of objects of development; neither ever considered them as subjects of a history of their own making.

The state as demiurge

The fact that we are dealing with two variants of a single model has long been clear from the hybrid that the UN and associated study groups more or less theorized for application to the 'developing countries'.[10] Adopting all the defining postulates of development and developed-country status, this synthesis involved a few basic components upon which nearly all the countries in question then drew. Industrialization was still the essential foundation, whether through the creation of import-substitution industries, industrial development projects in certain geographic areas, or, since the 1970s, the prioritization of manufacturing export industries. The state, representing the national collective and charged with the task of leading it towards development, was the great architect of such voluntarist policies. In the shape of central planning and administered economies, it was as present in countries claiming to be socialist as it was in the others. Everywhere in the South, or almost everywhere, it was the main industrialist and the main employer in the formal sector. It also acted as farmer and trader, to ensure control over everything that could produce wealth.

The state in the South was thus in tune with the era in which it was built. Pointing to the influential role they played in this, the socialist

states sometimes even claimed paternity and described aspiring emulators as 'countries with a socialist orientation'. The Western democracies
– which were then devilishly Keynesian, having nationalized part of
their economies at the end of the 1930s crisis or after the Second World
War – did not question the statism of their overseas disciples and even
saw it as a 'short cut' permitting them to reach the goal faster than they
had done themselves. The third-world planning state, especially when it
played at welfare, received all their favours; the drafting of national
development plans was one of the conditions required for them to receive
external finance. The World Bank hailed Tanzania's *ujaama* villages
(which forcibly grouped the peasantry into larger units) and its 'socialism with a human face' as one of the success stories of the 1970s. In the
1960s Tunisia's brief experiment with authoritarian socialist planning
and industrialization had similarly enjoyed its support.[11]

In this scheme of things, agriculture was worthy of interest only as a
part of large-scale development projects, whose modern character was
contrasted to the eternal archaism of the peasantry. In fact, third-world
peasants found it hard to understand that, in order to be modern, they
had to accept heavy state levies on their produce. In the case of export
crops, state agencies pocketed the difference between the world price
and the (always lower) price paid to producers; while in the case of
subsistence crops, the low prices paid to producers meant that from the
early 1960s the terms of trade between town and countryside systematically favoured the former in nearly every country in the South. The
main function of agriculture, then, was to fund the creation of state
apparatuses, national bureaucracies and large-scale development projects.
It was rural income levies, external aid and (in some countries) profits
from the energy and mining sectors which made it possible for statist
developmentalism to take shape during those years of illusion.

Previous history was simply overlooked in this whole affair, where
the mimetic myth soon came to serve particular interests, and economic
modernization of three-quarters of the planet offered fabulous opportunities to the industrial and technological apparatus of the North. Can
the totalitarianism of the development concept explain by itself the
amnesia that hit the elites of the North (convinced of the universality of
their model) as well as the South (filled with the catching-up myth),
causing them to overlook specific factors that had once made European
industrialization possible? They forgot Europe's long phase of accumulation boosted by two centuries of commercial capitalism and an agricultural revolution; forgot the relatively modest population growth at

that time (nearly 1 per cent a year, it is true, but bearing no comparison with the South's annual average of 3 per cent for more than twenty years from the 1950s); forgot the rapid development of highly labour-intensive industries that absorbed the surplus population from the countryside; forgot the unlimited possibilities for Europeans to emigrate to the four corners of the earth if they could not find employment or subsistence at home; and forgot the process of globalization that gradually extended the West's influence to the end of the earth. It was exactly as if the South was being asked to prove its modernity by following a recipe for which it had none of the ingredients.

Beneficiaries in the South

For the myth to become so quickly functional in the South, it must clearly have served some function there. First of all, its peoples believed in it. Although they quite soon became more sceptical about the endless speeches in which their leaders tried to ram home the correctness of their choices, they did mostly hope that the miracle in prospect would change their daily lives. Everywhere in the South people believed that a better life was no longer just a pipe dream, and this hope was baptized development. What Western developers or theoreticians could and would not see was that it coexisted in many places with a social conservatism that offered a shield against too-sudden change, even for people who hoped and prayed precisely for radical change. Westerners opposed tradition to modernity, but they did so without exploring the other kinds of relationship they might foster in the imagination and everyday practice of 'developing' nations.

On the one hand, then, dreams were given a name. On the other hand, third-world elites were won to the triad of development, all-powerful state and new international order, and made them the tools of their own ascent. Mostly fascinated by a West that had vanquished their forefathers and changed the course of their history,[12] they aspired to the modernity now presented to them as accessible – and outside which it was anyway pointless to think of joining the community of civilized nations. By the time of the Bandung Conference in 1955, they were taking up the term 'development' and proclaiming it an urgent necessity; they thought that everything remained to be done, preferably under their leadership, in countries left in the lurch by the Western withdrawal. But, without necessarily planning to instrumentalize development, they also saw it as a convenient means of securing a stable material basis – now that the mobilizing mystique of national liberation had exhausted itself – for the power monopoly they had hastily secured. To the new social layers (urban petty bourgeoisie, local assistants in the colonial administration, people marginalized by colonization) who had drawn from their leadership of liberation movements a collective claim to hegemony, independence offered the opportunity to haul themselves up to the upper reaches of the state. The next stage – the stage of development – gave them the opportunity to appropriate the state for themselves.

In nearly all the countries emerging from colonial domination, statist developmentalism soon became a technology that the ruling elites applied to extend their control over the whole of society – and to get their hands on revenue from its mineral wealth. The model proposed by Western mentors and launched by international backers seemed all the more attractive in that it remained silent about any political dimension of development, legitimating by default the wish of local elites to occupy the whole post-colonial political field, such as it was. In reality, the single party that spread throughout the third world from the 1960s until the late 1980s became the political equivalent of what development represented in economics.[13] The single political leadership had the task of making the single model a reality.

The 'new international economic order' – the third element of the triad – was supposed to lay the basis for a new division of global wealth between the countries that had always been rich and the elites in the South that aimed to become so. In addition, however, it gave development the moral dimension it badly needed to strengthen its legitimacy, and converted the rulers of the South into champions of justice and defenders of the oppressed. Even Westerners found it hard to deny the scandalous character of North–South inequalities and the need to remedy them. Finally, the demand for an order based on a kind of international democracy had the advantage of making people forget that its emergence had been blocked at national level.

But, if the ideology of development gave cover to powerful combinations of interests, themselves served by the huge aid machinery and development expertise, it was no less true that inequalities continued to sustain the gulf between North and South. What has been called the North–South dialogue may be read as an (aborted) attempt to divide up global wealth and power between new ruling layers in the South and power apparatuses in the North, the latter being in no hurry to abandon their privileges yet often prepared to come to local agreements over the joint exploitation of resources. The history of the 'development dec- ades' is, in part, one of convergent interests and conjunctural alliances between these new partners-cum-adversaries.

It cannot be reduced to that, however. It was also the history of a continental drift between Norths and Souths, an ever-widening gap between the living standards and wealth of the two regions, and a tight- ening of the bonds of dependence around the so-called developing countries caused by the very content given to the term. While the South desperately raced to reproduce the model, the North devised new strat- egies to modernize the foundations of its hegemony so that it would not have to yield any of its power. The resulting tissue of dependence, made up of imperial legacies as well as new networks, had effects that really demonstrated their potential in and after the 1980s.

SEVEN

The New Basis
of Hegemony

At the end of nearly half a century of development – a term that people have been shyer of using since the 1990s, so forcefully has it boomeranged on them – it must be agreed that any adjustments to the geography of global wealth have hardly redrawn the map. This does not mean that the world has not changed; indeed, the changes have been so rapid that they appear to some as revolutions. One example is the phenomenal expansion and redistribution of the world's population over the last fifty years. In the space of three generations, the total number of people living on earth has risen from barely 2 billion to 6 billion, radically altering the relations that human beings have with one another and with their surroundings. Only now are we beginning to realize the effects of this massively denser occupation of the planet.

Most of this growth has taken place in the South, and the countries grouped under this term now contain some 80 per cent of humanity. This new fact, which is one of the main challenges facing those countries, has not (yet?) changed the global relationship of forces. It is triggering new fears among the ageing populations of the North, who measure the demographic push by the nuisance value of inward migration. But the South does not carry any greater weight in issues affecting the fate of humanity: it does not play a larger role in decision-making bodies, and no new balance of global wealth covers the needs that are growing *pari passu* with its population.

The constancy of wealth

The map of wealth distribution is not, however, the same as it was half a century ago. The South has seen the birth of states with a very high

99

level of wealth derived from mineral and energy resources, as well as industrial economies based on the global relocation of labour-intensive manufacturing activity, but at the same time other parts of the third world have been hit by growing pauperization. This emergence of prosperous countries (whether idle or industrious) and sub-states reduced to begging is by no means a trivial matter, since it has blown apart the fiction of the unity of the South. Yet these shifts in wealth have occurred within the South itself and, while modifying its overall image, have not affected the global economy of its relations with the North. It is in other areas that their shock waves need to be traced.

The case of oil illustrates this continuity within change which seems to have marked the evolution of North–South relations over the last half-century. In 1973 and 1979, the two rounds of oil price rises were considered major shocks to the world's leading economies, and the oil-producing countries thought they had found a weapon that would last for as long as the old industrial powers remained dependent on the black gold. These powers, having rebuilt their economies after the war and regained their prosperity partly through easy access to cheap energy, were now forced to carry out difficult adjustments in the realms of energy and finance in order to regain the equilibrium disturbed by the price explosion. Not all did this in the same degree, however, as the North–South conflicts also served to settle some accounts within the North.

The United States, the world's number one oil producer until it decided to cut back on output and treat some of its deposits as strategic reserves,[1] gained more than it lost from the shock of 1973 and did little to dissuade its main allies in the most oil-rich region in the world, the Middle East. The rises of 1973 enabled American oil corporations (which then controlled the largest part of the market) both to quadruple their profits and to ensure profitability for a round of more costly prospecting.[2] Europe and Japan, on the other hand, which import nearly all their oil, were hit hard by the price rises and by the resulting weakness of their economies in the second half of the 1970s.

The new oil trends thus had a major impact in each of the two great divisions of the globe: in the South, the gap constantly widened between newly wealthy countries and others that were in no position to pay their soaring oil bill; while in the North, the influence and power of the United States increased to the detriment of its European and Japanese ally–competitors. But, apart from short-term tremors, the balance of forces between North and South did not radically change – on the contrary.

Once the first shocks had passed, the countries of the North devised counter-offensive strategies that were to reverse the early-1970s logic of oil dependence. Europe and Japan, having had their fingers badly burned, started to change their energy policy in the middle of the decade, with an ever greater use of nuclear power as well as various energy-saving measures. The United States, which refused to contemplate any such adjustment, assured itself of being able to satisfy its bloated appetite for oil by strengthening its political and military control over the world's major oil-producing regions. Finally, the intense activity of Western corporations led to new oil strikes and the emergence of non-OPEC producers that reduced the role of the oil cartel. Barely ten years were all that was required to bring prices almost back down to their 1973 level. In constant 1973 dollars, these moved from $2.25 a barrel in 1973 to $9 in 1974, then to $13 in 1979 (following the second shock) and $15 in 1982, before falling back below $11 in 1984 and down to $5 in 1985.

The fall that began in 1982 wiped out the illusion of the exporting countries that they held the fate of the industrial world in their hands. Of course, they had meanwhile grown considerably richer, and – whatever the market fluctuations – oil remained sufficiently important for them to continue to draw sizeable dividends. But we know today the damage that the rentier mentality caused to the economies of the major oil-producing countries. The most populous and the most endowed with an existence prior to that of their subsoil – from Nigeria to Algeria or Iran to Venezuela – used up their oil in a mad dash for industrialization and power[3] and a frenzy of ruling-class luxury spending that returned to their partners in the North most of the petrodollars they had managed to extract from them. As to the monarchies of the Arabian–Persian Gulf, they carried their rentier behaviour to the point of caricature. Once again, the impact of their new wealth was felt mainly in the South.

Saudi Arabia, in particular, used a not insignificant part of its assets to finance an amorphous band of ultra-reactionary political movements in the Muslim world laying claim to Wahhabi Islam, which were the main nuclei of Islamic radicalism in the 1980s. None of these movements would have been as influential as it was without the financial manna from Riyadh.[4] Nor was Saudi Arabia the only such player in the field. Iran's role in funding a rival Islamic International is well known, as are Libya's attempts to get Islamic radicalism off the ground in sub-Saharan Africa. In each case, it was in the South that the main shock waves were felt from the oil price explosion.

The debt economy

These trends had not been calculated in advance. But the influx of oil-fuelled liquidity into a world capital market in the throes of restructuring gave the signal for a radical transformation of North–South financial relations.[5] Within the space of a few years, a system based on aid gave way to one based on credit, heralding a debt economy from which the South, as a whole, has not yet emerged.

Since the 1950s, as we have seen, the countries of the South struggled to meet the high cost of reproducing a development model whose main feature was that it brooked no alternative. Official development aid (ODA) was scarcely a generous contribution (at no more than 0.34 per cent of GNP for the OECD countries in 1970, or an annual average of $6 billion in the 1960s[6]), but it was enough to maintain the spiral of financial dependence. For the other feature of mimetic development was that it was almost entirely imported from abroad; countries that tried it brought in factories and technologies at a high cost, and sometimes also the experts to run them. Thus, in the early 1990s, the cost of technical cooperation still represented a quarter of all aid to Africa, or more than $3 billion a year.[7] The structure of ODA shows the role it played in exporting the model and the vast field this opened for hungry Western corporations. In the 1970s, the financing of imports by recipient countries accounted for nearly a third of ODA,[8] and related administrative costs for roughly 13 per cent. Agriculture absorbed less than 10 per cent of the aid, mostly for large-scale projects, while industry received more in the way of funds than did health.

From 1973, however, as donor countries faced soaring energy bills and slower rates of growth, most of them began to reduce their aid, if not in absolute terms, then as a proportion of their GNP (even though this was not actually shrinking).[9] The developing countries had anyway not been developing at the expected pace, and the good intentions had begun to flag. Private capital, on the other hand, was ready and willing to step into the breach. In 1974 the financial surplus of oil-producing countries reached $60 billion, and in 1976 the official assets of OPEC countries represented a quarter of global assets. It is well known that the banks engaged in cut-throat competition to recycle the huge amount of excess liquidity. Many developing countries were then considered solvent because the general, if chaotic, rise in the prices of primary products soon swelled their monetary reserves. But official aid, which had equalled a half of their total debt in 1970, no longer covered more than 36 per cent by 1976.[10] The South's outstanding debt quadrupled between the two oil shocks: in a dozen countries it had shot past 50 per cent of GNP by 1979, while in twenty or so others it lay between 30 and 50 per cent of GNP.[11] The phenomenon soon became cumulative, as borrowers ran up further debts in an attempt to maintain their repayment schedule.

Accustomed to living on credit, unable to achieve the anticipated catching-up, the endebted countries of the South – both rich and poor – no longer had any room for manoeuvre by the end of the 1970s and would soon feel the full brunt of the mechanisms of dependence put in place during the first two 'development decades'.

The debt dividend

We cannot here analyse in detail the restructuring policies that began to be imposed on the South in the late 1970s.[12] But we should recall that the toughness of those policies, and the rapacity with which creditors demanded debt repayment, were proportional to the eagerness with which money had been lent throughout the 1970s. The major countries of the North may not have knowingly trapped their partners in the South, but they certainly made conscious use of the debt to reshape the world according to the new codes they were then elaborating. All through the 1970s, the industrial countries and the international finance organizations acting as their secular arm made it easier for the developing countries to borrow. Not only did this reduce the ODA requirement; it also served to boost their own exports to the South. Between 1970 and 1980, more than two-thirds of the money drawn from the IMF (which later built its reputation on toughness) were subject to very weak conditions.[13] In the second half of the decade, French president Valéry Giscard d'Estaing even came up with the idea of a 'trialogue' to make this flow of money a permanent feature of the landscape – that is, a three-sided partnership in which countries with a large oil surplus would play the treasurers, the industrial countries (duly rewarded by the latter) would supply equipment goods and services to the developing countries, and the developing countries would play the grateful recipients of aid that was supposed to make them developed. And it is true that the share of developing countries in French exports of equipment goods rose to 40 per cent in 1977 from 20 per cent three years earlier.[14]

During the years of rising prices for primary products, the countries which spent most lavishly on pharaonic ventures found themselves the most avidly courted. It would be tiresome to list all the 'white elephants', those exorbitantly priced projects, often useless or oversized in relation to needs, which hastened many a country's descent into bankruptcy – from the Inga dam in Zaire through the Ivory Coast sugar refineries to the Algerian steel complex at El Hadjar,[15] not to speak of the soaring military expenditure that helped a lot in recycling the petrodollars. From 1970 to 1977 the weapons markets of the South grew by an annual average of 13 per cent, and between 1971 and 1985 the developing countries purchased arms to the value of $286 billion (in constant 1985 prices) – that is, the equivalent of 30 per cent of the accumulated debt in 1985.[16]

From 1974, industrial gigantism in the South softened the OECD growth slowdown. According to the World Bank, the OECD countries would have lost an extra growth point in 1974 and 1975 if the developing countries had not had access to bank credit.[17] In the end, this accelerated the predatory drift of most of the ruling layers in the South, who found in it fabulous opportunities for enrichment.

The North's encouragement of breakneck industrialization, for no real purpose save that of filling its companies' order books, promoted massive corruption from which it stood to gain still further. Without retelling the history of 'Françafrique', we may note that the French state has continually covered up for the practices of French companies, which are past masters in the art of overinvoicing and hidden-dividend distribution to their clients,[18] and that the foreign trade insurance company COFACE has always had political blessing for its insurance of expenditure linked to corruption.[19] In the United States, the Federal Reserve has estimated that a third of the $252 billion by which the debt of Brazil, Argentina, Mexico, Chile and Venezuela increased between 1974 and 1982 was privately invested in the shares of foreign companies or personal bank accounts. In 1988 Latin American assets in the United States were thought to total $327 billion, of which $315 billion had originated in flight of capital.

Thus, the states and companies of the North have long enjoyed a twin benefit from their role as corrupter: they have gained markets that would not all have existed in more transparent contexts; and they have repatriated, in the form of private investments or luxury spending, commissions paid to decision-makers in the South.

This sharing of the dividend from excessive debt cannot be said to have applied to the disastrous final bill. Much has been written about the recession suffered by the North after the second oil shock in 1979, a recession from which it took years to emerge. Certainly there can be no denying the reality of a crisis which, with its massive contraction of demand, soon made itself felt all around the world. But we should also remember the many factors that lay behind it, and measure its scale not by the exceptional growth of the preceding period but by the recessions that hit the rest of the world at the same time.

The short-term rise in the price of energy sources, minerals and agricultural products played only a modest role in the loss of impetus in the industrial heartlands. The main factors were the exhaustion of the post-war growth regime and the destabilizing shift from strictly super-vised global circulation of capital to deregulated money markets. There had been more and more signs that a change was under way, but it seems to have taken the soaring fuel prices to illuminate a process to which people had previously tended to turn a blind eye. Western demand for consumer durables, after a quarter-century of spectacular advances, now underwent a certain contraction that was not offset by growth in parts of the South expected to achieve take-off. The first-generation manufacturing activities of the industrial revolution, so far concentrated in the old bastions of Western Europe and the United States, began to migrate to the new workshop countries of the South, while third-generation industries came to the fore in the North – a trend that lay at the root of a radical change in production structures and the organiza-tion of wage labour. These tremors occurred in a climate of monetary instability and high inflation, in which the rising prices for primary products did play some role.

Finally, the crisis gave the signal for a turnaround in the economic and monetary policy of the industrial countries, one so far-reaching that it soon looked like a revolution for which the theoretical foundations had been laid in the previous years but which had not produced all its effects. The crisis therefore ran deep, and people soon realized that it would last a long time. Yet, whilst redrawing the architecture of the global economy, it did not threaten the North's hegemony over the rest of the world or reduce the imbalance between North and South, whose scale and structure remained similar to what they had been before the approach of the fin-de-siècle. In fact, although the Western countries were momentarily destabilized by new initiatives in the South, they turned to their advantage the predictable outcome of the debt spiral, which suddenly became apparent in the Mexican bankruptcy of 1982 and the Western drive to purge global finances and put an end to further dreams of a new deal. The shattering collapse of the socialist bloc in

1989, then the implosion of the Soviet Union itself, greatly assisted the West by giving the *coup de grâce* to an already seriously devalued socialist rhetoric, and by rendering obsolete the alliance blackmail that some leaders in the South had made their specialty.

Crisis and adjustment

There is much to be said, and much has been said, about how people in the South faced the brunt of adjustment to the new-look global economy in the 1980s, and how people in the North underwent the same process less intensely, in different forms and with different names. Although the shocks were severe in both cases, they were clearly not of the same order of gravity. The North – or anyway Europe, which lacked its own oil reserves – experienced a recession that was quite minor in comparison with those affecting Latin America, Africa and parts of Asia (only East Asia soon recovered from a crisis that had struck a little earlier than in the rest of the developing world). Between 1981 and 1990, the OECD countries recorded average yearly growth of 3.2 per cent, whereas Latin America and the Caribbean notched up 2 per cent, sub-Saharan Africa 1.9 per cent, and North Africa and the Middle East 0.4 per cent (the rentier countries of the region suffering the worst effects of the oil shock in reverse).[20] Asia, carried along by its dragons (first and foremost China), mostly had growth rates in excess of 5 per cent. But these averages obscure the fact that during those years many experienced negative growth or growth below 1 per cent. This was the case in 22 countries of the South, more than a quarter of the 82 major economies for which statistics were available[21] – a list that included such large American economies as Mexico or Argentina, but none in the North other than Portugal, then still considered a developing economy. Belgium's 1.4 per cent over the period from 1980 to 1988 was the lowest in the North, while the United States and Canada outstripped Europe with yearly advances of 3.3 per cent, and Japan profited from the Asian dynamism to consolidate its own growth.

The gap between the world's two divisions was even wider if we take into account their different population trends. Whereas the North – with the exception of countries with inward migration, such as the United States, Canada and Australia – experienced something close to demographic standstill, the South saw its population increase more slowly than in the previous decade but still at a high average rate of 2 per cent. In many countries of the South, the slow progress of GNP therefore meant an actual decline in per capita GNP.[22] According to the UNDP,[23] in the course of the 1980s 59 countries in the South out of a total of 107 for which figures are available saw a decline in per capita GDP, whereas between 1976 and 1990 all Western countries – even those worst hit by the crisis – chalked up a significant increase.

The differential evolution of real per capita GDP tells us even more about the reality of the three 'development decades' from 1960 to 1990, for the gap between North and South widened in 62 of the 90 countries for which the UNDP has figures.[24] Several countries in Latin America which had almost reached the level of Europe in 1960 fell further and further behind over the next thirty years; China and India, for all their progress real or alleged, also saw the gap widen between themselves and the developed world; and although the Asian wonder-economies managed to move up closer, they still – with the atypical exceptions of Hong Kong and Singapore – had a long way to travel before catching up their models. In 1990 South Korea, the most advanced of the so-called dragons, still had a real per capita GDP less than half that of the countries of the North.

If the crisis affected various parts of the world in different degrees, this was also because they were not all handled in the same way. Once the Western countries had regained the initiative, they inflicted upon their debtors in the South a treatment that they were far from having applied to themselves. This is not to deny that there were profound changes in the Western economies, or that the neoliberal revolution, begun in the United States and Britain and extended ever more zealously to the whole of Europe, delivered a sharp social shock to the weakest sections of the population – all the more scandalous in that these countries continued to grow wealthier, albeit at a slower pace than before. Nor am I forgetting that, in the world's richest countries, there was growing absolute poverty – that is, larger numbers of people altogether excluded from employment and therefore (in the developed world) from social existence. The passage from economically Keynesian and politically social-democratic management of the Western countries to a universal (if differentially paced) deregulation was expressed in a degree of poverty which, during the post-war golden age, had been thought safely consigned to the museums.

Nevertheless, even if the unions and other agencies of social mediation lost some of their strength and often concentrated on defending the gains of the old wage-labour aristocracies, the negotiated settlement

of disputes and, at least in Europe, the existence of real if inadequate
safety nets did something to soften the fall. The workings of democracy
may not have thrown up an alternative to the neoliberal turn, but they
did mitigate some of its effects and – to an extent that varied with the
country's wealth and degree of deregulation – kept absolute poverty at
the level of a relatively marginal phenomenon. In 1995, at the end of
fifteen years of deregulation, 16.5 per cent of the population of the
United States, the most inegalitarian of the developed countries, were
living on an income less than half that of the national average. Other
centres of deregulation had poverty levels of 15.2 per cent (Ireland) and
15 per cent (Britain), while Sweden's 7 per cent was the least
calamitous.[25]

In most of the South, the shock to the urban popular classes and
lower levels of the middle classes was so violent that it can scarcely be
compared to that in the North. Those excluded from the system represented a far larger part of the population.[26] And for millions upon
millions, structural adjustment had massive consequences in their daily
lives: sweeping redundancies in the public services, including hundreds
of thousands of permanent staff sacked with little or no compensation;
liquidation of numerous state corporations, whose employees were
thrown onto a usually saturated labour market; erosion of real wages
through inflation in nearly every country in Latin America, or an actual
reduction in nominal wages that went as high as 30 per cent (as in
Cameroon); abolition of the subsidies on staple items that had allowed
the poorest sections in many countries to feed themselves; cuts in education and health budgets, leading to higher charges and, in many
African countries, to declining rates of school attendance and health
cover.

No Western government, unless bent on suicide, would have dared
impose such medicine – some were punished at the polls for much less.
Yet budget and trade deficits, or state companies so profligate that their
very existence owed more to politics than to sound use of public money,
were by no means a peculiarity of the South. From the gaping US trade
deficit of the 1980s to the Italian public-sector waste worthy of a
Courteline farce, there is no shortage of examples of 'unsound' management in the North – to use an expression dear to the IMF. Although
monetarist dogma and market expansion at the cost of deregulation
everywhere imposed similar measures, the North and the South did not
experience these with the same intensity or the same speed, and their
peoples did not feel the effects with the same violence.

In the North, adjustment to the new liberal order widened social inequalities more than it impoverished society as a whole, and it was the glaring nature of the contrasts that caused the loudest outcry. In the South, too, structural adjustment policies worsened inequality – all the more since the welfare state either did not exist or took the form of clientelist redistribution. But the changed rules of the economic game also gave decision-makers in the North (who had made up the rules) an opportunity to offload onto the rest of the world some of the bill for neoliberal 'reforms', so that the blow was softened in the developed countries through the worsening of global inequalities. People in the debt-riddled South thus suffered from the new international conjuncture of the 1980s and their declining economic weight, while also being forced by their ruling layers to bear the brunt of IMF measures foisted upon their semi-bankrupt economies.

The main aim of IMF-sponsored restructuring was to make these economies again capable of debt repayment. In many cases, the new context of falling prices for the whole range of primary products turned this programme into a veritable nightmare, as countries with high levels of debt saw their solvency savagely reduced. At the same time, anti-inflationary measures in the United States and then the European Union greatly increased the outstanding debt: tighter controls on the money supply translated for the South into sky-high interest rates (again largely positive in real terms by the early 1980s) and a credit squeeze that drastically curtailed the scope for refinancing.

Although the international financial organizations recognized the crucial role of exogenous factors, they set out to eradicate only what they deemed to be the internal causes of debtor-country default. The twin pillars of the first adjustment package were thus a reduction in local demand and government spending, and a prioritization of exports to generate the foreign currency for debt repayment. Despite frequent rescheduling and a plethora of derisory debt-reduction schemes,[27] the 'adjusted' countries met their repayment deadlines more punctually than it is often believed. In any event, conditions attached to new (public) loans did not leave them with any choice in the matter, making them net exporters of capital all through the 1980s. Between 1982 and 1989 the high-debt countries – that is, almost all countries in the South – repaid $1,180 billion in interest and principal and received $774 billion in public and private funds from the North, so that the transfer from South to North amounted to $405 billion.[28] The World Bank estimates that between 1982 and 1990 gross debt-related transfers from South to

North were as high as $1,345 billion, and that between 1984 and 1989 Latin America alone paid $153 billion more than it received.[29] Since the debts could not be rescheduled, the IMF and World Bank became throughout the second half of the 1980s what bankers' jargon calls negative net lenders: that is, they received in repayments from debtors a total sum greater than that of the new loans they granted.

The South may not have paid cash on the nail, but it continued to reimburse a debt which, far from disappearing, kept on growing through the magic of interest rates and expensive rescheduling. In 1979, just before the crisis broke, its aggregate debt stood at $457 billion; by 1991 it had more than tripled to reach $1,478 billion, and by 1998 it had passed $2,000 billion.[30] The poorest of the poor are still repaying. So it is a little cynical to claim – as a whole chorus of voices do in the West – that the countries of the South will never pay back their debt, that the sums officially due are effectively lost to creditors, and that cancellation involves a profit-and-loss calculation on anyway irrecoverable debt. Listening to these fanfares, one would think that they were announcing humanitarian gestures to lift the poorest countries from the abyss. Only rarely does a commentator point out their extremely limited scope and the draconian conditions attaching to them, with the result that public opinion is fed on the idea that the West's civilizing mission is continuing in different forms. After the tough but ultimately beneficial colonial period, after the help given for them to catch up with the Western model, the time has supposedly come to forgive the poor the disastrous effects of their prodigality and to put them back on the right track by wiping out part, but only part, of their debt.

Technologies of constraint

The refusal of creditor states and organizations to take any responsibility for the bad financial practices of the 1970s removed any possibility of joint (not solely Western) management of the accumulated debt, while the lure of debt relief as a way of salving public conscience and keeping debtors hopeful ensured that the file would not be closed. In fact, the South's debt has proved a useful tool for creditors to keep debtors dependent on them and to impose conditions in line with the second aim of adjustment programmes: that is, the dismantling of regulatory frameworks as part of a global return to liberalism and all-round competition among the world's economies.

One point should be clarified here. My long experience of countries in the South makes me rather cautious about the kind of out-of-hand condemnation of adjustment that one sometimes hears in the West, in circles of people filled with the best intentions. For everything depends upon the precise content. The (relative) clean-up of high-debt economies, including in most cases a curbing of the state's bloated prerogatives, has dried up a few rentier deposits and sometimes put a brake on privatization geared to the profit of ruling teams or families, or the scarcely larger layers of people living on sinecures. Nor is there any reason to regret the end of the overinvestment policies best illustrated in Latin America, which, though theoretically designed to speed up development, had little or no effect on the general standard of living. Similarly, the modification of the internal terms of trade between town and country to be less unfavourable to the latter, especially in sub-Saharan Africa, and the halting of the pathological increase of parasitic bureaucracies (most grotesque in Congo-Brazzaville, where in 1980 there were 80,000 state functionaries for a population under two million), cannot be regarded as underhand blows against hapless victims. History offers many examples which show that the state is just as capable as the market of suffocating society. In principle, a redrawing of its functions and taxation powers, without penalizing the population at large, could have helped many economies in the South to end their drift into rentierism.

Nevertheless, the few secondary positive effects of adjustment policies seem to have been due more to chance than to any intentions on the part of those who launched them. Their first and often only aim was to get the debt repaid and to sweep away any obstacles to a full opening up of national economies. With privatization and the retreat of public authorities into their so-called regalian functions, the market-opening removal of customs barriers and obstacles to the movement of commodities and capital became a central requirement for any country wishing to benefit from new and costly gifts.

The changing conditions attached to Western aid policies are evidence of the new concerns. Until the 1980s, the only conditions were political in nature: the country in question had to choose sides in the cold war whose battlefields were dotted around the continents of South. The state – that is, the ruling group – was then the only valid interlocutor for financial backers, since it alone could swing the country to one or the other side of the strategic line dividing the world. 'Civil society' never entered the picture. Most of the movements which stood in for it

were thought to have been corrupted by Marxism, and were treated as
fifth columns for the Red menace. Especially in Latin America and
Asia, the main priority of US assistance was to reduce them to silence;
aid money came with hardly any economic or financial strings, and the
greatest laxity was the order of the day in such matters. Subsequently,
however, the shift to terms and conditions defined in terms of economics is further evidence that this came to overlap with politics in a new
strategic horizon for the West. Logically enough, it was in the economic
sphere that the West rebuilt the foundations of its hegemony after post-
war geopolitical recomposition and intellectual questioning had made
the old ones partly obsolete.

Over time, the new conditions for aid became a kind of box of tools
for spreading norms established in the North to the rest of the world.
Those directly concerning the economy left the South's rulers with the
scantiest room for manoeuvre, turning them into adjustment managers
even as they dreamed up countless stratagems to get round their obligations. In the 1990s, however, political conditions started to reappear in
new guises.[31] Since the full opening of national economies to the market
required a favourable institutional framework, 'good governance' became the central pillar of a now multivalent system of constraints. Wise
management of public affairs, struggle against excesses of corruption,
establishment of a legislative, regulatory and fiscal framework to favour
economic growth, encouragement of free enterprise and foreign investment, respect for a minimum rule of law: these were the main components of the model sketched out a decade or so ago.[32]

Again, let there be no misunderstanding. I am not scorning attempts
to curb the corrupt or arbitrary practices that people remote from the
corridors of power have had to endure in the countries of the South.
But if exhortations to good governance may have had some positive
effects, their main aim was to make the state an effective instrument for
the promotion and protection of a liberal economy. In Africa, the World
Bank argued, the state should be content 'to instal basic infrastructure
and social services, to run the legal and judicial apparatus that a market
economy requires, and to protect the environment. Even in these areas,
the public authorities should appeal as much as possible to the private
sector – for example, through adjudication procedures.'[33] The major
international organizations had a similar conception of the war on corruption. For the OECD, which in 1997 sponsored an 'agreement on
combating the corruption of foreign public officials in international commercial transactions', the task was 'to create a level playing field for

companies wishing to obtain markets abroad, by prohibiting the payment of bribes to foreign public officials. As the agreement will assist more efficient allocation of economic resources, it will also benefit nationals of the countries that allocate these markets.'[34] The institutional recasting is considered important only in so far as it appears to be a condition for the success of neoliberal economic reforms.

Most countries of the South, being prisoners of the technologies of constraint developed in the aftermath of independence, had no other choice than to occupy the position allocated to them in the new international division of labour and wealth. Only a few gained sufficient room for manoeuvre to negotiate on the matter, and even they lacked the means to turn the hazards of financial globalization to their advantage and were forced to submit, at least partially, to rules that mainly served the interests of those who had decreed them. This was the case of the emergent Asian countries, whose dynamism was supposed to keep the Bretton Woods organizations at arm's length, but which were forced to turn to them in the financial crisis that devastated their economies in 1997.

Worldwide uniformity, under the auspices of the information revolution and financial globalization, has come to appear such an unyielding law that today the worst prospect for a country is to be excluded from the planetary dynamism. For the 'useless' fringes of the Western labour force, as for countries of little economic and financial interest and the most insecure sections of their population, exclusion has become, together with long-familiar exploitation, one of the figures of inequality between and within nations. The chimeras of autarky or disconnection have had their day – and whenever they came true they took on nightmarish features. Since alternative forms of globalization are still out of the contest, though we must still try to believe that they have a future, the only remaining choice – a purely theoretical one at that – is between high-risk solitude and a perspective of insertion which, probably less dangerous, may also carry an exorbitant price.

EIGHT

The Privileges of Power

The costs of globalization would certainly be lighter if all (consenting or constrained) partners in the building of a unified world market for the twenty-first century were in the same boat. But since time immemorial, the privilege of the powerful has been to escape the rules they are able to lay down. Thus, within the international arena serving to enforce deregulation, the North campaigns for total freedom for itself (with a few safeguards or periods of grace before full implementation) in trade with its interlocutors in the South, but continues to do as much as it possibly can to protect itself from any competition that appears harmful to its interests.

Making use of liberalism

When it comes to trade, the more the countries of the South seek to comply with neoliberal injunctions, the more they seem to suffer from the asymmetry between what the North imposes on them and what it applies to itself. In a field where survival of the fittest is still the prevailing law, the two main levels of international commercial relations contain three groups of protagonists – although there may also be ad hoc alliances or shifts between them. Best known and most widely covered in the media is the long-standing conflictual relationship between the United States and the European Union, since it concerns the main players in world trade which are at the same time the major world powers.

The American hyperpower regards its export performance not only as a crucial source of income, but also as one of the tools ensuring its preponderance in the world. Whilst opposing any access restrictions on its own services and commodities in the European market, the United States uses a battery of laws contravening freedom of trade whenever it sees a threat to its own interests. Since the start of the Uruguay Round in 1986 these Euro-American differences have regularly been in the headlines on both sides of the Atlantic, but this has tended to push out of sight the third group of players in world trade, the countries of the South. The interests of these countries vary as a function both of their productive apparatuses and of their position in the international division of labour, but the countries of the North have similar attitudes to them, and in this respect there is nothing much to choose between Europe and the United States. Proof of this is the fact that the US non-energy trade deficit with its principal partners in the South is far greater than that of the EU, the region of the world that achieves the largest trade surplus.[1]

Since the shrinking of the world turned trade into the principal human activity – between 1948 and 1998 trade in goods rose 14-fold while world output increased 5.5 times over[2] – and made its expansion the official index of global prosperity, all countries (or nearly all) have tried to make the most of their export capacities. All the neoliberal updaters of Ricardo's theory of comparative advantage – and, following them, all organizations charged with applying liberal norms, from the Bretton Woods institutions through the OECD to the WTO – have promoted export growth to the rank of an economic imperative.

The monetarist requirement of macroeconomic equilibrium – whether expressed in the constraints of structural adjustment or the obligation to comply with the Maastricht convergence criteria – has made a veritable obsession out of the usual concern of governments to achieve a positive trade balance. Any surplus is publicly presented as a sign of good national health, any significant export order as a report of victory over the rest of the world. In the 1950s and 1960s, the recentring of most of the world's economies upon their national or regional space made people forget that the capitalist powers first asserted themselves as traders on the world market. Today, once more, the power of a nation is largely measured by its capacity to sell its products in the four corners of the earth.

In today's free-for-all, therefore, the point is to export at any price and to import as little as possible, to use any means to penetrate external markets and keep out overzealous competitors, while jealously protecting one's own market. And, as in every free-for-all, the most powerful are able to have their way. Over the past few decades, the large developed countries have put in place a whole arsenal of measures to open up other markets while leaving their own barely ajar. Protectionism is here their most effective weapon, even as they compel their partners in the South to open their frontiers to competition. Although free trade looms as a sacred cow in the speeches of those in charge, the policies of the main trading powers have for years had the colours of a strange liberal mercantilism that imposes infinitely variable regulations on the rest of the world, in accordance with the idea that their rulers have of their interests at any particular moment and the power of various lobbies to defend a particular sector of the national economy.

Anything goes when it is a matter of keeping imports within tolerable limits, especially if these come from emergent countries whose dynamism is still feared as a threat. Of the anti-dumping procedures introduced by the EU in 1997, most of which refer to largely imaginary dumping and serve mainly to enlarge the EU's protectionist arsenal, 26.6 per cent concern the major exporters of the South (Korea, Hong Kong, Indonesia, Malaysia, Taiwan, Thailand and Brazil) and 20.8 per cent China alone.[3]

The countries of the South, however, traditionally protectionist for a mixture of good and bad reasons,[4] were forced by adjustment programmes and an unfavourable balance of forces at the start of the Uruguay Round to remove more and more of their protective barriers. Once the major trading powers had defined market access as a key imperative, the rule of mutual advantage replaced the principle of compensatory non-reciprocity that had been dominant in the 1960s and 1970s. All the North–South trade agreements signed in the 1990s – from the North American Free Trade Agreement (NAFTA) to the agreements between the EU and Tunisia and Morocco – prized open the borders of the South, with only the LDCs (the 'least developed countries') benefiting from any compensation. Even more of a new departure was the insistence that each country signing the WTO's Marrakesh agreement should guarantee import access to the value of at least 3 per cent of internal production for all products – an opening of its market, therefore, even in sectors where demand was fully met internally.

In order to gain the further trading advantage of captive markets, the Western states also used the Uruguay Round talks to ring-fence their monopolies in technological capital. The TRIPS part of the Marrakesh Agreement, which concerns intellectual property rights, strictly guards patents and licences in every area where new products and applications multiplied in the 1990s. Since 1995, for the first time in human history, the movement of scientific and technological innovations throughout the world has been regulated by the market; free loans of technology have no longer been an available option for the furthering of development. The countries of the South eventually signed the TRIPS agreement only in return for an explicit undertaking that all obstacles to trade in textile goods would be lifted within a period of ten years. By the end of 1999, the United States had removed just 13 of its 750 quotas and the European Union 14 of its 219 import restrictions on such goods.[5]

The loaded dice of free trade

Financial clout gives the major countries of the North a further capacity to control their overseas markets, in ways that reinforce the mercantilist logic of their trade policy at the expense of the liberal creed they serve up to their partners. For example, by converting the world market in grain and meat into a clearance sale for the colossal surpluses generated by their productivist agriculture, they have secured a virtual monopoly such that the USA, EU and Canada alone control three-quarters of world grain exports. But, in order to undercut any competition while ensuring stable incomes for their national producers, they have generalized the disastrous practice of direct or indirect export subsidies. Having made abundant use of food aid to open external markets to their products, they now engage in extreme forms of the very dumping that they tirelessly block at their own frontiers. Both practices have the effect of encouraging agricultural surpluses at home and holding back subsistence agriculture in the countries that receive their exports.

For at least two decades, food aid served to prop up world prices for grains and dairy produce, by allowing a part of output to be sold on the margins of commodity circuits; it reduced the size of Western food mountains and gradually turned aid recipients into regular customers for Western products. The flood of so-called humanitarian disasters around the turn of the century has tended to obscure the fact that emergency relief has never been more than a small part of food aid, and that the bulk of it has always consisted of long-term contracts with recipient countries, usually large grain consumers (such as Egypt or the Maghreb) and only rarely among the world's poorest. At the end of the 1970s, food accounted for more than 10 per cent of official Western development aid and more than a third of the aid disbursed by the

European Community (for which it was then a major plank of agricultural policy).[6] In 1984, the thirtieth anniversary of the enactment of America's 'Food for Peace' legislation led the Reagan administration to draw up a balance sheet upon which no comment is needed:

> The Food for Peace program has accomplished multiple objectives: to combat hunger and malnutrition abroad, to expand export markets for U.S. agriculture, to encourage economic advancement in developing countries, and to promote in other ways the foreign policy of the United States.... Eight of our top ten agricultural markets are former recipients of Food for Peace aid.[7]

Although imports under the food aid rubric were also intended to help the trade balance of, and stave off social disorders in, many countries allied with the United States, the free handouts or low-price sales in major urban agglomerations deprived local farmers of their national markets and discouraged any effort on their part to increase subsistence crops.

Export subsidies had a similarly negative impact on food-importing countries in the South, as institutional food aid began to fall away in the late 1980s because of supply-side policies in the West and the growing number of emergency relief operations. In 1990, government support for agriculture in the countries of North America and Western Europe averaged 41 per cent of the total value of agricultural production, or approximately $150 billion.[8] Although, during the Uruguay Round, the United States had openly sought to liberalize agricultural trade and thereby counter the EU's high-subsidy export dynamism, support for agriculture has not diminished since the signing of the Marrakesh agreement on the WTO. According to the OECD, the level of support for producers actually increased in 1998 in all the major exporting countries.[9]

The abortive WTO conference in Seattle in November 1999 was the scene of a Euro–American dispute over figures for agricultural aid. But in reality it is not the size of the aid but only its forms that differ: the EU's main priority is export subsidies (although it has undertaken to reduce them in the future), whereas the United States prefers to disburse aid directly to producers. For years the world's two major food-producing powers have been fighting it out with each other by means of subsidies and discounts, to capture third-country markets in the East and South by keeping world food prices artificially low. In November 1992, at the height of the agricultural battle within the Uruguay Round, what was then still the European Community announced export refunds of 82 ecus (roughly $80) per tonne of wheat to cover sales of 250,000 tonnes to Algeria and 600,000 tonnes to Egypt. A fortnight later, the United States sold Morocco 530,000 tonnes of wheat with a subsidy of $47 per tonne.[10]

Importing countries value such practices as a way of reducing their food bill, but the effects on their own agriculture are most often disastrous as producers are unable to match the prices of the world's most productive and heavily subsidized agricultures. Since the 1980s there have been more and more cases where dumping has destroyed whole chains of local production. The EU, for example, has long been flooding African countries with low-grade beef at knock-down prices, undercutting local produce and thereby preventing the development of a profitable cattle sector.[11] In the Philippines, the lowering of customs duties on a wide range of agricultural goods, combined with the effects of American subsidies, has made the price of imported US maize 20 per cent lower than locally grown produce, and the price differential is set to rise to 39 per cent by 2004.[12]

At the same time that they discourage imports, therefore, the major countries of the North have been constantly refining strategies to increase their global market share. Of course they share this aim with every other market economy, but only they have had the means to achieve it and to impose on the rest of the world the contradiction they have cultivated between what they say and what they do. Less ambitious exporting countries are not always happy to see the big trading powers flout the rules that they themselves support within international bodies: the 'Cairns Group', spanning both North and South,[13] calls for the elimination of all export subsidies or assistance and the complete liberalization of world trade.

Having neither the wealth to promote dumping policies nor the political clout to impose their own views on trading partners, these countries have become the promoters of a level playing field in the shape of fully liberalized markets, which, in their eyes, are the only framework that can ensure fair competition among the world's exporters. But the United States and the European Union have so far paid them little heed, apparently intending to remain the sole or principal suppliers in every sector except raw materials.

Now, it is not exactly new for trading powers to impose a policy that removes barriers to their own exports while retaining a protectionist option whenever free trade does not seem certain to work in their favour.

Britain, at the height of its power in the nineteenth century, was the great apostle of opening borders to competition, and the colonial powers generally demanded freedom to export to their possessions (while closing their own markets to colonial manufactures or discouraging production there through a variety of authoritarian measures) and forced those states which remained formally sovereign to reduce or abolish their customs duties. For the weakest countries, historical periods of free trade witnessed a flattening or decline of production, whereas the Western countries protected themselves during every phase of their industrial expansion. What is new today is that they operate a protectionist and a liberal strategy simultaneously, attuning them to each sector and the needs of the hour.

The impressive arsenal at the disposal of the major countries of the North explains why the faster growth of international trade (which is one of the most striking features of 'globalization') has not dented their commercial hegemony. Once again, the effects have been felt mainly in the South, through a new distribution of the cards among its constituent regions. Whereas East and Southeast Asia has asserted itself as a rising economic force and some countries of Latin America have also increased their market share, huge areas of the world – most notably, sub-Saharan Africa – no longer occupy more than a marginal place in world trade.

Asian dynamism threatens in the coming years to alter the balance of world economic forces, but it has not yet overturned the hierarchy of commercial power. In 1995, at the peak of Asian expansion and before the crisis that hit the region, the developing countries together[14] accounted for no more than 20.7 per cent by value of world exports and 21.9 per cent of imports; the so-called high-income countries made up the balance of 79.3 per cent and 78.1 per cent respectively. Among the latter, the four pioneers of Asia's economic growth shared 10.3 per cent of world exports and 17.2 per cent of imports, and the world's seven leading economic powers (G7[15]) 49.1 per cent and 48.1 per cent, respectively. In all, moreover, 61 per cent of commercial transactions in the world are conducted between high-income countries. Not only do these figures confirm the overwhelming supremacy of the major Western countries; they also put into perspective the threat that they are supposed to be facing from the aggressiveness of newly industrialized countries. Taken as a whole, the old developed nations export more than they import, and their trade with the South shows a surplus in their favour.

Some more equal than others

The asymmetrical conditions of market access imposed by Western mercantilism are designed to ensure that trade remains weighted in favour of the North. But, as well as being convinced of its mission to flood the world with its own products and to restrain their development elsewhere, the North draws endlessly upon the resources of the planet as if it were a big supermarket. With no problems in its path, this limitless expansion of consumption came to seem a synonym for progress. Over the last quarter of a century, however, as demographic pressure has grown more constricting and awareness of the planet's finiteness more acute, the consumerism of the rich countries has gradually ceased to be a model and turned into a scandal. Guzzler of air, water and space, producer of all kinds of noxious waste, shameless grabber of non-renewable common goods: this is how the North is perceived in the rest of the world, even when the resulting level of comfort is still an object of people's aspirations.

There may no longer be the same fear that humanity will soon start running short of raw materials and energy sources, but the prospect of changed conditions of human existence, as a result of man's own actions, no longer belongs to the realm of fiction. We know that none of the elements permitting life on earth has an unlimited potential for regeneration. To relieve the pressure on the ecosystem, now rightly considered a common human heritage, has become a major theme in international relations and in the repeated clashes between countries of the South – which wish to secure their future by gaining a fairer share of non-renewable resources – and rich nations braced to defend and extend their privileges.

Contrary to what speeches about crisis and stagnant consumption might lead one to suppose, the West today enjoys a larger share of global wealth than it had a decade ago; the consumption gap, far from closing, has continued to widen. In 1998 a fifth of the world's population, nearly 85 per cent of it living in Europe and North America, accounted for 86 per cent of all the consumption in the world – consumption which had doubled since 1975 and increased sixfold since 1950. Over the same period, mass consumption grew much more slowly in the developing countries, even if there was remarkable progress in a few of them. Thus, at the end of the 1990s, the richest 20 per cent of people on earth had an income roughly sixty times higher than that of the billion poorest (whereas in 1960 the ratio had been 'only' 30:1), and the world's richest countries cornered four-fifths of global income.

To guarantee a standard of living and consumption that its own sixth of the world's population was not willing to forgo, the North consumed at the turn of the century 60 per cent of the energy, 75 per cent of the metals, 85 per cent of the wood and 60 per cent of the foodstuffs produced on earth; it was home to three-quarters of the motor vehicles, produced three-quarters of all the solid waste, and poured into the atmosphere 54 per cent of the total quantity of carbon dioxide.[16] In 1995 one person in the United States discharged some twenty tons of this gas into the atmosphere, nearly ten times more than a Chinese and twenty times more than an Indian. Average per capita daily consumption of water is 600 litres in the USA but no more than 10 litres in Chad.[17] In 1995 one Indian consumed 260 kg of oil equivalent, one Frenchman 4.2 tonnes, and one inhabitant of the USA nearly 8 tonnes.

Each statistic, each conference, each new report confirms that these inequalities are worsening and that the North–South gap will probably widen further over the next quarter of a century. The World Bank estimates that, between 1999 and 2008, average per capita consumption will increase by 1.3 per cent in Latin America and the Caribbean, 1.4 per cent in North Africa and the Middle East, and 0.9 per cent in Africa south of the Sahara. Only Asia is likely to do better. In a number of cases, given the disparities among countries in the same region and within each country, actual retreats lie concealed beneath these meagre advances. In 1999 already 43 countries in the South – against 23 in 1996 – recorded a decline in per capita GDP. The economies of the North, on the other hand, experienced remarkable growth rates in the second half of the 1990s, and seem to have profited from the Asian crisis of 1997–98.[18]

It is not necessary to continue with these examples to grasp that, in the eyes of the rest of the world, the main distinctive feature of the West is that affluence is there a collective form of life rather than the privilege of a few. The density of infrastructure (compared with the scant material capital accumulated further south), the habit of luxury revealed in trivial attitudes to consumption, the central position occupied by products that three-quarters of humanity consider surplus to their needs: these are some of the things that divide the planet into two hemispheres so far apart from each other. The inhabitants of the North probably cannot understand the fascination that their lifestyle holds for other human beings, cannot understand that the most maligned council housing, the most perfunctory medical insurance, the trolleyload filled with the cheapest goods, or simply a tap that gives out running water, are elsewhere treasures beyond reach. Despite the crises and the increasing precariousness of existence, despite the social ravages due to the retreat of the welfare state, the citizens of the North are solidly and collectively implanted in a wealth so normal that they no longer realize how exceptional it is.

So long as the illusion lasted that the Western way of life would gradually spread to the rest of humanity, it did not seem illegitimate to those who did not yet benefit from it. But they eventually had to face the fact that, since its underlying modes of production and spatial occupation could not be extended to the eight billion humans of the twenty-first century, it would remain the prerogative of a minority. However much concern was intoned in the ceremonies of international conferences, the rich nations were not prepared to change this aspect of the world order, and no one – except for a few minorities with little influence – seriously thought of challenging what the population in the North saw as a natural and legitimate lifestyle and level of consumption. It is true that politicians strengthened people's sense of being in the right – by failing to abandon any of the postulates of the golden age of post-war industrialism or to seek a viable alternative to the dominant models of growth. Indeed, these models continued to present higher levels of consumption as essential for the higher levels of production that constituted the horizon of Western economies and societies.

The leaders of the North never tired of repeating to their fellow-citizens that the West, and the West alone, would be the salvation of economies shaken by the transition from the manufacturing era to the service society. Any flagging of the appetite for consumption, they argued, meant a lack of civic virtue that had to be instantly remedied through vigorous reflationary measures; only the dynamism of the growth–consumption tandem could restore full employment twenty years after it had ceased to exist. What this overlooked, however, was that the society of full employment – which corresponded to the boom in consumer goods industries – was a brief phase in the West's history as well as a geographical exception in a world of underemployment.[19] To maintain such a system, there have been constant attempts in recent decades to reduce the life cycle of ordinary objects and promote disposable goods, multiple packaging and other forms of waste, to convince people that having more things is more gratifying than having better things, to increase supply (as in the case of energy) in order to boost demand, and generally to turn incidentals into essentials.

The almost obscene satisfaction that political and economic leaders display over the slightest rise in consumption indices, an investment structure that favours the wasting of time, space, resources and non-renewable goods in order to boost production and growth rates, the reluctance to internalize social and environmental costs, are for the moment removing all credibility from those who claim to have been converted to less predatory use of the planetary capital.

Not only does the economy of the North rest upon the fastest possible turnover of ordinary material goods – as one can appreciate by imagining how disastrous it would be if cars or household appliances gave loyal service for twenty years – but its structuring ideal of consumerism has become a cultural fact as powerful as the belief in its entitlement to rule the world. Of course, the rise of ecological movements and consumers' groups suggests that these certainties are beginning to waver. But there is still a great distance between vague intimations that less waste or more responsible consumption is possible and acceptance of different patterns and specific measures to limit the excesses of consumption. Too much zeal in these matters would be politically suicidal in the democracies of the West, as the German Greens discovered in late 1998 when their proposals to limit greenhouse gas emissions through a sharp rise in petrol prices led to a decline in their popularity. In the United States, a number of opinion surveys in 1997 and 1998 showed that Americans were really concerned about environmental damage to the planet but remained unwilling to accept any price rises for a fuel that cost them next to nothing. The strong reactions to oil price hikes in autumn 2000 confirm that public opinion is in no mood for compromise.

Growth, then, is today considered not as a means to well-being but as a kind of categorical imperative – with no real challenge in sight. Although there have been periodical outcries since the Club of Rome's *Limits to Growth* report in 1972, those who dare to question the content of growth and the sacred aura surrounding it soon find themselves sidelined as neanderthals. Just as the North set up its own evolution as a model for all, it now promotes the idea that its own economic growth is a key factor in global prosperity, since it alone is capable of stimulating the world economy; more of the same is needed if living standards are to be raised for the whole of humanity, and any fetter on the development of its own wealth could end up penalizing the rest of the world. The locking of economic thought on to these few simple ideas has made it possible to ignore the fact that growth is far from benefiting all who are supposed to profit from it, and to take account of global imbalances only in so far as they might threaten world stability. The developing economies, for their part, are handed over for treatment by the Bretton Woods institutions or for the exotic attentions of a few battalions of NGOs; only the emergent countries most strongly linked to the dominant economies arouse any interest among Western economists.

A huge bill

Officially, however, the rich nations recognize that the time has arrived for more rational management of the ecosystem. At the end of the 1980s, their think-tanks came up with the notion of 'sustainable development', as a way of reconciling the wish of countries in the South for development with the desire of those in the North not to call a halt to their own growth. Sustainable development was also supposed to mark an end to the ultra-exploitative approach to exploitation of the planet, and to restrict future extraction to levels that would no longer compromise the reconstitution of natural resources. Indeed, in all the international agencies, the Western states began to champion natural conservation and the use of clean technologies, and did not hesitate to stigmatize a good number of states in the South that were not showing enough concern for the environment. Buoyed up by their new awareness, they tried to convince the various regions of the South not to follow their own example and to adopt instead development policies more respectful of the ecosystems that have suffered from Western depredations. With the whole planet now a common human heritage, the Western states even assumed a right to inspect how the South drew upon its wealth.

The truth is that the North does not feel completely easy about how the globalization of its growth model and economic system will work out. Risks to global equilibrium threaten to come from swiftly rising energy consumption in countries such as China, India or Brazil,[20] the success of road transport and car ownership as an outward sign of affluence, and also the auctioning of natural resources to slake the unquenchable thirst for foreign currency in a world where exports are necessary to survive. The needs of the South are themselves expanding as a result of population growth and collective aspirations to a better life. But it is not possible to imagine – unless one consciously plans for catastrophes – that billions of people around the world can attain the same consumption levels that the inhabitants of Europe and North

America have achieved, and by the same methods. To preserve the future of the planet, therefore, different growth models must be adopted as quickly as possible.

That is where the shoe pinches. For, at the same time that it speaks of sustainable development, the North continually demonstrates that it is incapable of reversing its own growth logic and applying its own prescriptions. A good illustration of this are the interminable negotiations on the global warming issue since the early 1990s – from the international convention on climate change at the Rio Earth Summit in 1992, through the Kyoto protocols of 1997, to the Bonn follow-up conference of 1999. Is it a question of thoughtlessness, cynicism, or impotence before the totalitarian short-termism into which economic and financial interests lock Western societies? These three components of immobility influence in different proportions the policies practised on each side of the Atlantic.

The cynicism mainly radiates from the United States, which differs from Europe in refusing to make any energy adjustment whatsoever if this even marginally affects the American way of life. Despite a few *mea culpa*s concerning the irresponsibility of American consumption, such as Bill Clinton's speech at the UN 'Rio + 5' conference in June 1997 in New York,[21] Washington has developed a series of arguments to dilute its own responsibility and to blame others for global warming. According to its experts, uncontrolled population growth in the South and deforestation in the tropical countries are doing more than New York traffic jams to lead the world to ruin, and the methane emanating from Asian rice fields contributes more than exhaust fumes to global warming. It is hardly surprising, then, that the United States refuses to take on its share of the 'ecological debt' of the old industrial world, or that it is willing to reduce its greenhouse gas emissions only if the countries of the South immediately do the same. In the same spirit, it demands that the countries of the world should be classified only according to their total emissions, without any reference to the size of their population – a procedure that made China appear the second worst polluter in 1995 and India the sixth worst.

Representatives of the South have denounced the bad faith implicit in such arguments and pointed out that, in per capita terms, their energy consumption and emission of polluting gases are the lowest in the world. They have also called for a distinction to be made between survival emissions (including rice field methane) and comfort emissions (including the car and air-conditioning culture of the world's industrial heartlands).

The Europeans appear more inclined to compromise with developing countries that wish to have their own share of a now-fragile legacy: they have recognized the 'common but differential responsibilities'[22] of countries around the world for the degradation of ecosystems; and they have agreed to consider compulsory curbs on their own emissions while leaving the late-industrializing countries of the South a longer time to adjust to the new facts of life. In reality, however, even if Western Europe[23] and Japan devour less energy and cause less pollution than North America, no industrial power has yet been capable of reducing its emissions except through massive recourse to nuclear energy (which creates problems of its own). Studies linked to each of the international gatherings on this strategic issue show that energy consumption has continued to grow in those regions.

Figures published on the occasion of the Kyoto conference in December 1997 showed that, despite the promises made at Rio, all industrial countries increased their discharges in the first half of the 1990s. In the space of five years they leapt by 8.8 per cent in Japan. And in just one year, from 1994 to 1995, the increase was 3.4 per cent in the United States and 1.7 per cent in the European Union. The sudden flurry at Kyoto, when 38 countries in the North undertook to reduce their emissions by 5.2 per cent between 2008 and 2012 in comparison with 1990,[24] never came to much. No country has committed itself further down that road, and the regular meetings on the issue simply record the differences between advocates of market regulation of pollution and supporters of compulsory measures. Now that researchers are quite clear about the reality of global warming, no one actually disputes the need to tackle the causes. But there is no agreement on who should make the first sacrifices.

Eager to see cuts in global emissions without having to change its own production and consumption patterns, the United States has worked out a market negotiation mechanism whereby each country would receive an 'emission permit' for a certain quantity of gases and could, if it did not reach its authorized limit, sell part of its entitlement to another country that had already used up its own permit. The world's largest per capita polluters, which are also the world's richest countries, would thus be able to avoid cuts in their own emissions by buying entitlements from less well-off countries. In a parallel move, the United States also proposed that any reduction in discharges by a country in the South or East that was due to funding by a donor in the North should be credited to the donor country and increase proportionally its right to pollute.

Such mechanisms would enable the major industrial countries to maintain the same level of atmospheric discharges while subscribing to the aim of cuts in global greenhouse gas emissions.

Seeing that the struggle against global warming made little sense without the United States, the European Union and countries in the South eventually accepted the principle of a pollution entitlement market, but only on condition that an emissions threshold was set at the same time for each country. As Washington rejects this, no further progress has been made on the issue and everyone has profited from the standstill to delay any cuts of their own. With a bad faith almost as great (if more discreet) than that of the American superpower, neither Europe nor Japan has actually considered changing its policy without waiting for the elusive international consensus.

The needs of growth and consumption are obviously such that there can be no question of the North's taking the first step. Although the countries in question express concern about the environment, they reject any ecologically motivated constraints and prove to be incapable of translating their much-hailed sustainable development into reality. Significant action against greenhouse emissions would indeed have a more direct effect than climate change itself upon most interest groups in the polluting countries. Awareness of the future risk is not sufficient to motivate a struggle against the logic of short-term profit – especially as it would not hit every region in the world with the same intensity.

Studies carried out by the Intergovernmental Panel on Climate Change (IPCC)[25] show that the earth's intertropical belt will be more seriously affected than its temperate zones, and that many islands and coastal areas in that part of the world face flooding as a result of rising ocean levels. Rainfall will decrease there by a significant amount, whereas it will increase in temperate and cold regions; the latter will also become more suitable for agriculture because of milder temperatures. Finally, global warming will lead to more frequent and violent meteorological disturbances – cyclones, floods, recurrent drought – and indeed these have already started to ravage the tropical and arid zones more than the temperate zones. These forecasts, confirmed by each new study, hardly encourage the less vulnerable richer countries to question practices that have already demonstrated their damaging potential.

This resistance to change is all the graver in that some ruling layers in the South use it as a pretext to continue for as long as possible the depredation of their country's natural resources. Injunctions from the North that warn 'Do what I say, not what I do!' give them the opportunity to defend questionable practices with the help of rather less questionable arguments. It is partly due to such a rhetorical play on Western contradictions that Brazil, Malaysia, Indonesia, Zaire and a few other countries have been able to maintain the principle of unrestricted exploitation of the tropical forests. When this was held against them at Rio in 1992 and they were threatened with international inspection of their forest management, they could turn each of the North's arguments against it to reject any limitation of their own sovereignty.

Do the tropical forests play a vital role for all of humanity by trapping huge quantities of carbon gas? Yet the aim cannot be to turn them into sanctuaries so that the North can continue with its all-for-the-car policy; it is at home that the North must start the cleaning up. Should deforestation be considered one of man's negative actions against nature? Yet Western historians treat Europe's great periods of forest clearance as so many progressive advances. Have not the countries of the North, so ready to lecture others, allowed much of their remaining forest to be killed off by acid rain? Those who are opposed to internationalizing the issue of the tropics[26] have countered with the idea that all the forests on earth, tropical as well as temperate and cold, should be placed under international scrutiny. Yet the states of the North are as ill prepared to suffer scrutiny as any run-of-the-mill country of the South, and in reply to such arguments they have quickly closed the file and recognized the primacy of national sovereignty over the quest for the common good. States in the tropical belt therefore happily continue stripping their forest to meet foreign demand, or, as in the Brazilian case, encourage landless people to do the same as a way of dispensing with agrarian reform.

The struggle against Western interference has become a favourite theme of the South's most predatory rulers, who cloak their acts of pillage in a new anti-colonial rhetoric. The determination of the Northern powers to dictate everyone else's pace and mode of growth while themselves displaying the most grotesque forms of waste has unfortunately won them some popularity at home, although public opinion is taken in less and less as the years go by. In point of fact, many countries in the South have recognized the need to adopt forms of sustainable development, and the most industrialized among them see the North's resolve to push them into it as an opportunity to carry out an indispensable reform of their productive apparatus.[27] But the strength of a Western model to which no one has found an alternative, combined with the rentier interests and behaviour of most of the South's ruling layers, has made movement on this question as slow and as faltering as it is in the countries of the North. The latter do not all take the same positions on the thick file of environmental issues, and one should not underestimate the divergences between Europe (which still believes in the virtues of public regulation) and the United States (which holds it up to public contempt). But America's clearly expressed refusal to give up the privileges of power is echoed by Europe's reluctance to deprive itself of the comfort that power provides.

Immigration, memory and amnesia

Such are the powers of this world. Having the means to do it, they force their weaker partners to liberalize their trade yet partly exempt themselves from a similar opening. Rightly fearing that human predation will use up the planet, they refuse to rein in their appetites and to question the forms of growth that opened the way to today's plight. Exhorting the rest of the world to develop as they have done, only to do it faster, they place the necessary knowledge and technology beyond its reach by patenting the least of their inventions or products. The countries of the South are urged to open up to exports from the most productive and highly subsidized economies on earth and to take the development road themselves, yet to do so without wasting resources that are supposed to belong to humanity as a whole. They are even compelled to pay a high price for the modified seeds of their own crop varieties. And the forced residence of their own population, which is not permitted to move abroad, is yet another prescription with which they have to comply.

Nowadays everything is supposed to travel and be exchanged in order to produce wealth, every barrier is meant to disappear so that commodities, capital and services can move around as freely and rapidly as possible – only the movement of people does not come under the same freedom that is at the heart of globalization. Never have their travels been as tightly controlled as they are in this epoch so hostile to regulation. In seeking to curb international migration and identify it as a major problem, those who run today's world are breaking with the whole previous history of humanity.

An analysis of the Western approach to migration should begin by underlining the complexity of the issue. First, national withdrawal is not a peculiarity of the West: most states around the world use a host of measures to prevent foreigners from settling on their soil, and since the early 1980s there has been an increasing number of mass expulsions of non-indigenous populations. In Africa, Nigeria and Gabon have specialized in ruthlessly driving out tens or hundreds of thousands of people who had settled there. Libya receives or expels immigrants from Egypt and Tunisia in accordance with the ups and downs of its relations with those states. In 1997 the authorities in the Dominican Republic forced back across the frontier thousands of Haitians who had fled their devastated country in search of work. The next year, Thailand and South Korea tried to weather their economic crisis by expelling tens of thousands of clandestine immigrants. In the best cases, foreigners are still accepted in a trickle after being carefully sorted for their likely future performance. Countries whose modern population is descended from immigrants – such as the United States, Canada or Australia – have not yet sealed their borders, but they have installed more and more filters to block the entry of anyone considered 'unnecessary'.

There are many reasons for this tendency of countries to withdraw into themselves. It is well known that times of crisis, real or perceived, fuel the search for scapegoats, and that everything different becomes the emblematic Other that collectives have always felt a need to exorcize. It is also known that the combination of xenophobia (a universal feeling) with political demagogy can carry this rejection of the Other to the most tragic extremes. In many civilizations, there have always been only 'bloody foreigners', accepted or tolerated when they performed key services to the community and sent back as soon as these no longer seemed so necessary. Human beings have always had only a limited inclination to share their possessions, and when these appear to be shrinking foreigners are seen as parasitic consumers of what does not belong to them. The final factor is the unprecedented growth of the world's population over the last half-century, which has fuelled people's fears and helped to make an invasion from relatively overpopulated regions seem a plausible scenario.

Western leaders are by no means the only ones to exploit such feelings for political ends, by playing up to popular fears when they cannot find solutions to the problems of the hour. Indeed, the position of foreigners in the West today is undoubtedly less precarious than in other parts of the world; official humanism and a long-established rule of law for the moment keep xenophobic lurches within strict bounds. And, however summary they may be, measures to get rid of undesirable aliens are less brutal than those one might encounter elsewhere.

Once again we see that the West is a place of paradox. It turns people away, but it has to handle the legacy of past openness. It engages in protection, but foreigners are no longer completely alien in its big cities. The streets of New York, London or Paris have become flamboyant microcosms of human diversity. If you go for a walk one evening during the Paris music festival, when summer pushes outdoors young people from the four corners of the earth, or one Sunday morning in Central Park, or one late afternoon in London when people from the old Empire or their children throng the pavements, you can feel how deeply rooted this diversity has become, how inexorably Western capitals have been transformed into metropolitan centres where the fine word cosmopolitanism, so detested by all breeds of nationalism, might again find a meaning. Perhaps they are laboratories where, in spite of local tensions and political demagogy, the paths to post-nationalism are being discovered and opened up – often amid violence, but also in an effervescence of different cultures.

Since the Western countries are not alone in closing themselves to others, and since non-indigenous populations have been able to settle there on a permanent basis, why is the new frontier cordon the object of such intense debate? Why do sections of public opinion find it more scandalous than what happens elsewhere in the world? Three factors account for this specificity. In the eyes of formerly dominated nations, the way in which Europe handles this issue – history having left different traces in North America – is at once incoherent, amnesiac and rooted in racial criteria. The weight of the past, which they seem to want to deny by turning their territories into protected reserves, together with the eternal split between what they say and what they do, explain why the attitudes of Europeans to migration appear more as a special privilege of power than as an all too banal consequence of collective fears in a time of uncertainty.

Europe's affluence, which has no equivalent anywhere else in the world, also stamps its withdrawal tendencies with the mark of illegitimacy. When people leave the land of their birth, they go in search of space or riches as well as freedom – and there is hardly a single case of large-scale migration that departs from this rule.[28] If Venezuela, the Dominican Republic, the Ivory Coast or South Africa have attracted and continue to attract people from neighbouring countries, this is because they are richer and offer more secure ways of earning a living. But although the income disparity between people from the Ivory Coast and Burkina Faso is enough to encourage the latter to cross the frontier, the difference between the comfort of some and the wretchedness of others is here only a matter of degree. There is not a huge gap between the region's well-off and the less fortunate periphery, especially as their income does not generally rest on a solid base and could easily melt away. It is usually in lean years that they close the door to immigrants. In the South of the world, the geographical frontiers between wealth and poverty are liable to shift with the economic conjuncture; it is only within each country that they are becoming more settled, as divisions establish themselves between emergent social classes. Thus migration within continents – which, we should remember, is by far the most frequent case – leads the very poor towards less poor areas, where they are sent away once poverty strikes again at the shaky foundations. Such movements have often involved a major swing of the pendulum, in time with changing regional fortunes.

This reading of short-distance population movements is not meant to obscure the nationalist or ethnicist manipulation to which leaders of countries with inward migration often happily resort, in the knowledge that it can deflect the frustration and anger of their fellow citizens. Rather, it seeks to show that in this respect, too, the richest countries occupy a special position, since their wealth is not time-specific and is sheltered from conjunctural fluctuations. The egoism of far-off lands that seem to have everything seems even less justifiable than the capriciousness of close neighbours.

Westerners throw up barriers when it is to their advantage, and the rigidity of their stand on migration is the polar opposite of their enthusiasm for open economies. Protectionist here, liberal there, they do not fear self-contradiction when it serves their interests, and refuse to see that their very incoherence creates further reasons for people to emigrate from the poorest countries. On the one hand, they are unwilling 'to cater for all the world's poverty'[29] for fear of having to share their wealth; on the other hand, they do little to bridge the gap and restrict the opportunities for people in the South to grow rich in their own countries. In fact, as we have seen, the gap is continuing to widen. More than poverty itself, this growing inequality operates as a powerful force driving further migration, since it deprives millions of individuals of any prospects in their own country. The powers of the North contribute to this lack of perspectives, by protecting themselves from both the products and the nationals of the so-called developing world, by refusing to alter the patterns that pile up their advantages from wealth and power, and by compounding the numerous endogenous factors with exogenous ones that multiply the causes and effects of poverty. This is the context in which their closing of borders and their refusal to recognize migration as a bone of contention for the South continue to cause an outcry.

Furthermore, a dual historical amnesia in the North seems intolerable to peoples who formerly lived under the colonial yoke or were driven from their homes by European expansion. After 1945, when there was a need for foreign labour, many European countries appealed to their overseas subjects to make up the shortfall – and it was in the name of ties resulting willy-nilly from a long imperial history that men and women continued to go and settle in the metropolis. Many are the Indians, Pakistanis and West Indians who fill the streets of English cities, many the North Africans or black Africans who populate the French suburban sprawls, many the Indonesians or the Surinamese from former Dutch Guiana who have their home in Amsterdam, many too the Zaireans who have grown used to living in Brussels.[30]

History shows that one cannot close its chapters by decree and that its effects are felt well beyond the events which punctuate its course. The establishment of permanent extra-European communities in the old colonial heartlands is part of a continuum that Europeans first began, then continued through wars to satisfy their land hunger, and for the consequences of which they now refuse to accept responsibility. Always eager to claim longstanding ties when it is a question of consolidating their economic or political influence on missionary lands in the South – France, in particular, has specialized in such invocations to give its African policy a hazy historical legitimacy – they are quite prepared to conceal historical realities when the modern sequel is not to their liking. European leaders have spent a quarter of a century harping on about the immigration threat and the difficulty of integrating people too alien to European culture, but not one of them has dared to mention that today's movement of population from South to North has something to do with the waves of North–South migration that broke over the nineteenth century. Here the amnesia remains total.

It is forgotten not only that Europeans once had a 'visa-free presence' all over the world,[31] but that their great exodus turned many lands into extensions of Europe. Silence covers what it meant for the old continent to have 60 million of its people depart in little more than a century – a massive transfer which enabled Europe's most populous countries to soften the impact of the demographic changes and economic revolutions through which they were passing. Europe made the planet a safety valve for its entry into the twentieth century. And the least one can say is that it prevents others from following its example amid the shocks of the contemporary world.

European politicians brandish the immigration issue whenever they need a simple explanation for a problem they cannot control. Worse, on the right – but also on the left – a process of demonization has identified it as a breeding ground for crime that needs to be tackled in similar ways. Thus, under the heading 'The fight against illegal trafficking', the first French contribution to the debate on the renewal of the Lomé convention groups together 'drugs, counterfeit money and illegal immigration' – as if the latter were on a par with the most dangerous sectors of organized crime.[32] All the EU texts on harmonization of immigration rules repeat this stigmatizing rhetoric, which is scarcely likely to make the presence of foreigners in Europe a routine matter of fact.

Barriers against the Other

Judging by the warnings of danger, one would think it was a massive presence. Yet it remains a small-scale phenomenon, in comparison both with the percentages of outward migration from nineteenth-century Europe and with the present-day population of the continent. The alarmist discourse does not correspond to numerical reality. Between 1960 and 1980, at the height of the immigration wave, Western Europe received altogether approximately a million foreigners per annum. At the end of the 1990s, the European Union had approximately 18 million official immigrants (or some 2.5 per cent of its total population[33]), of which two-thirds were from countries outside Europe. In France, on the widest definition that includes people who had acquired French nationality and those who were born there, it has been estimated that the population 'resulting from immigration' numbered 6.1 million in 1990, of whom 40 per cent were born on French soil.[34] Thus, leaving aside people of Italian, Spanish or Portuguese origin,[35] the number of non-Europeans resulting from immigration was less than 7 per cent of the total population of France.

The proportion of immigrants from continents other than Europe is below 10 per cent in all Western countries; in 1996 the United States, still the world's primary pole of immigration, counted 24.6 million foreigners of all origins, or 9.3 per cent of its total population. Only Australia exceeds this figure, with immigrants accounting in 1990 for

nearly a quarter of the total population.[36] The presence of illegal immigrants is a minor factor: in Europe they account for 10 to 15 per cent of the total immigrant population,[37] while in the United States the immigration department calculated in 1997 that they were 4.5 million in number, or 18 per cent of the total foreign population.

Should these quite low figures be attributed to the restrictive policies of Europe and, to a lesser extent, North America? Or does the threat of massive migration exist only in the paranoid minds of the well-to-do? Although the tightening of border controls has undoubtedly caused a fall in migration,[38] the threat of 'invasion' is not really there – especially as, whatever the public may believe, the countries of the North attract not so much the impoverished masses as elites and groups of young people for whom their country of origin is unable or unwilling to offer a future. In the second half of the 1990s, highly qualified workers accounted for more than three-quarters of official immigrants into the United States and nearly half of those into Britain and Canada, where they are much in demand; the proportion was considerably lower in continental Europe, especially France, where it was only 15 per cent.[39] The West may not be as afraid as one is led to believe by those political leaders across the spectrum who tirelessly seek to deflate the far right by implementing part of its programme;[40] but it is afraid none the less.

The fear is mainly of those who count as irredeemably 'other'. The countries that present a 'high immigration risk' are all in the South; their nationals are the ones for whom the borders are closed. It is they who, for the briefest stay, have to wear themselves out at Western consulates that make the most ordinary trip to the North seem like an obstacle course. Policemen in the more ill-famed districts of big cities look for giveaway signs on the faces of those who enter as illegal immigrants – unless the net is cast wider through spot checks on those who have the misfortune to be ethnically or racially identifiable. Everywhere skin colour, looks or accent are more reliable indicators of foreignness than a passport or place of residence. Everywhere barriers are in place to defend jealously guarded wealth against would-be participants whose presence might shatter the homogeneity of Western nations – even if, as we have seen, the precise degree of closure depends on the country's past history, the influence of the far right and the political uses made of the immigration issue.

The United States, which has built up the American myth largely around its self-definition as a nation of immigrants, has less restrictive laws than those of the European countries. The long presence of sizeable ethnic minorities, such as the black community, also makes it more difficult there to distinguish foreigners and nationals by how they look, and strong multicultural roots in society have made it easier than in Europe to maintain a flow of migration of non-European origin. Questions linked to the very real ethnic–racial hierarchy are therefore more an issue for national debate than a problem arising out of the presence of foreigners. Nevertheless, just as it operated quotas for more than half a century to curb non-Anglo-Saxon immigration,[41] the United States has for some years been trying to protect itself from what it increasingly judges to be undesirable Latin American immigration. To stem the flow of some 300,000 people (mostly Mexicans) who enter illegally every year, the authorities have been working since 1994, at the rate of seven miles a year, on a frontier wall thirty metres high.

Europe is not building such physical barriers, for the Mediterranean is in itself one for people from North Africa and south of the Sahara. But the Fifteen have installed a veritable shield of laws and regulations to keep their frontiers sealed. Countries with a traditional outward migration, such as Italy, Spain or Portugal, have gradually fallen in with the tougher line of France and others, and EU harmonization on this issue has generalized the most restrictive practices of member states. Since any non-Western foreigner is now looked upon as a potential immigrant, permission even for short stays is carefully doled out. In France, the number of short-term visas granted to sub-Saharan Africans fell from 106,000 in 1987 to 79,000 seven years later, and in the case of Algerians from 800,000 in 1989 to 40,000 in 1996.[42] Similarly, the number of foreign students enrolled in French universities has been constantly falling since the late 1980s. In 1995 it was a third lower than in 1991, with fewer and fewer nationals of France's former colonies. In the case of students from Algeria the decline was quite dizzying, as numbers plummeted from 3,662 in 1991 to 545 in 1996 – smaller than the Japanese enrolment for that year.[43]

On the issue of immigration, the Socialist governments that came to power in most major European countries in the late 1990s confirmed that ideological splits are relatively unimportant in comparison with the solid political consensus. In Britain, France and Germany, previous policies were only marginally altered. In France, Socialist interior minister Chevènement gained considerable popularity on the right as a result of his smug campaign in 1997 to regularize the situation of foreigners, his violent attacks against advocates of a more liberal policy, his tacit encouragement of a more restrictive interpretation of official guidelines, and the determination of departments under his control to expel illegal immigrants. In Germany, SPD Chancellor Gerhard Schröder played up to popular xenophobia as soon as he took office by promising to deal firmly with undesirable aliens.[44] Then he lined up with the most conservative sections of his electorate by introducing a law on naturalization which, though ending the central role of *ius sanguinis* in defining German nationality, only timidly opened the door to immigrants already settled in the country.

Apart from the fairly small fringes around civil movements and left-wing Greens, the European political elites stand in a straight line of descent from the certainties of the colonial epoch, which raised with a good conscience an impenetrable barrier between their 'race' and 'inferior' peoples. Today, people who would once have been called white men can travel or reside wherever they like in Europe or America. Others do not have the right to cross certain frontiers: not being the same, they cannot demand to be treated as equals. It is true that no one outside the far right openly talks of being racist. Indeed, most European politicians are sincerely convinced that they are not, and consider the term to be an insult. Yet they have no compunction in classifying foreigners according to their affinity with Europe. In the contemporary West, 'inassimilable groups' have replaced 'inferior races', all the more dangerous in that they live in the centres of civilization and threaten to distort it.

Vagaries of the right to asylum

The true foreigner, who is not recognized as a neighbour and is accepted, if at all, only from necessity, is even more remote when he or she is poor. Mother of all the vices in the bourgeois imagination, poverty is always suspicious and can be tolerated only when confined to its original locality. Poverty, together with difference, therefore presents a dual danger. Of course, fear of beggars is not a Western peculiarity in a world where social ties are coming apart and the sharpening of inequalities pushes crime and poverty together in the big cities. In each continent, although the rich foreigner can also be scapegoated, he or she causes less of a problem; it is from impoverished others that protection is sought. What distinguishes the West, however, is its readiness to sacrifice on the altar of its fears or interests those very principles which it claims most securely to uphold. The vagaries of the right to asylum provide an example of this Western ability to enclose universality within frontiers that shift according to its perception of real or imaginary enemies.

The granting of asylum, an age-old custom of protecting the hunted from their persecutors, received the blessing of the law when the Enlightenment set itself the task of combating tyranny. Whereas the United States set itself up from birth as the sacred land of freedom, the nations of Europe began to welcome refugees after the defeat of absolutism and the replacement of arbitrary power with the rule of law. Reproaching themselves for a few infringements during the Second World War, Western states subsequently adopted clear and fairly generous laws that permitted the right of asylum to reach its apogee during the cold war years. Freedom fighters escaping from the Eastern bloc were received with open arms on both sides of the Atlantic. The United States allowed tens of thousands of anti-Castro Cubans to settle in Florida over a period of thirty years; as many as 160,000 arrived between 1959 and 1962 alone,[45] mostly from the island's rich and well-educated white elite. Famous or unsung heroes of the struggle against communist dictatorship were all welcome, and in the mid-1970s France granted more than 95 per cent of the 20,000 or so requests for asylum.[46]

The fall of the Berlin Wall in 1989 and the collapse of the socialist bloc gave the signal for a change in Western asylum practice. Refugees from the East, no longer being a political card in the West's hand against the USSR and its satellites, were especially undesirable as they swelled the numbers of those claiming refugee status in order to circumvent new restrictions and to settle in the eldorados of Europe. Freedom fighters had become economic refugees that West Europeans did not want at any price. Indeed, it was no longer the same people who were knocking at the door of the Union. Representatives of the Central and East European elites, whose social and intellectual proximity made them genuine cousins, had been replaced by indistinct masses whose social status turned them into unacceptable foreigners. On the other hand, the vagaries of the post-cold war transition to democracy in many parts of the South, which sometimes involved authoritarian backsliding and the spread of civil conflict, threatened to increase still further the influx of refugees. The Western powers were not willing to accept these new-style exiles, who were not fleeing communism and came mainly from the South.

Since the 1990s, then, a political discourse centred on human rights (even wars are fought in their name) has coexisted in the West with ever more restrictive attitudes to the right of asylum that see it as potentially opening the floodgates to economic immigration. The European Union first took action to stem the flow of refugees from the former Eastern bloc, which reached a peak in 1992 with nearly 700,000 requests for asylum. Then it slammed the door shut on the increasing number of refugees from the South. In 1994 Britain granted fewer than 15 per cent of requests for asylum, and in 1995 France let through 16 per cent – that is, 4,742 applications against 15,000 in 1991.[47] Several times in the course of the 1990s, the United States ruthlessly turned away thousands of Haitians fleeing acute social distress and political chaos who were socially and ethnically less presentable than the anti-Castro exiles.

Many Westerners know that a complete end to South–North flows is no more than a fond hope, and that it would not even be desirable for countries whose population decline can be checked only through fresh immigration. They also know that they really should get used to the people already established on their soil, even as they require them to melt invisibly into a majority that daily reminds them of their otherness. But Westerners also want to protect themselves against the possible effects of a disparity between high fertility rates in the South and low or zero growth of populations of European origin, and to do this without remedying the global imbalances that drive people to leave the South.

A model in question

All in all, it seems that the recent history of North–South relations is summed up in a strange ambivalence. On the one hand, as we have seen, there is a single evolutionary model. The hegemonic position of the West has enabled it to erase the specificity of its experience and to theorize it as the only way towards universal progress, with itself as pioneer and guide. To be sure, the model has been attacked for as long as it has existed – but its basic logic has not been challenged. The different versions of socialism and what is known as third-worldism have not disputed the primacy of growth (which is confused with development) or found a theoretical alternative to the almost linear succession of stages that are supposed to lead to it. Heavy industry may have lost its glamour, but arguments still refer explicitly or otherwise to the necessity of catching up, and the universal standard of well-being remains the mode of production and way of life for which the West sets the tone.

The new awareness of the finiteness of our planet, and the ecological revolution in our ways of thinking and acting in the realms of politics and economics, may perhaps herald the exhaustion of a model whose specificity would then immediately be recognized. But that is not where we are at now. The developing countries – whether poor or emergent, advanced or less advanced (a term, by the way, that further illustrates the certainty of a single model) – are still asked to imitate the West by striving to follow the paths that it has already mapped out.

What is not said is that these paths are closed. In reality, the countries of the South find it impossible to take the journey that made of the North what it is. Once again, we should not look here for some Machiavellian design – indeed, the West's strategists do not even have a very clear picture of what they are imposing on the world. The real problem is that they do not wish to see the inconsistency of both presenting themselves as an example to the rest of humanity and forbidding it (in the name of their own interests) to use the formulas with which the West amassed its fortune. If there is a Western deception today, it is this compulsion on others to take historically unexplored paths to end up the same as the West; this, after all, is the meaning of development in all senses given to the term.

Whereas Europe and North America used to be protectionist, and still are in sectors where they feel weak, the countries of the South are forced to open up to the kind of general competition which the West's own history shows never to have served as a lever for 'take-off'. Whereas today's rich took the liberty to subjugate the planet and to draw endlessly upon its resources, the countries of the South are required to explore unknown paths to a distinctive and sparing growth, but also to achieve results at least as remarkable as those of their mentors. Whereas Europe made emigration a key tool of growth and of its own expansion, the inhabitants of the South are confined to their place of residence and expected to find at home, and only at home, the means to a better life.

Let us make no mistake. The Western growth model that has hitherto served as revealed truth cannot be extended to the whole planet, and the time has come for human beings to invent other ways of satisfying their needs and aspirations. It is time to question the goals of a growth that has not paid out its much-trumpeted dividends to the whole of humanity. The peoples of the South – but not their elites, often the only ones to benefit from the dictatorship of the single model – would probably have everything to gain in social and human terms from novel initiatives of their own to break out of the mimetic impasse, without waiting until new stipulations force them into it. But only if those with the power play the game.

For, unless force is used on a systematic basis, it is impossible to compel virtually the whole world to respect the 'do what I say, not what I do' rule. It is impossible to offer people the model of comfort and modernity represented by the motor car, while at the same time preventing them from buying cars of their own and enjoining them not to discharge noxious gases into the atmosphere. It seems difficult to forbid the South to follow in the steps of the West, while continuing to present the latter as the future for humanity. The deception consists not in asking others to act differently from now on, but in requiring them to remain faithful copiers even as they act differently.

In order to end this deception, the West would have to clear up another of its contradictions. If it wishes to convince people in the other half of the world that its prescriptions are just, it must first review from scratch the growth processes that made its fortune, and whose reproduction it now fears outside its own frontiers. It is by invalidating the model it defined as universal that it can persuade others not to aspire to it. This implies a truly vast programme, and one which neither the populations nor the elites of the West would currently endorse. As we have seen, only small minorities in the North have tried to move beyond critiques of the model's perverse effects to question its overall relevance. Rejection of its globalization, which is starting to become visible in the rich countries, does not in most cases imply a challenge to its validity; rather, it suggests fear of a shipwreck of which the North could be the first victim. In the eyes of many Westerners, the purpose of blocking globalization of the dominant model of growth and consumption is to ensure the continued existence of that very model in the chosen lands which have seen it prosper.

NINE

The Beginning of the End?

The most remarkable of the privileges of power is the freedom to load the dice against one's prospective partners. The North, a consummate expert at this game, has nevertheless watched the world change and is not always able to ensure that each new development is in its favour. Hegemony can no longer be decreed in the same way as in the age of the imperial division of labour. What is called globalization – a catch-all term whose content should be more clearly specified – has shaken the traditional economic hierarchies by making the movement of goods more important than their production, and by establishing financial capital as the driving force of the economy. Its effects in the political domain are equally important, since the gradually emerging transnational and post-state forms of regulation seem to involve a crumbling of state power and a challenge to the idea of the nation.

But under whose aegis are these new classifications being introduced? Who profits and who suffers from the upheavals? Who fears the re-compositions that the turn of the century announces, and why? Is the North really giving up part of its power, or is it once more establishing it on new foundations? Unless we force a definition, we do not yet know much about what this process of globalization will mean, but might it not have the potential to end the North–South divide by preparing the way for a global ruling class freed from the constraints of geography? Will the future centres of the world be the same as yesterday's? On this question hangs the fate of the old Western supremacy. The world is certainly changing, but it is not so certain that it will be gone with the wind.

Hegemony wounded

The North gratifies some countries in the world with the title 'emergent' – that is, officially emerging from underdevelopment.[1] There is many a rambling argument about whether their performance is due to precise following of the model's guidelines or to a capacity to give it national forms. Western analysts, true as ever to their culture of supremacy, are in the habit of attributing the success stories to mimetic talents and the failures to unconquered cultural specificities. The World Bank has hailed the miraculous advance of Asian economies as hard evidence of the superiority of liberalism over its ideological rivals,[2] while others have found in it fresh material to defend the role of the state in national economic construction. Only the storm that hit them in 1997 would appear not to have had an exogenous model, as the same theorists essentially limit the role of speculative capital to one of illuminating endogenous defects. Having arrived late to bring their competitive advantages to bear on the world consumer-goods market, the new industrial countries of Asia have in any event carved a not insignificant place for themselves – and they intend to make it bear fruit, however much they may have to suffer from the vagaries of the economic conjuncture. Following the original four dragons,[3] the whole of East Asia has successively asserted itself as a frontline player in world trade.

The commercial strength of the region began to make itself felt in the 1980s. In 1986, for the first time, the world's developing countries as a whole derived more income from manufacturing exports than from primary products. But ten countries achieved 80 per cent of these exports, and five of them (Taiwan, South Korea, Hong Kong, Singapore and Brazil) nearly three-quarters. For a third of a century, the Far East has notched up results that earn it a mixture of envy and fear from a North worried about the potential threat to its own positions. The whole of developing Asia accounts for roughly a quarter of world trade, and in 1998 Chinese exports alone accounted for nearly 3.3 per cent of the world total.

Elsewhere in the South, other powers have thrust themselves forward – not so much through their actual results as because of their demographic and economic place on a global stage where they are no longer willing to play minor parts. India in South Asia (whose GNP growth rate oscillated between 4 per cent and 5.5 per cent from 1974 to 1995[4]) and Brazil in Latin America (whose growth, as in the rest of the continent, was more chaotic) are no longer content with the regional power status to which the truly great and powerful have hitherto consigned them. Forecasts of the international economic and financial organizations give the leaders of these countries some grounds to believe in the future. In 1997, the World Bank announced that a new hand of economic cards was being dealt to the benefit of five 'big powers': three in Asia (China, India and Indonesia), one in Latin America (Brazil), and one ghostly return in Europe (Russia). Between 1992 and 2020, China's GNP appears set to rise from 1.4 per cent to 3.9 per cent of the world total, India's from 1 per cent to 2.1 per cent, Indonesia's from 0.6 per cent to 1.5 per cent, and Brazil's from 1.7 per cent to 2.5 per cent. The old Asian dragons (South Korea, Singapore and Taiwan) will continue their advance, since their combined GNP will rise over the same period from 2.3 per cent to 3.8 per cent of the world total, and the young tigers (Malaysia, the Philippines and Thailand) will also increase their weight as joint GNP climbs from 0.8 per cent to 2.4 per cent of the world total. In 2020, still according to the World Bank, Asian GNP will thus represent nearly 15 per cent of the world total, up from 6.7 per cent in 1992. The countries with very high income will account for 70.9 per cent of the total in 2020, down from 84.2 per cent in the early 1990s.

This projected advance is even more remarkable if one calculates the economic weight of a country by purchasing power parity. By this method, in 1995 Asia already accounted for 24 per cent of global GDP and Latin America for 9 per cent, and in 1997 the IMF forecast that the Asian economies alone would represent 30 per cent of world output by the year 2000.[5] Tomorrow's G7 may therefore not look the same as today's: it may well include such nations as China or India which seek to become the powers they once were in the past.[6] In 1820 the world's two most populous countries might well have been considered its two leading economic powers. In the early twenty-first century, if the crisis does not persist, Asia will do no more than regain the position it had two centuries ago, when it accounted for 32 per cent of world production.[7]

The first consequences of these trends are already visible. In the international negotiations that punctuated the 1990s on a number of issues – from trade to the environment – these future powers spoke up and more than once disturbed the North's carefully laid plans to keep control. As the major countries of the South also successfully increased their military nuisance value, they have more than one card capable of thwarting the diktats of their erstwhile masters.

These trends may well be considered among the major events of the last quarter of the twentieth century, but for the moment their impact on Western hegemony is only marginal. Quite soon the weight of emergent countries will be far from negligible, and they will consolidate their position in a number of manufacturing sectors to achieve a near-monopoly that drives out the old industrial nations. Some are doing even better. South Korea, for example, has left the lower category of a workshop country and worked its way up the chain into new specialist fields; its 'inventiveness coefficient' is among the highest in the world, as it occupies second place in terms of the number of applications for new patents proportional to the size of the population.[8] In Singapore, Bangalore or Canton, Asia has created high-tech poles that allow it a modest place in the international competition for the control of knowledge. The rapid pace of growth in certain parts of the world suggests that the 'catching up' so often predicted by development economists may now actually be taking place; and that relocation within what used to be the third world, where the least sophisticated segments of manufacturing industry are now migrating further to the least developed regions, may be one of its most evident signs.

Do these new phenomena, together with the demographic hegemony of the South, amount to a force that is redrawing the map of the centres of power? It will be difficult for power to retain the same contours as before, and those with some basis for their aspirations will doubtless have more say in the matter, but for the moment nothing indicates that the map is fundamentally changing. Although the spatial distribution of industrial activity and world economic growth is real enough and has raised the profile of a number of countries, it has not (yet?) brought about a redivision of global power. For we must weigh correctly the southward relocation of first-generation industries, now that world economic activity is divided into two increasingly dissimilar categories. Concentrated in the South are the whole range of low-value-added manufacturing industries that are large consumers of more or less skilled labour – industries that the North has progressively abandoned in order to focus its energies and finance on designing and producing the new knowledge and communications sectors in which it enjoys a monopoly position. Everything suggests that the migration of traditional industries has actually made it easier for the powers of the North to embrace the third industrial revolution.

In the new international division of labour that has established itself over the past thirty years, many of the now-industrialized countries of the South do seem to have abandoned the one-crop agriculture to which they were previously assigned for various kinds of 'industrial monoculture' involving the making or assembly of consumer durables. The fact that 60 per cent of exports from developing countries now consist of manufactured goods has not by itself redistributed the cards of world economic power. Rather, the main consequence of the new international division of labour has been to accelerate the processes of differentiation with the South, so that while some areas – such as sub-Saharan Africa or parts of Latin America and the Caribbean – continue to specialize in the primary production of energy, agricultural goods and minerals, others now figure among the world's leading manufacturing regions. This industrialization, with its exorbitant social and environmental costs that should never be forgotten, has undoubtedly changed many things: it has brought partial solutions to such crucial problems as unemployment, permitted a fairly rapid increase in living standards, favoured the development of urban middle classes and important domestic markets, changed the face of the emergent South that would like to live differently, and widened the gap with a south of the South that is stuck with functions inherited from the old imperial division of production.

Yet the Mexican *maquiladoras*,[9] the giant Chinese toy factories,[10] the television and personal computer assembly lines of Taipei or Seoul, and Nike's Malaysian or Indian footwear plants are not enough to change the old relationship of forces profoundly. Some twenty years from now, Europe, North America and Japan will still carry the weight of more than half of a structurally modified global GNP,[11] and will most probably have consolidated their position in areas of economic activity with a very high value-added. Even in sectors left to the South, they have kept or regained the cutting-edge branches such as high-grade textiles or high-quality food. Their preponderance remains overwhelming in the service economy, where they account for 80 per cent of global exports (tourism included).[12] Still occupying a central place in everything that produces wealth, they are simultaneously laying the basis for the future preservation of their power.

It is in the North, and for the moment only in the North, that economic power is concentrated. The rise of transnational corporations does little to change this. Their activities are scattered around the globe, and their plant constitutes an ever larger part of the industrial fabric of the South, but their directors, owners, headquarters and laboratories have escaped any tendency to relocation: 94 per cent of the world's top five hundred companies, with a combined turnover in 1995 representing 47 per cent of world production,[13] belong to the so-called 'triad' and achieve three-quarters of their value-added in those core countries.[14]

From Boeing to Airbus and Microsoft, there is not one company whose activities are considered strategic which does not have its origins and the bulk of its operations there. Novartis, the first of the world's top twenty pharmaceutical corporations as well as the main developer and producer of biotechnologies, is Swiss; Merck, the second in this field, is American; and Glaxo Wellcome, the third, is British. Ten of these twenty colossi are American, two Swiss, three British, three German, one Swedish, and one Franco-American.[15] From AOL to the German-American Bertelsmann or the French Hachette, the key communications sector is also entirely controlled by Northern corporations.

The large global corporations therefore have a nationality. The profit imperative may, if opportunity knocks, trigger a strategic choice to send whole areas of their activity roaming the world. Yet their original countries are the main ones to benefit from their prosperity, hosting most of the return on their investment and enjoying the effects of their enrichment, market strength and power.[16] The governments of the North well understand this and do everything they can to increase the influence and market share of 'their' firms, while also protecting them from foreign competition at home.

In fact, the rise of the transnationals has so far worked as a huge device for the further accumulation of wealth by those who already held the reins of the world economy. Horizontal global networks may be replacing the old vertical hierarchies, and the communications revolution may possibly be making information more accessible, but the computer terminals that are changing the face of the world are situated in the North. As things stand, then, the new architecture of global power does not seem to involve a crumbling of traditional hegemonies. At the most, a few large countries in the South are exchanging their old position as objects of domination for the less humiliating and more profitable one of partners with which the North will in some respects have to reckon.

A grouping of enemies

The trend is important, but hardly spectacular. What it has done is give beneficiaries of the old status quo a glimpse into a less favourable future. Are these short-lived worries, or do they herald revolutions to come? The reactions of 'others' to the West's hegemony have long been part of its history: collective memories recall that imperial conquest met with resistance, and that subject peoples revolted more often than the school textbooks would have us believe. People also remember that in its hey-day the 'third world' challenged the relations of domination that tied it to its former masters – a challenge perceived at the time as a threat to the established order. Ways were found of stamping it out.

The dangers are now of a different nature. Whereas the clamorous demand for a new world order eventually became part of the game, the countries of the South that are now considered the most threatening are those which seek to insert themselves into the global system by accepting its rules, and which profit from any openings to undermine its hier-archies and its more or less stable balances. The good pupils who follow the endlessly trumpeted model now inspire more fear than those who reject it. Western societies experience as so many traumatic shocks to the system even the moderately growing strength, and the increased visibil-ity and competitiveness, of the South's most industrialized countries. The southward migration of economic activity over the past three decades appears as an unacceptable encroachment on a kind of natural industrial monopoly, and as an equally scandalous transfer of wealth.

As it breaks down the barriers that used to shelter the old industrial countries from newcomers, the opening of the world economy is often blamed for promoting 'unfair' competition.[17] Relocation – that early and especially pernicious manifestation of globalization – was held responsi-ble for all the evils that began to destabilize industrial societies around the middle of the 1970s, at the moment when the Asian dragons were spitting out their first flames. In addition to trade-union attacks on the new competition, political leaders regularly branded the new industrial countries as disturbers of their fellow-citizens' wage security. In both Europe and the United States, all the political and social players placed the issue of relocation at the centre of debate on the seemingly in-exorable trend of rising unemployment that affected all the major industrial countries, with the exception of Japan, throughout the 1980s and early 1990s. In 1993, under the presidency of the French Socialist Jacques Delors, the European Commission published a 'White Book' with the evocative title *Croissance, competitivité, emploi* (Growth, com-petitiveness, employment), in which the emergence of manufacturing economies in the south of the world was presented as one of the main reasons for the explosion of unemployment in Europe. In the same year, a French parliamentary report found that relocation was to blame for the removal of job security.[18] In 1994, the annual report of the Davos World Economic Forum also dwelled on the threat posed to Western economies by competition from the new industrial countries.

Those who use such language are prey to more than one contradiction. The Western trade unions, while declaring their solidarity with people in the South striving for a better life, protest in fine unison against any transfer of activities that might raise employment levels there. Thus, in the debate that preceded ratification of the North American Free Trade Agreement in 1993, the AFL–CIO justified its hostility to recomposition of the world labour market by invoking fears that US manufacturing industry would emigrate to Mexico. Rightly concerned at the rising unemployment, the unions point to the low wages and poor conditions that Western firms impose on their workforce in the South, but they remain silent about how production and work – and related income – should be distributed in a world where the soaring active population means that exclusion from the circuits of employment is an evil more feared than exploitation.

Representatives of European and American agriculture speak in similar terms, citing the need for national protection against Southern competitive designs but also, in the face of government attempts to limit surpluses, never missing an opportunity to promote their own exporting 'mission' and its supposed benefits for the whole of humanity. Western leaders, who mostly support a growth in world trade and act as travelling salesmen for their respective corporations, have no greater hesitation about blaming exports from the South for structural unemployment in their own countries.

Troubles in the North

This convergence of views has lent great weight to the idea that industrial migration to the South lies behind deindustrialization and its social ravages in the North. In ceasing to produce masses of consumer goods at home and turning to cheaper opportunities abroad, Western Europe and North America are said to have programmed the death of their own industries. But this thesis loses some of its credibility when we recall that in 1997, after twenty years of relocation, the European Union, United States and Japan together imported manufactures to a value of $514 billion from the South and the East Central European countries – that is, 10 per cent of the total value of world trade in goods and services.[19] It is estimated that, between 1972 and 1992, these imports reduced the demand for unskilled workers by 3 to 9 million, or less than 4 per cent of their total labour force.[20] In the United States, the most pessimistic forecasts in 1993 envisaged that half a million jobs – or 0.5 per cent of the domestic total – would disappear in the ten years following application of the NAFTA accord.[21]

Since then, of course, manufacturing industries have continued to shed jobs. In 1998 the EU's textile and clothing sector lost a further 2 per cent of its 2.2 million workers, who represent some 10 per cent of the manufacturing labour force in the Union.[22] But neither the relative opening up of trade by the industrial powers nor the cumulative effect of all the relocation can alone explain the existence of 35 million unemployed in 1998 in the countries of the OECD. France, for example, saw a tripling of unemployment between 1975 and 1995, whereas the degree of openness of its economy increased by just 3 per cent as imports rose from 18 per cent to 21 per cent of GDP.[23] Deindustrialization of the old industrial countries also appears in a clearer perspective if one bears in mind that they continued to figure among the world's largest producers of manufactured goods. Although China has raised itself in twenty years to the rank of the world's leading exporter of clothing, and although Turkey has managed to occupy fifth place in the league table, the third and fourth places are still taken by the European Union and the United States. As to textile goods, the EU in 1998 was still the second largest exporter in the world.[24]

It is true that, despite attempts by developing countries to woo investors with attractive investment codes and a low level of social or fiscal obligations, firms in the industrial countries have directed to them only a small proportion of their overseas investment and continued throughout the 1980s and 1990s to allocate some 80 per cent of it to the OECD. NAFTA has meant that between 1994 and 1998 Mexico received $18.1 billion in direct US investment, while Canada attracted more than double that figure, $39.6 billion.[25] In 1997, all the countries where direct foreign investment was greater than 5 per cent of GNP belonged to the OECD (with the exception of Singapore).[26] The rich countries, then, experienced neither disinvestment nor wholesale deindustrialization during the decades when part of the South was itself entering the industrial age.

All the same, structural unemployment was a feature of their economies in the last quarter of the twentieth century,[27] as was the deindustrialization of regions that pioneered the first industrial revolution. And neither statistics nor rough-and-ready explanations based on images of communicating vessels have much importance for the tens of millions suffering unemployment. Just as immigrants were seen as wrongly taking work away from nationals within the various countries of the North, so are the (typically female) workers of Asia, Latin America or North Africa seen as depriving Europeans or Americans of their jobs when they place themselves next to a sewing machine or an assembly line. Such perceptions hardly brighten the prospects of jobseekers from the South: they find themselves forbidden residence in the North, yet are supposed to refrain from industrialization at home in order to preserve jobs in the old manufacturing countries. The truth is, however, that the redistribution of industries around the world only partly explains why several million wage-earners have been expelled from the jobs market in the North, and that technological advances carry a not insignificant share of the responsibility. Productivity gains due in part to computerization and artificial intelligence,[28] conversion of Northern industrial plant to the production of intangibles, growing strength of communications and knowledge-based industries, the explosion of service activities: all these trends have increased the demand for skilled workers and massively reduced the supply of unskilled jobs.

In demanding the constant growth of corporate profitability, stock-exchange capitalism has made cuts in the wage bill the main variable in cost-cutting strategies and thereby also contributed to tighter jobs markets. Manufacturing sectors have not escaped the general downsizing. No doubt relocation has helped to marginalize sections of the unskilled workforce in the North and to intensify the downward pressure on wages; indeed, those sections are the only real losers from the changes in the world industrial map. But the other factors in that marginalization considerably reduce the relevance of the wage-earner nationalism which is the choicest rhetorical morsel for defenders of the world industrial status quo.

Inhabitants of the various regions in the South, whether they wish to emigrate to the eldorados of the North or to find work at home at any price, have provided a useful outlet for the frustrations of those left to fend for themselves by the latest industrial revolution. This has enabled Western decision-makers to postpone any real analysis of their inability to mitigate its social consequences. The changes of the last few decades have not caused the North to lose its prerogatives: its control over the future of the planet remains almost complete, and it has been able to reassert its power through a monopoly of the new technologies. All it has lost – with the consent of its elites[29] – has been the monopoly it held for a little more than a century over world manufacturing production.

This loss, which is largely offset by increased activity in the branches of the future, has been endured by (especially female) unskilled workers and felt by sections of the population as an intolerable attack on the supremacy that was for centuries part and parcel of Western identity. Since the beginning of the industrial era, the West – later joined by Japan – saw itself as the workshop of the world and, when necessary, tried to prevent others from developing their own industrial production. It is too often forgotten that the first relocations in modern history operated in a South–North direction, in many cases through the use of force. The dismantling of the Chinese porcelain industry and then of Indian textile production are the best-known examples of this migration in favour of European manufacturing. The contemporary industrialization of the South has nowhere been able to rely upon the powerful proto-industries that some of these regions had before they were systematically destroyed in the nineteenth century, and that made of India and China, among others, great exporting nations.

The incarnation of evil

Even if the North is not losing out, the period of its industrial monopoly is now coming to an end. This brings down with it the social orders and ideological corollaries stemming from the industrial revolution, and delivers a fatal blow to collective imaginations based upon the old myth of working-class power. The fears bound up with such wrenching changes require some definite cause to be identified and labelled. And so globalization, as a kind of hidden deity, serves to condense all these upheavals of the past twenty years, which are seen by their victims as so many calamities. For its assorted opponents, globalization is self-evidently the cause of all the world's evils.

There has been no end of analysis of a phenomenon which, according to one's point of view, is either only just beginning or nearing its final phase. It is not really known what it contains, what it encompasses, what it destroys, and what it creates. But its manifestations are everywhere. The least modification of the economic landscape is attributed to it. Everything new originates in it, and the future is being shaped by it alone. For the first time in modern Western history, however, the future is suspected of no longer bearing the constant progress expected of it. Does the rejection of globalization stem from this fear? But who is actually rejecting it, and why? An indisputable reality and a convenient scapegoat, this object that people still have trouble defining does not mean the same everywhere or for everybody; the term refers to a set of

different events whose concomitance makes them appear a single phenomenon. It is a catchword denoting all at once: the continuation of
trends that can be traced over a long period of history; a break with the
most recent and therefore most familiar phase of capitalism and international geopolitical relations; and the consequence of technological innovations that are shaking not only modes of production but the very
organization of societies and relations among them. In the eyes of the
public, this multiplicity of meanings makes globalization a total phenomenon from which nothing escapes.

Despite all this ambiguity, we must try to determine not its multiple
reality – that would be asking too much – but the functions it has in
collective imaginations and the political instrumentalization of its al-
legedly totalitarian quality. Globalization is often depicted as a kind of
earthquake that took place around the turn of the 1980s, halting the
chaotic yet assured forward march of humanity and giving the signal for
regression on an ever broader front. In this view, it is less the cul-
mination of a process unfolding over several centuries than a radically
new phenomenon constituting a break in the familiar order of the world.
Yet it is just as much part of the old as of the new. From the late
fifteenth century, European conquerors, empires and trading networks
carried ever further their occupation of the inhabited world, and from
the sixteenth century 'the power of Europe was enough gradually to
deprive other areas of any possibility of an independent history of their
own'.[30]

We know the episodes in that early globalization through which
Europe, and later its North American offshoot, steadily consolidated
their supremacy over the world. Sole beneficiaries of this unification of
the planet, they remained in control during every stage, at least until
the onset of decolonization. Neither the elites who led the globalization
nor the nations which profited from it came out against the principle.
Socialist alternatives born in the wake of the industrial revolution countered the imperialist variant with proletarian internationalism – a high-
minded but Eurocentric messianism that was incapable of theorizing
multiplicity yet was supposed to free the human race from capitalist
oppression. The national capitalisms born amid the crises of the 1930s,
which for the next half-century recentred the industrial economies on
their own territories and markets, did not forgo the advantages generated by the imperial or post-imperial projection of Europe and the
United States. Access of all the world's regions to sovereignty in international law and a theoretical possibility of deciding their own future

did more to accelerate than to slow down the unification of the globe under the aegis of the West.

This whole process, so long the cherished goal of Western elites, today appears to be reaching completion. We shall return to the effects that this closure is having on world-views, and to the new beginnings that it may herald. First, we should recall that the phenomenon now denoted by the name of globalization is part of a history that made it largely predictable.

But the present context also gives the term a different content from that of the recent past. The communications revolution has opened the way by shrinking the world and making it possible to speed it up, while the neoliberal turn has also contributed by opening wide all the frontiers. Consequently, ever since globalization became known as such, it has been perceived as the most visible, and therefore the most questionable, solvent of any social harmony painfully constructed over the past century. Whereas the world needs rules, global deregulation appears as the most fearsome weapon of a freedom that serves only the rich and powerful. The victory of an eminently volatile and uncontrollable financial capitalism over industrial capitalism, and thus of profit over labour, is one aspect of the process; others are the weakening of national protection and the supposed crumbling of the national state under the impact of globalization.

We should certainly not underestimate the close links among the three aspects: the rise of industries producing non-material goods, economic liberalization, and globalization. Globalization has undoubtedly made huge strides since free movement of capital became the rule, enabling money to be invested anywhere and moved around at the speed of the computer. But it cannot be reduced to its economic and financial dimension, or dissolved into the neoliberal revolution that has carried away the post-war edifices – a confusion very common among those who blame it for all the negative trends of the last few decades. Some maintain that the downsizing policies evident wherever rentier capitalism is in command, including in the non-competitive sectors, have their origins in globalization. The former top European official Riccardo Petrella has held it responsible for 'the massive and widespread reduction in the life expectancy of goods and services',[31] overlooking for the sake of his cause that the waste culture was born in the thirty-year golden age of full employment. The French editorialist Bernard Cassen reproaches it for structural adjustment policies that have axed public expenditure.[32] The Observatoire de la mondialisation, a French NGO created in 1996, argued in a leaflet to be handed out at its demonstrations that globalization was the root cause of 'the growing political dangers' represented by 'the breakdown of social cohesion, the threat to the rule of law and citizenship, the erosion of politics, and the rise of extremism of every stripe'; it did not wish to recall that attacks on the rule of law and the principle of citizenship were already legion before the ravages began. In Latin America – admittedly with the addition of the epithet 'neoliberal' – globalization has appeared as a vampire responsible for all the social and political catastrophes in the region;[33] many articles speak of it in anthropomorphic terms, as a real person, cynical and cruel, who spreads unhappiness wherever he goes. These are the attributes of the scapegoat, the incarnation of evil in uncertain times when the traditional points of reference become unreliable.

The rulers of the earth are themselves not averse to blaming it for crises in their respective countries, and in large parts of Europe politicians on both the left and the right make uninhibited use of the term. In December 1999, when the flood of comment peaked with the organization and then failure of the WTO conference in Seattle, French prime minister Lionel Jospin underlined the threat that globalization posed to the environment and the public health system,[34] without also mentioning the dangers of corporate productivism – encouraged by all governments, including his own – and of the consumption levels of his fellow-citizens.[35]

Nor do the leaders of the South lag behind. Also in late 1999, the Brazilian head of state Fernando Cardoso accused globalization of worsening the concentration of income,[36] and pretended to forget that record levels of social inequality had long been part of his country's profile. Similarly, Venezuelan president Hugo Chávez blamed globalization for the poverty of his fellow citizens but forgot to point out that, thanks to its oil, Venezuela had for decades been one of the richest countries in the region, with a per capita GNP of $3,500 in 1997.[37]

As to the IMF and World Bank, which public opinion around the world regards as the secular arm of globalization, they continue to be held guilty of all manner of exactions. 'In Somalia and Rwanda', writes an Amnesty International activist, 'there was virtual food self-sufficiency in the 1970s for the former and until the late 1980s for the latter ... until the point when the IMF stepped in.... These structural adjustment programmes have plunged the whole population into extreme poverty and exacerbated internal tensions.'[38] The dictatorship and then clan warfare which devastated Somalia for three decades and held its population to ransom, as well as the Rwandan genocide of 1994, are implicitly included on the debit side of structural adjustment policies, without any mention of internal political causes. Nor is there any reference in either case to the events that shattered an already fragile economic equilibrium: the two decades of raging drought in Somalia – a country, by the way, which has never implemented an adjustment programme – or the demographic trends that exacerbated conflicts in Rwanda. 'In Brazil we choose our enemies, and ours is the IMF', noted Brazilian writer Fernando Morais, as if echoing the thoughts of his president.[39] Such stigmatization of the hydra-headed international financial institutions is far in excess of their real responsibilities for economic liberalization and the growth of global inequalities.

Many are those who hold globalization in contempt, but they do so for often very different reasons and can ally with one another only if these are not clearly spelled out. Whereas some challenge the very principle behind it, others consider that it is too selective. Whereas some wish to change the rules, others wish to limit the effects. The confusion is compounded by ambivalent alliances between certain countries in the North and the South, between governments in the South and NGOs in the North, between nationalists and inheritors of the last socialist Internationals, or between supporters of the all-embracing state and champions of civil society. This mixing of banners – which dispenses with any analysis of the 'global lurch', to use Michel Beaud's expression[40] – makes it impossible to work out what is really at issue. For, as we have seen, there are as many rejections of globalization as there are contents given to the term. If we leave aside for the moment the kind of cultural rejection that sees the process as (in the case of the South) a Westernization of the world or (in the case of Europe) an Americanization of the world – hence a fatal thinning down of human diversity into uniformity – we are left with a few broad categories.

Nostalgia for the state

Two characteristics of globalization make it especially threatening for broad sections of the population in the North. In the redistribution of power that it implies, the state is no longer the only incarnation of power and, more particularly, the Western state no longer has a complete monopoly. Global power today is shared among the large states that remain undisputed powers in the world, plus a few emergent powers in the South, the largest transnational corporations, and the major international financial operators. The novelty of the situation appears all the more dangerous in that it breaks with the Keynesian phase of capitalism, which, since the bankruptcy of 'actually existing socialism', has been the only historically credible alternative to liberalism. By shattering the framework that maintained some discipline for half a century, globalization has helped to draw a line under the only period in which the dominant system was able to appear a bearer of justice. But neither working-class memories, with their justifiable nostalgia for national full employment, nor the inheritors of a political generation that limited its horizon to consolidating the redistributive functions of state capitalism wishes to see that that epoch was an exception in the long history of the expansion of capital. The liberal restoration and economic opening of the last twenty years are part of a much longer continuum, and the construction of alternative globalizations to the one now imposed by the holders of capital offers more for the future than does a search for national alternatives to globalization.

People regret the weakening of the protective state and attribute it to external attack. This is the context in which we should interpret the systematic amalgam that political leaders make between globalization and the dramas accompanying the current round of economic restructuring. In this way, they can not only escape blame for failing to deal with challenges that have left people on the rubbish heap of neo-liberalism but also minimize the role played by governments in the liberalization of the financial sector. If we were to believe these leaders, they are powerless in the face of diktats originating from the markets or the Bretton Woods institutions, in the face of an externally determined withering of the state that robs them of the means of action, and in the face of uncontrolled competition resulting from the opening of the world economy.

Although the new division of the globe has diversified the sources of power, it has by no means caused states to lose all of theirs. Nostalgia for the welfare state often makes people forget that the international financial and commercial organizations are only emanations of national states and themselves have only limited autonomy. It is the states of the North, and they alone, which dictated to those institutions the policies they should follow in the countries of the South and the conditions they should lay down. It is they which have refused for two decades significantly to reduce the debt burden of the South. It is they which have seen a general opening up of the world economy as the best means of enlarging the field of action for their corporations, and which have introduced more and more measures in their own countries to alter the relationship of forces between labour and capital. With certain shades of difference between Europe and the United States, they have all gone over to the customized liberalism that is the dominant ideology of our times. Apart from its more extreme fringes, this ideology does not repudiate the state but demands that it mainly serve the interests of those who own capital, that it make it easier for capital to move around, and that it continue to guarantee the socialization of losses and the privatization of profits.

What is called globalization does not therefore go hand in hand with disengagement of the state. In nearly all the developed countries, compulsory tax levies remain above a third of GDP. But public expenditure goes more today on assistance to companies or the most vociferous lobbies than on what is left of welfare services. And, even if orders from abroad leave them with considerably less room for manoeuvre than in the North, the leaders of the South also make improper use of globalization as a bogey for internal consumption.[41]

It is hardly possible to speak of a disappearance of the state, then, except perhaps in those areas where it was never fully constituted. A large part of sub-Saharan Africa, for example, served as a testing ground for the sorcerer's apprentices who pushed their neoliberalism a long way in that direction. They seem to have concluded that it could continue to serve that purpose but that it would be dangerous to go right to the end. After the liberalism with totalitarian hues that marked the 1980s, the next decade saw some evolution in dominant thinking about the roles of market and state: some think-tanks are not far from the view that the former is incapable of self-regulation and that the latter must keep large prerogatives, albeit completely different from those of the Keynesian epoch.[42]

Although the state remains a key force in international life and has kept most of the regulatory power at national level, a host of new international, global and local players have come forward to dispute with it, and the rise of transnational economic powers as well as the emergence of civil society[43] have contested its monopoly over political speech. This new hand of cards has produced many losers. Those excluded from the 'new economy' place all their hopes in a return to the protective state. And in the political domain, hankerers after an idealized image of the nation-state – an individual as symbolic and anthropomorphic as the globalization to which they counterpose it – have become spokespersons for the victims, in order to defend the income guarantees at the basis of its now-threatened monopolies.

So it is that in recent years we have seen surprising points of convergence between European nationalisms of the right and movements of the far left that have passed from revolutionary internationalism to mere defence of the gains of national wage-earners. In attacking globalization, the former can disguise their systematic support for economic liberalization and new social compromises more favourable to capital. In making globalization synonymous with American hegemony,[44] the latter can rejuvenate the vocabulary of anti-imperialism without touching any of their icons – which accentuates a little more their drift towards a popular conservatism disconnected from the new international issues. These two tendencies come together in rejecting any attempt at global regulation: for the nationalist currents (including part of Western social democracy), this threatens to blunt the edge of the sovereign state and damage a sacrosanct national identity; while for those on the left nostalgic for former divisions, it threatens to modernize the armoury of the old imperialist enemy.[45]

Winners and losers

What is new in the present stage of globalization is that, although the North is a net beneficiary of the recomposition taking place under its direction, it is no longer the sole beneficiary. Whole sections of its population have, for the first time, something to lose, while others elsewhere have derived some profit from the migration of industry that goes by the name of relocation. Fragile though the so-called emergent countries still are – the stock-market collapses of the late 1990s, triggered by footloose Western speculative capital, brought home the narrowness of their room for manoeuvre – these new trends have modified their status and level of wealth. Although it would be wrong to speak of a global transfer of wealth, some wage-earners and labour representatives in the North see this aspect of globalization as an unacceptable change to the status quo. It has indeed been a harsh blow to a planetary aristocracy of labour long accustomed to drawing dividends from Western expansion and convinced by its elites that the West's mission would last for ever.

The new situation has blurred the once-so-clear frontiers between North and South. It is exactly as if the North has suddenly ceased to be watertight against global misery, as if two spaces that were never meant to meet have run into each other. Making a spectacular return to latitudes from which it seemed to have been definitively banished, large-scale poverty has brought the South to the very heart of the North, to its great city centres and their scarred peripheries. The most evident causes of this are the redundancy of unskilled workers in the world's richest nations; their competition in sectors where they are still needed with the more plentiful and less demanding labour force of the popu-lous South; the downward pressure on wages due to the simple threat of joblessness or reduced compensation in branches that escape foreign competition; and the quest for maximum short-term profits by firms that benefit from a loosening of social legislation.[46] Sometimes, the poverty takes on the true colours of the South, by fixing itself to mi-norities from those parts of the world. The teeming metropolises of the North had forgotten that human beings could beg, or that they could be deprived of medical treatment because of a lack of money to pay for it. Now there are again people who have nothing. The penniless and home-less are becoming identifiable groups, geographically closer than at any time in the past century. The charity that had seemed reserved for the ultra-poor while others enjoyed welfare entitlements is again coming to the fore as the state concerns itself with matters other than the allevia-tion of social distress.

Globalization, then, means disturbance of the world, mingling of places, return to the image of barbarism contained in poverty. No matter that it never disappeared beyond the frontiers of the so-called developed world; what is abnormal is that it is resurfacing at its core. To say this is not to blind oneself to the reality of extreme poverty, which is all the more scandalous since the means exist to eliminate it. It is to recall that the North had grown used to a geographical apartheid which divided the earth into prosperous continents and deprived regions. The former are no longer safely sheltered. That is what causes such an outcry.

In the South, globalization does not arouse the same rejection or the same expectations, and people are more concerned to change its rules than to stop it in its tracks. If it does not get a good press, this is because it is mainly seen as a modernization of centuries-old domina-tion, and because its chief manifestation is the propensity of the world's major powers to universalize their diktats. The elites of the South there-fore demand, first and foremost, that the same constraints and freedoms should apply to all partners in the world economy, that the states of the North should open up to the South's products instead of adding more and more import barriers, and that they should agree to the same kind of protection for weak sectors of its economies that they apply to themselves. Seeing the asymmetry of international economic relations and regulations as proof of the North's refusal to yield an inch of its hegemonic positions, these elites plead for an 'equitable' globalization that does not merely place the power of the North on a new basis but offers their own countries new opportunities for development.

Such language goes down well in the cities of the South, where industrial relocation is generally thought of as an expansion of national jobs markets, although it is also true that (when repression is not too relentless) people increasingly question the working conditions of the sub-proletariat in the developing world. Peasant populations tend to be more hostile to the whole process, since the opening of frontiers to agricultural products from the North and the influx of agribusiness multinationals (especially in Latin America) create skewed conditions in which their own internal markets are lost and marginalization and impoverishment ensue. Nevertheless, at least in the economic field – culture is a different matter – there are not the same isolationist inclinations in the South that one finds expressed in North America or Europe. The fact that national resources are often not sufficiently large or abundant to create the basis for prosperity silences the sirens of autarky and opens the way to projects of regional integration. As to the social movements, many try to forge relations with their counterparts in the North in order to win support for an essential goal of their struggles: that is, elimination of the terms imposed by the Bretton Woods institutions and the establishment of less unbalanced North–South relations.

This has been the basis for alliances with civil movements in the West which are convinced that globalization should shake off the neo-liberal model that makes it a machine for crushing the majority of humans on this planet. Nevertheless, the tactical links between these movements and certain governments in the South rest upon a series of misunderstandings. Whereas associative movements representing a kind of new internationalism argue for global regulations that will put an end to the processes of exclusion and impoverishment, the leaders of the South demand freedom for themselves to reproduce the model through which the North built its present wealth. Did old Europe and the United States send their children to slave away in mine shafts and textile mills? Did they divert rivers and poison or exhaust their soil in order to extract the greatest possible wealth? Well, the South should be able to do the same, without having to face sanctions based on moral principles or reminders of the alarming state of the planet. For, in this view, such warnings are just the hypocritical clothing of a North which, for all its liberal professions of faith, has by no means renounced protectionism as a way of safeguarding its interests.[47]

Leaders of the most powerful or dynamic countries of the South (from India through Malaysia to Brazil) have often expressed their determination to make whatever use they like of the competitive advantages of unbridled capitalism – which would seem to contradict their wish to see a certain equity prevail in world economic relations. The paradox is not new, and none of today's protagonists is free of contradiction. Decision-makers in the North, for their part, do have some of the protectionist reservations attributed to them, even if they sincerely believe that ethics and the future security of the planet make it necessary to dissuade the South from following in their footsteps. Leaders in the South refuse to accept this, however, or do so only if they are forced into it.

The North is thus trapped by the very attraction of its model. The obstinate resolve of interlocutors in the South to follow the same path, even if it is questioned by those who first took it, is the source of new fears. Once again, the reproduction elsewhere of a specific historical experience – an experience always given universal value and a key element of globalization – seems to have turned against its apostles. Through its sensitivity to the fate of Amazonia or its alarm at wide-spread pollution in the South, public opinion in the North expresses its unease that one day the whole planet may suffer the consequences of a predatory mode of growth that is unable to reduce its capacity for harm. Perhaps globalization will begin to produce 'boomerang effects'[48] that shake Western prosperity to its foundations. Such apprehensions are not so profound as to raise the question of real lifestyle changes in the North, which are the only thing that might give legitimacy to the warn-ings addressed to the South. But they are a further sign of mounting uncertainty in a part of the world that has for centuries been accus-tomed to never paying the bill for its actions.

Finally, there are those in both the North and the South who seek to define the conditions for a new kind of planet-wide regulation that takes account of the shrinking of the world, and that remembers that global-ization has a history without taking refuge in objectless nostalgia. This is undoubtedly a challenging idea for anyone who wishes to think about the future. For the point is not to go back to earlier forms of regulation – which were less equitable than they are sometimes said to have been – but to find new forms that can halt the present drift and ensure proper ways of handling the problems facing the planet, which cannot be solved only within national frameworks.[49] Such forms of regulation would again impose limits on the market – though at a different level – and thereby prevent the crushing of the weakest both within each country and worldwide. In this way, the general interest would no longer be sacrificed to the race for rentier profit and the particular interests of the strongest. But, of course, it would also be necessary to reach agreement about the contours of the general interest.

This vast programme is barely in its infancy, for although, in the West at least, the international dimension has long been a focus of reflection, globality seems everywhere to be a new idea. In the South, it is hard to imagine that anything more than ad hoc alliances can be forged with the North – a North which, for many, is still the hereditary enemy. In the West, only rare currents try to construct discourses around a social universality that is not confined to simplistic abstractions, or seek ways of jointly tackling the extreme plight of the South and the poverty of the North. To venture in this direction, it is necessary to agree that the struggle against global inequalities cannot dispense with a fresh look at the privileges of the rich world, and that is something for which its citizens are not yet ready. In each hemisphere, attempts are made here and there to throw bridges across to the other, and it might be possible to build something around them. But they too are few and far between.

Meanwhile, the still hegemonic North has launched a massive reconstruction of its supremacy and is acquiring the means to cordon off the future for its own profit. There have been times in the past, however, when it was more self-confident. Although many of its citizens remain convinced of the legitimacy of their privileges and do not even experience them as such, they do have an awareness of the existence of others that is growing less and less hazy. More than ever, they fear that those others will disrupt a system which has been established for such a long time that it seems to be part of the natural order of things. Every new trend that appears to escape the control of those in power is perceived as a threat. Thus, the demographic dynamism in the South may pose insurmountable problems essentially at a local level, but the fears it arouses are all the more intense in that the North is aware of the rapid ageing of its own population. As regards the worsening social divide that seems to be carrying the two hemispheres ever further apart – the affluent islands in the South mirroring the acute poverty now present in the core of the rich world – it is rightly perceived as the focus of huge frustrations that might result in unpredictable kinds of revolt.

Is the supremacy of the West in danger of being swept away by the force of these currents? How far will the shock waves travel from these global jolts? In a confused manner, without clearly formulating things that still belong to the realm of the unthinkable, a part of the West is asking itself questions about the future of its central role. Although recent trends do not seem to herald its end, the advent of a new globality based on the shrinking of space may well be leading the globalization process to dissolve the Centre into a rhizomatic system that attaches less and less importance to geographical space. Then the old really would bring forth the new. Would the completion of the West's project of encompassing the whole world within its frontiers herald a world in which it lost itself? Would the triumph of the West ultimately be a Pyrrhic victory containing its final paradox – that is, a globality generated by its thirst for power but nevertheless escaping it?

We have not reached that point. But, in this murky world where rapid changes fuel the fears of some, the frustrations and aspirations of others, and the uncertainties of all, everyone tries to find points of reference through the building of myths or new citadels. By forcing everyone to recognize the other's existence, the shrinking of the world has also made more sophisticated the forms of its own negation or demonization. Never have antagonistic constructions of identity had so much mutually reinforcing success. The worlds that unequally share an ever more open planet confront and meet up with each other at the same time, redefining each other but also overlapping. Can anything be born of these reciprocal fantasies, these warmed-up hatreds, these new detestations, these encounters that are always beginning over again and shaping the current geography of human relations?

PART THREE

The Two Sides of the Mirror

Mostly impassable, more or less visible according to time and place, rooted in both consciousness and geography but riddled with hybridizing flaws, a frontier does indeed exist between Norths and Souths – and for the moment not much seems to have the power to overshadow it. Of course, it is not the only separator of peoples and territories. Within each of the two entities that it sets face to face, other divides are sometimes more profound; they can also produce greater violence than anything created by the boundaries enclosing the West. Recent history gives a hundred examples. To mention just one, the world map of identity distinctions is far from coinciding with the frontiers between the two hemispheres.

On the other hand, similar currents pervade the Norths and the Souths. That which unites extremist movements within each of the religions claiming universality is much more important than that which separates them. Although each claims a monopoly of salvation, their servants have in recent years more often formed alliances to oppose the two main dangers facing humanity – women's emancipation and secularization – than they have fought each other for the triumph of their God.[1] On both sides of the *limes*, however, public opinion attaches greater importance to manifestations of the familiar divide between Muslim East and Christian West than to convergences around new ways of bringing religion into politics. In any event, the former inspire more fear than the latter among the citizens of the North.

Here, as in so many other cases, it is the North–South stand-off that really makes sense; the space defined by its shadow still – perhaps more than ever? – structures the perceptions that each has of the other. And

167

that vast space encompasses both a history – whose accounts have, with rare exceptions, not been settled – and contemporary realities that have widened the gaps and frozen the splits. On each side, the shrinking of the world makes it impossible to ignore the other, while the disparity of forces rules out any direct confrontation. But every move is watched, every opportunity taken to measure the other's capacity for harm. In the South, people nervously gaze at the new weapons that those in power are developing to renew their hegemony. In the North, people shudder at the idea that crowds of beggars might take power, or demand a share of it, simply because of their numbers. These mutual suspicions rise up like walls. To protect themselves, both sides eagerly assert what they are in order to exorcize the spectre of being swallowed up into the other. Demonstrations of identity are, in fact, much more common than one might think. And again it is by turning to a new-look universality that the West seeks to redefine itself and to relegitimate its supremacy.

On the other side, attempts are certainly made to establish a clearly demarcated identity, but the main reaction is to oppose the West's power projection and to challenge its rule. The contemporary period in the Souths may be read as one long history of reactive tensing in the face of the West's injunctions and norms of enforcement, and the discourse of their intellectuals as the inverted image of a dominant way of thinking from which they are unable to free themselves. Whereas the West can see the other only when it sends back a reflection of itself, the other often looks at itself only in the mirror held up by its former master. Whereas universality remains a prisoner of its limitations, as it has ever since it was invented, those on the other side exist first of all in opposition to it, before they begin to explore other self-definitions.

Is any exit possible from these deadly mirror-games? The West feels no real need for one, since its main purpose is to uphold its own centrality by remaining the only issuer of norms. In the South, those who wish to escape the reactive trap and to acculturate universality by making it universally appropriable usually run up against the concern of Westerners to retain their monopoly on the production of meaning, as well as the indifference or hostility of compatriots who have been seduced by other discourses or imprisoned by various constraints. Nevertheless, some scope does exist: it tells us that the world is changing and that we should perhaps look at it differently.

TEN

The New Look
of Universality

Universality has never before seemed in such good shape. The six billion people on earth are part of the same humankind, and only the tiniest groups in the West would dare to express in public a belief in the inferiority of certain races. In most countries such statements, or acts of racial discrimination, are anyway punishable offences. There are no longer human beings 'still at a rough stage', as Gobineau put it, and at least in this respect equality reigns all over the globe. Indeed, human rights are idealized as never before: since the end of the cold war the democratic powers have officially made respect for them one of the preconditions of aid; some speak of 'human rights' as the conquering ideology of the new century. Although violators do not necessarily suffer punishment, they at least face reprimand and expose themselves to opprobrium.

Most states in the world verbally revere this set of rights which define the human condition. They have signed, and often ratified, the numerous UN conventions, and they have written into their national legislation the Universal Declaration of Human Rights to which every country joining the UN theoretically adheres. In this context, the white male is no longer the only subject of natural law who enjoys the integrity and liberty codified by the Enlightenment; universality seems to have swept away the barriers that for so long made it the promised land for only a small band of the elect.

Does this mean that the West no longer claims a monopoly of universality, and that at the end of a long road it has agreed to accept the principle of absolute equality of all who represent the human race? Theoretically, yes. We should certainly not discount the importance of this formal recognition of universal rights. And yet those who ascribe the invention of human rights to their own collective spirit have not given up claiming something akin to usage or seniority rights, whereby they can decide what is and what is not included in universality, or judge how the principles issuing from it should be applied. In agreeing to enlarge the territory without abolishing the frontiers, they retain the dual privilege of modernizing a closed domain and making themselves its sole managers – even if this means that others can exploit the persistent confusion between globalization of universality and Westernization of the world.

As God or science (at least for the North, in the first case) has failed to produce certified truths, contemporary manifestations of the Western culture of supremacy are more complex and sometimes more ambivalent than those which appeared in the age of absolute certainties. But the distance between them is not all that great, and they follow similar logics to those of the past. The glorification of universality still does not prevent the exclusion of the 'other', even if the reasons given for it have evolved over time. The West scarcely thinks of giving up the privilege of defining by its own lights who should have access to the real humanity, the one most like itself. It also determines, in its own interests alone, who should enjoy and who should be excluded from the rights attached to that humanity. In this respect, the world still functions as a club in which one can be enrolled if its founder members give the nod.

A new geography of law

After attempting to spread the blessings of civilization to the rest of the planet, even to the forces most reluctant to embrace their own happiness, the Western democracies gave themselves the mission of establishing the rule of law. Once the colonial wars that cast a veil over the principles had come to an end, the West waged its major battles for the defence and spread of freedom. This was the banner under which it fought the Soviet Union and eventually saw off the embodiment of totalitarian evil, and it was also the ostensible reason for its spectacular adventures of the 1990s. Western states now conduct their external operations as if they had a duty to extend to the whole of humanity the benefits of basic personal and political rights.

It is a truism to say that the energy with which they pursue this goal is directly linked to geopolitical and economic imperatives. Throughout the cold war, the political instrumentalization of these rights took on the familiar forms of caricature: unflagging support for South American and East Asian dictatorships, constant backing for the regional security policies of the apartheid regime in South Africa, and assistance to the bloodiest African regimes happily coexisted with enthusiastic cheers for the slightest glimmer of democratic opposition in the socialist countries of Europe. It was a real war – politicians said later, as they admitted the persistent application of 'double standards' during those times. They soon got over the deaths under torture on the right side of the iron curtain, since the war had, after all, ended in the triumph of Good.

After the collapse of the Soviet empire, although Western advocates of realpolitik would have regarded it as suicidally naive to make the issue of rights the main criterion in choosing future allies, many people thought for a brief moment that it might weigh a little more heavily in the balance, alongside the West's own interests. It is true that there was more talk of such matters, but the ritual incantations of the 1990s did not give them the expected weight, and there were as many ways of instrumentalizing them as in the days of the cold war.

One approach has been to ignore the issue – or timidly to give an impression of interest when the interlocutor is too powerful to be intimidated from taking it further – and at the same time to denounce violations in less significant countries. China, for example, benefits from an indulgent attitude for which it is envied by many smaller states that are regularly taken to task. With impressive harmony, North America and the European Union utter discreet sighs when the tension rises too high in Tibet or the repression of dissidents goes beyond reasonable bounds, but these brief flurries subside as soon as Beijing speaks up. In fact, when Western leaders are asked for their opinion, they like to mention the democratic advances of the Chinese state to justify closer links with potentially the world's number one market.[1] Niger – whose allowance was cut off in April 1999 for the sterling reason that mutineers had killed the official president – had no right to the same understanding, and the army had to rush through elections to gain the ear of the country's funders.[2]

A perfect example of selective blindness and attention is the Western attitude to various Islamic states. Everyone knows the consideration shown to Saudi Arabia, and no official in Washington or Paris would dare voice the slightest criticism of a regime that barbarously applies the most obscurantist reading of Islam. Neither the absolutism nor the bloodletting of an archaic monarchy without equal in the world ever moves the chancelleries of the West, which are so quick to hand out their good and bad marks. The Islamic Republic of Iran did not benefit from the same indulgence before it embarked on its equivalent of the Thermidorian period following the French Revolution. The totalitarian and misogynist regime which took power in Iran in 1980, also based on an ultra-regressive version of the sharia, was blackballed by most democratic governments for its human rights violations and the scale of its repression of opponents. Those who continued trading with it did so almost on the sly, for fear of drawing the wrath of their peers. An obscurantist religious dictatorship, it was said, could not have a place in the concert of nations – a praiseworthy attitude, no doubt, but one that would have been more credible if Western officials had waxed equally indignant at the execution of an oppositionist or the butchery of an adulterous woman in Riyadh as in Tehran.

It soon became necessary to face facts: the West's tolerance threshold in relation to political Islam directly depends upon the camp it chooses. It was less their religious roots than their militant anti-Westernism which earned the Iranian leaders of the Khomeini period such intense hostility. But the campaign against them was at least partly waged in the name of values that were promptly forgotten as soon as it was a question of the oil monarchies or even of Baghdad, whose bloody leader was held up at the time as an enlightened despot. Islamic Iran, rightly felt to be unsavoury, was classed among the world's evildoers, whereas the Saudi regime continued to enjoy the solicitude that the West reserves for its closest allies, especially when they are also its biggest customers.

The United States excels when it comes to moral selectiveness: whether in its support for the Afghan Taliban, its protection of Congo President Laurent-Désiré Kabila in 1997–98 (when the United Nations and humanitarian agencies present in the country accused him of covering up the massacres of Hutu refugees), or its virulent condemnation of the Cuban regime. The Europeans do not lag behind, and were quite able to show simple discretion when Moscow called upon them in autumn 1999 not to interfere with its reconquest of Chechnya. Far from rising clear of cruder interests, the West's handling of human rights has essentially meshed with its strategies to defend them.[3]

Without dwelling on the precise instrumentation, we must at least attempt a general review of the issue. Some think that the use of all available means, verbal as well as others, is an inevitable part of the exercise of power. In general, however, power does not burden itself with principles and relies only on its own authority to assert or consolidate itself. Today, as in the past, the West is alone in placing its actions under the auspices of universal human law; it covers up violations of that law as often as it appoints itself to guarantee it, thereby continuing the split between words and deeds which has long been its custom. Just as systematic violations used to be the rule anywhere beyond the frontiers of Europe, so does flexibility on principles now allow a line of demarcation to be drawn between the same and the other. This line establishes a kind of computer image of the peoples or individuals deserving to be part of the limited universality that seems a hallmark of Western modernity.

One cannot deplore enough the tragic consequences of this double language, this simultaneous resort to noisy condemnation and deafening silence in accordance with the place and interests of the moment. Emptied of meaning, universality becomes unintelligible to those who suffer its effects and ends up as the West's ultimate ruse of self-justification. Those in the South who uphold the primacy of such universal law over often regressive local specificities face ridicule whenever the actions of a democratic power devalue the very principles that it utters. Those who oppose democratic universality, fearing that it would spell the end of their rule and the systems on which it is based, find in the Western game arguments for why their fellow countrymen should condemn such a dangerous body of values. Although the West is not alone responsible for the identity convulsions shaking so many regions in the South, nor can it be considered free of blame; a good number of its actions simply make it impossible for the local people in question to believe in the virtues of a universal law that it claims to represent. Nowadays, the West sometimes even conducts its wars in the name of that law, when in reality its choice of enemy involves considerations at least as complex as in the past.

Selective morality

The Gulf War is a good example of the disasters to which manipulation of the law can lead. We cannot here go into the history of the first international conflict after the end of the cold war, but we might try to interpret it in the light of the West's discourse of justification. The prologue was the bloody conflict of the 1980s, when Iraq tried to profit from the weakening of its hereditary enemy by attacking Islamic Iran. The violent anti-Westernism of the Khomeini regime meant that the

West lost no time in taking the side of Baghdad, a further factor being the danger of revolutionary contagion in the strategic monarchies of the Gulf, and potentially in a wider Arab world not insensitive to the radical Islam that Iran claimed to be transforming from utopia into a political project. But as enlightened self-interest was not enough to justify the scale of financial and military support to Iraq,[4] other arguments were summoned to fill the breach. All Western leaders liked to see the Baghdad regime as an embodiment of progressive nationalism, which, though little concerned about freedoms, was closer to their own values than the Iranian theocracy that sent its children to die for the glory of God.

Saddam Hussein, whose throne already rested on piles of corpses, was then a valued partner with whom it was good to be seen. According to the received wisdom of the time, this authoritarian modernist was a convinced secularist,[5] and commentators pointed to the building of factories, hospitals and schools as evidence of this. Western intellectuals, with the European nation-state in mind, certainly found it easy to convince themselves that signs of material modernization indicated a choice of modernity on the part of nationalist movements in the South. What they did not wish to see was that nationalism in the Arab-Muslim part of the world had also drawn upon a religious register as a tool of legitimation, so that, for example, in Saddam Hussein's Iraq the code governing the position of women continued to be largely inspired by Muslim law, polygamy was a permissible option, and conjugal repudiation remained a male privilege.[6] Nor was it recognized that the Iraqi dictator had done his utmost to worsen the tribal and religious fragmentation of his country and reverted to the most archaic clan procedures to strengthen his hold on power. Human rights organizations could reel off a long list of his misdeeds – nothing was ever done.[7] Until 2 August 1990, it remained perfectly acceptable to be seen with Saddam Hussein.

The tune changed as soon he launched his invasion of Kuwait. From the beginning of the crisis, demonization of the West's former ally went far beyond what was required to defend international law and to restore the sovereignty of the country under attack. Saddam was soon the incarnation of evil, and with rare exceptions Western politicians and journalists trotted out analogies *ad nauseam* (the Saddam = Hitler equation being the most memorable) which precluded any real analysis of the regional situation and made negotiations impossible. For, as Munich had shown, you can't negotiate with Hitler.[8] The aim was no longer to make a dictator see reason, if necessary by force, after he had gone beyond the limits; it was to wage war for the triumph of Good. The declared objective of protecting the international legal order from an overweening tyrant – and, less vociferously, of recovering the oil wells – turned into a moral crusade so that the Law should have the final say.

Since, however, legality is not defended with the same vigour in every part of the world, the disproportion in the Iraqi case made it possible for Saddam Hussein to brand his enemies as duplicitous and, by posing as victim, to win a large part of Arab public opinion to his side. After several decades in which nationalists and then Islamicists had continually raised the pitch of anti-Westernism, and an even longer period in which its intellectuals and leaders had sustained the myth of Arab unity, the broader public did not have to make a great effort to embrace Saddam's positions. But the West's chosen line of argument was also a powerful spur. Was the conquest of Kuwait a violation of international law? Well, it was asked, why did the United Nations not call for the use of force at the time of Israel's annexation of East Jerusalem in 1968 and the Golan Heights in 1981, or in response to the invasion of Lebanon by Syria in 1976 and by Israel in 1978?[9] Was the international coalition fighting to defend freedom against a dictator who kept his people under a terrible yoke? Well, why did it not move against Kuwait or Saudi Arabia in the name of the same principles? Western opinion-makers had little idea of what people thought in the Arab world, and never understood the degree of antipathy that the Gulf princes aroused from Rabat to Cairo. Too rich and arrogant, they set up their quarters in Arab capitals as in conquered cities, shamelessly feasting there at the same time that they imposed a pitiless moral order in their own countries. Ordinary people had come to loathe these coarse types rolling in money who did not deserve their oil, and rejoiced to see Saddam Hussein teaching them a lesson.[10]

Social frustrations in the most populous Arab countries also led people there to approve the takeover of the Kuwaiti oil reserves, which they saw as the first step to a regional redistribution of wealth. In this view, if the US-led international coalition acting under the UN umbrella wanted to punish Iraq in the name of principles that experience had shown to have no more than the label of universality, then the principles were bad and should be rejected. In early 1991, most of the population in the Arab world was convinced that the moral arguments put forward by the United States and its allies served only to mask their intention to keep control of the Gulf oil and to prop up unsavoury dynasties that were under its heel.

A war for oil or a war for law? Although a concern for legality was not absent from this war for oil,[11] its instrumentalization released shock waves that are still felt today. The ravages produced in the Arab intelligentsia left their mark, as supporters of a legality based upon universal principles (who were already in a minority) found it extremely difficult to continue upholding them or to insist, however intolerable the Western hypocrisy, that the Iraq dictator remained indefensible.[12] On this and other occasions, the Western elevation of diktat, silence and doctored argument to the status of strategies helped to strengthen the worst identity withdrawal in the South and to weaken local pioneers of endogenous modernities based upon a belief in the universality of freedom.

Logics of interference

The end of the cold war did, however, mark a break. Having triumphed over the last totalitarian variant of modernity in the name of a polymorphous liberty, the Western democracies sought to establish fresh legitimacy for their hegemony by posing as global protectors of the same values[13] for which they had waged the struggle against communism. In order to guarantee the primacy of law, as they said they wanted to do in the Gulf War, they had to ensure the protection of certain rights – mainly individual and political ones, subject to the higher imperatives of geopolitics. But that was not all. Communism, itself heir to an old tradition of social messianism more resonant among the masses than respect for the democratic ideal, had made justice the supreme value before which liberty had to lower its guard. The neoliberal turn of the 1980s banished all talk of equity, but the Western powers, aware that extreme poverty involved a denial of the rights they sought to promote, tried to mitigate those glaring forms which most shocked public opinion. Finally, the fragmentation of federal states linked to the great secular ideologies, as well as the destabilizing effects of economic openness and the resistance it provoked, gave a new intensity to the question of minorities, who were often the first victims of the weakening of multinational, multiethnic or multireligious entities. Western states sought to lend weight to the idea that their now undivided hegemony was the bearer of progress for those who submitted to it and acquired fresh duties as a result.

Already in the 1980s, the new official doctrine – which involved more open and more frequent references to human rights, the addition of a social dimension, and the attachment of democratic conditions to Western aid for the weakest countries in the South – began to link up with demands formulated by younger generations since the 1960s. Tired of waiting for change in an unjust world order, eager to act then and there to relieve people's actual sufferings, a new breed of activists demanded that their governments put an end to the most flagrant breaches of human rights – a reinvention of the idea of humanitarian intervention, at a time when the Western states were seeking to redefine their modes of operation in a world from which their most serious rival had been removed.

This convergence of aspirations and interests gave new life to the idea that respect for the law required certain parts of the world to be placed under watch, and that morality dictated intervention when other human beings were in danger. The rhetoric was not new. Europeans had employed it more than once in the course of their imperial history, perhaps most notably in the second half of the nineteenth century, to justify intervention in support of Christian minorities in the Middle Eastern provinces of the Ottoman Empire. As we can see, the use made of human rights is a problem at the heart of the modern history of the West.

The end of the twentieth century witnessed a series of military–humanitarian campaigns, whose official aim was to save people from (often interlinked) famine and violence. The first of these, in late 1992, was the disastrous 'Restore Hope' operation in Somalia, led by a United States eager to be seen as a benefactor in the South after its recent stick-wielding in the Gulf region. Then came the French decision in June 1994, when Rwanda was already strewn with corpses, to launch Operation Turquoise in response to public demands and in support of allies in headlong retreat. From the protection of Iraqi Kurds (those in Turkey not being deemed in danger) to crisis-management in the former Yugoslavia, all these operations pursued objectives often very remote from the concerns that officially lay behind them. More than once, humanitarian demands served as a pretext for governments seeking to justify their actions.[14] In making the duty of assistance to individuals and nations a moral imperative, and in campaigning for international law to take precedence over national law, advocates of intervention have nevertheless publicly raised a number of crucial issues. Authoritarian regimes certainly treat as dangerous enemies these sworn opponents of the dogma of state sovereignty, who in recent decades have inflicted harsh blows on it in the name of principles equally valid in all places.

My purpose here is not to analyse the ambivalent relations between supporters of humanitarian intervention and those who use it for their cynical realpolitik, but to show that, in order to give substance to a doctrine involving recognition, hypocritical or sincere, of the primordial value of the human individual, it has been necessary to develop something of a theory of intervention. Though drawing on different, sometimes opposite sources – from official political structures to the amorphous social movements of the Western world – discourses that advocate a duty of assistance or a right to sanction the lack of basic freedoms invariably display the same certainty that the West alone is suited to exercise that duty or right.

Is it conceivable for Americans that any action of the United States might be judged by a South American or African court? asked an *International Herald Tribune* editorial during the debate on setting up an International Criminal Court with worldwide jurisdiction.[15] Internationalization of the UN's public function has certainly brought some exotic faces into the ranks of global diplomacy, but their task is to apply the norms not to define them. In the world as it is today, the right of intervention operates in a single direction. To be sure, given the relationship of forces governing international relations, it is hard to imagine that any states in the South might ever punish a breach of the law committed by any state in the North. But the point is that the very scenario belongs to the realm of the unthinkable for an overwhelming majority of Western citizens. Much as they used to possess the truth and assumed the mission of spreading it, they have now set themselves up as sole guardians of principles.

France has built a reputation as the homeland of human rights, and most of its population adheres to this self-image so often presented by politicians as well as by intellectuals and the media.[16] Similarly, the United States is the homeland that Good has chosen for itself and therefore the only country really entitled to defend it; politicians are fond of upholding this belief among a population whose whole culture prepares them for it. More generally, the values underlying human rights are supposed to be part and parcel of Western existence, possessing a quiet certainty that disdains political divisions. The highly internationalist Daniel Cohn-Bendit, for example, wrote during the 1999 European election campaign that 'the division between communitarian ghettoes or the split between ghettoes of luxury and ghettoes of poverty is contrary to European civilization'.[17] A peculiar reading of the history of the continent, one might think.

On both sides of the North Atlantic, the dominant discourse is built around a soothing rhetoric that serves to establish a kind of timeless identity between humanism and the West. In this view, the West cannot be suspected of scorning values so close to its heart, and if one of its own strays from them he can only be judged by his peers. Although 'the others' must convert and show allegiance, they will never be more than novices or join the guardians of the temple. Carrying Good within itself, the West has a natural responsibility to ensure that the rules are everywhere respected.

Of course, the chaos of war, poverty-stricken suburbs, countrywide prisons are more numerous in the South than in the North.[18] Human rights are more widely abused in these grey zones of the South, where famine often rages or law barely exists, and the far from glorious state of the world compels action where the need for it is felt. But the very idea of reverse intervention in suitable cases seems to Westerners totally inconceivable, and it is hard to imagine a Senegalese or Indian investigation of conditions in French prisons or American penitentiaries. At most, these apprentices are allowed to do some tidying up among their neighbours, on condition that their regional intervention is not harmful to Western interests.[19] Not everyone who wishes it can decide how the law is administered. Once again, this unwritten postulate of unilateral intervention strengthens the barriers that the West raises between itself and others; once again, it reinforces the frontiers within which the West encloses universality.

ELEVEN

The Same and the Others

In the West today there are several ways of approaching the existence of others. Ranging from a simple denial of otherness, through stigmatization or appropriation of elements thought to be similar, to a recognition of otherness decked out with false equivalences, these appear as so many strategies to rebuild the founding hierarchies of Western superiority in new ways and by means of new images. It remains the case, however, that universality is embodied in a single form given it by Europe and its various extensions around the world. Even if the criterion of race or civilization is replaced with the more respectable one of common respect for basic rights, closeness to the reference model is the only real security asked of apprentices. Anyone who does not try to match it on every point forfeits any claim to be following its resultant principles – in the eyes of those who hold a monopoly on their proclamation.

In recent years, this requirement has often led a copy to be taken for genuine respect for principle, elections for democracy, or verbal praise of the model for a sign of its triumph. Invited to comply with it, the dictators of the South soon learned the art of producing imitations – and their mentors in the North seemed happy enough. Yet the guardians' mimetic injunction places non-Westerners in an impossible position. If they refuse to conform or fail to strive for sameness, they give proof of their incapacity to join the sphere of universality and find themselves cast into alterity, at worst a locus of regression, at best a worthy yet frozen place from which nothing new can ever emerge. But if they seriously try to make their likeness perfect and to join the Western realm where universality has its home, they are soon – with very rare exceptions – told that their efforts are in vain. The Other can never become the Same.

Colonial history and the contemporary epoch offer many examples of such refusals, which expose the repeated talk of integration as so much fraud. The British or Belgians, for instance, are in the habit of contrasting the distance they kept from their colonial subjects with the French determination to assimilate them; whereas the French like to counterpose Anglo-Saxon community-centred thinking to their own universalist egalitarianism. Although these variants draw on different sources – a sanctification of cultural differences or a wish to erase them – and although they may lead today to different ways of handling non-indigenous minorities in the West, they are less far apart than one might think in their actual effects. The influence of the Enlightenment on intellectuals in the British Empire was no less great than on those in the French colonies; Shakespeare is as well known (or as little known) in India as Molière is in North Africa, and Britain, the Netherlands and Belgium have as high a proportion as France of citizens originating in their former overseas possessions. Similarly, it is by no means certain that the barriers which France has created between those who do and those who do not manage to become full citizens are easier to cross than the lines between communities in the British model. Loudly as its heralds may trumpet the French policy of assimilation, it has proved as miserly with integration as other courses pursued elsewhere in the West.

Colonial subjects found this out a long time ago. In Algeria – which, as we know, used to be France – the mother country's nationality was always granted most parsimoniously to a population which for many years hoped to accede to it. In 1936, when the Popular Front government agreed once to grant non-transmissible citizenship to 21,000 particularly deserving individuals, the president of the Ulema Association, Abdelhamid Ben Badis, expressed pleasure at the advance and hoped that universal suffrage would allow 'straightforward integration of the Muslim collectivity into the great French family'.[1] Ferhat Abbas went further at one point, challenging the very idea of an Algerian nation and calling for equal rights between the indigenous and French populations. For decades a majority of the elites believed that France represented the future of Algeria. But, except in words, the guardian power did everything it could to discourage them. In 1947 there were 58,000 Muslim French citizens out of a total Muslim population of 7,800,000.[2] Awareness of the obstacles to assimilation did a great deal to push the 'Frenchified' elites towards the cause of independence.

Decades later, when it faced the challenge of integrating on its own soil a new wave of people from overseas, France came up with the idea of a 'second generation' who inherited the qualities of immigrants, no longer really foreign, but not French either. It mattered little that they now had French nationality. If someone belonged to the second generation and had too exotic a name, nationality was no guarantee of integration: it opened no doors to employment, or to a ring-fenced political world that admitted children born to foreigners only if they were of European descent.[3] Whether they remain in their country of birth or decide to emigrate, non-Westerners can achieve a fully human modern status only if they metamorphose and become identical with the model to which they are supposed to aspire; but it is precisely this which they are given to understand is impossible. What Cornelius Castoriadis calls the 'essential non-convertibility of the other'[4] means that they are unable to fulfil the condition required of them to express universality. Different from their parents because they have willy-nilly entered modernity, some non-Westerners try to escape the trap by building reactive identities, in the hope that these will replace what they no longer are and what they are unable to become. Islamicism is one such option, which reinterprets a tradition that is no longer supposed to be in working order, and opposes head-on a West that is too distant to be really accessible. We shall return to this below.

The re-emergence of the Other...

The forms of universality, then, are not open to negotiation. But who is this Other, summoned to fit into moulds where the quality of otherness will no longer be discussed? Has much changed since those Modern Times when Europe turned its discoveries into conquests and forged the instruments to legitimate them? Does contemporary Western identity feed on the same oppositions, more or less touched up over the centuries, or has it agreed to renew itself by drinking from other sources? More cautious because of their loss of numerical superiority,[5] but still confident of their strength, where do today's Westerners draw the frontiers that distinguish them from the rest of the world?

Sometimes they appear to be in two minds. Although the United States has always barred undesirable aliens from its El Dorado, it considers that an empire can also be measured by its power of attraction and encourages a degree of cosmopolitanism in its big cities and among its elites, as a stage in the Americanization of the world. On the periphery of the Western world, Australia is discovering the constraints and opportunities of its geographical location, as it asks how far it can become part of Asia, officially declares itself to be multicultural (like Canada, the other land of migration in the far North[6]), and expresses its wish to integrate Aboriginal survivors into a nation still in the course of defining itself. Europe, for its part, wonders where it should stop in order to remain itself. Should it bring in Turkey, which aspires to become a European power?[7] Are the Muslims of the Balkans the last dross of the Ottoman Empire, abandoned outside its historical and therefore geographical reach? Are they aliens in a continent cemented together by its Christian heritage, or themselves Europeans who should be defended against anyone who disputes it? Can Europe ensure its demographic future without rethinking the frontiers between itself and others?

For many different reasons, which range from their changing relations with the world to enlightened self-interest, Westerners are beginning to convert what they used to see as other into a part of themselves. But there is no guarantee that this is a harbinger of something larger. The old culture of supremacy, given a new lease of life by burgeoning anxieties as well as by recent advances in economics and technology, has not finished structuring people's thinking and attitudes. As it adapts to new global configurations, it reformulates its underlying paradigms and defines new divisions that consolidate the older frontiers. Reaching into political, intellectual and popular life, the culture of supremacy continues to booby-trap the relationship between Westerners and the rest of the world. It still dictates who are other and how they should be seen.[8]

Let us be clear that it is not a question of blaming Westerners for their feeling that they are different from others. The sense of belonging to a particular civilization is not itself a problem, and is anyway shared with the rest of humanity. What some rightly hold against globalization is, after all, that its market logic casts the whole of human diversity in the same mould and prepares the way for a lethal unification under the banner of the dominant subculture, which would appear to be a contradiction in terms. All the disciplines that concern themselves with human reality have taught us that it is the existence of the Other which controls our recognition of ourselves. Yet the Western culture of supremacy, carried along by a centuries-old hegemony, does not place itself on this terrain. Tragically lonely in its ancient self-assurance, it still seeks to define by itself the conditions of access to a modern universality.

The real issue today is very different: it is to make universality intelligible, and therefore appropriable, for one and all, by finally fleshing out the definition that the West's thinkers gave of the inalienable rights of the human individual. To that end, how is it possible to develop a political, social and moral contract in which all the components of human society recognize one another? This is certainly a vast programme, at the opposite pole from all the different kinds of 'cultural exceptionalism'. But we should not forget that one such exceptionalism is the variant in which the West remains too self-confident to allow any place for others in its constructions – unless it can recreate the other in its own image, or shut it up within its alterity, thereby sorting the wheat from the chaff.

...and the return of threats

Once communism had been safely laid to rest, once that enemy sibling whose seductiveness went far beyond the lands of its birth had carried its rival universalism down with it, the West gave a new twist to divisions that had partly faded within the alliances of the cold war and brought back into fashion a more culturalist reading of the world map. In the early 1990s, soon after the publication of his *Clash of Civilizations*, Samuel P. Huntington's new 'civilizational' geography of global conflicts began to exert the influence that we know upon Western elites and strategists.[9] One of the effects of its essentialist view of the real or supposed splits tearing the world apart was to push other factors into the background, including world social and economic inequalities, and to free the West of blame for any resultant worsening of tensions.

Coming after the narcissism of the 'end of history' thesis, presented a few years previously by his fellow-American Francis Fukuyama,[10] the simplistic character of Huntington's view certainly made it the object of attack. But it still provided a theoretical foundation for exclusion, on the convenient grounds that the Other constituted a real danger.

For Huntington, Islam poses a problem of a special kind, and the greatest danger is that of an 'Islamic–Confucian link-up' between two entities deeply hostile to what the West represents.[11] On both sides of the Atlantic, Islam is seen more than ever as a barrier. The far east of Asia is politically powerful and economically threatening, but in its self-assured otherness it seems to have no other pretension than to assert its differences and its autonomy; and Africa is wrapped up in wars, which are evidently a sign of regression to precolonial barbarism. Of course, the North may well be afraid of both, since the Asian powers wish to gain a political status more in keeping with their position in the economy, while it is always possible that Africa will export its nuisances, especially its poor and its AIDS virus.

Nevertheless, these risks seem more controllable than the one posed by an Islam once more dressed for conquest. Is the religious revelation underpinning it too close to be really alien? Is this very proximity (however much denied on both sides) more dangerous than distant alterity? Many factors have contributed to the situation where the epithet 'Islamic' condenses everything that the other side finds uncomfortable. The states, elites and public opinion of Muslim countries are, as we shall see, far from innocent in an encounter involving reciprocal demonization, which draws in each case upon a highly instrumentalized historical repertoire. But the aberrations of what Maxime Rodinson calls, on the Muslim side, the 'culture of resentment' have given rise in the West to all kinds of amalgam and the threatening image of an inherently alien Other.

A few years ago, on the 8 o'clock television news in France, a report on a recent attack by bearded commandos somewhere in the world carried the bold-lettered headline, 'Islam'! It would have been inconceivable to see the label 'Christianity' over pictures of a strong-arm attack by fundamentalist anti-abortion protesters on a European or American clinic. Although the Algerian writer Achour Ouamara, in contrast to most Arab intellectuals, rightly argues that 'Islam should be compared not with the letter of the Koranic verses but with the political practices that enlist them in their support',[12] it is worth looking more closely at the way in which the West conflates the great majority of Muslims with the radical movements that lay claim to the name, or identifies the latter as its main enemies of the hour. In fact, over the last twenty years, the West has put together a syllogism whose pertinence needs to be carefully examined. It goes like this: Islamicists are dangerous, every Muslim is a potential Islamicist because his religion carries extremism as a cloud bears rain,[13] therefore every Muslim is dangerous.

The new main enemy

No one, except their sympathizers, would deny that radical Islamicist movements have a capacity to inflict harm and are ready to use force to hoist themselves to power.[14] The problem is not so much the fact that they threaten established regimes – which, in nearly all the Arab and Muslim countries, would not necessarily be a bad thing – but the nature of what they preach and seek to achieve. Fiercely opposed to liberties, xenophobic, intolerant, misogynist, eager to impose a totalitarian order on their peoples and to justify violence for that end, they may be said to belong – even if they cannot be reduced – to the broad family of fascism which, in different continents, haunted the twentieth century. Under Western eyes, moreover, they are all the more dangerous because their ambitions cover the whole of the vast *Dar al-Islam*, which includes the Muslim diaspora living in the West.

Such de facto internationalism, which they base upon the universal value of Koranic revelation, has placed them in direct contact with a West whose interests and stability they have the capacity to threaten.[15] This does not mean that the West does not cultivate all manner of ambivalent attitudes towards them: it can get them started if that is of use in the geopolitical conflicts of the day (as it was in Pakistan and Afghanistan throughout the Soviet military presence in the latter country[16]); or it can adopt a benevolent neutrality if they do not show open hostility to it and are prepared to integrate into the dominant system at least by embracing economic liberalism. These new players have to be reckoned with in the world arena, and Western capitals are often unsure whether to opt for alliance, neutrality, containment or open struggle. Certainly they have more than once preferred to accept the order they bring rather than risk chaos in a sensitive area of the planet.

However opaque the attitudes dictated by an ostensible realism, the public message is always the same: everything to do with radical Islami-cism, armed or unarmed, seeking power through the ballot box or the gun,[17] is considerably higher on the scale of threats than other political dangers from which democratic states have to protect themselves. Only those who support relativism – which is equally to be criticized, though for different reasons – speak a less unambiguous language.

Let us remember the hue and cry over the victory of the Islamic Welfare Party in the Turkish legislative elections of 1995. At the time, forgetting that Necmettin Erbakan's party had won only a quarter of the vote and could form a government only by exploiting divisions among other political forces, Western governments worried about the political drift in an important ally and did all they could to break the coalition between the Islamicists and a party of the right. Four years later, after fresh elections, that party chose as its new coalition partner the Nationalist Action Party, a showcase for the fascist Grey Wolves movement whose violence had helped to bring the army back to power in 1980. But no one in America or Europe then expressed public alarm at the inclusion in government of a far-right formation at least as fascistic as the Islamicists who had been driven into illegality. We should also recall how swiftly the American authorities blamed Islamicists for the bloody terrorist attack at Oklahoma City in 1995, before discovering that the real perpetrators were members of a completely indigenous fundamentalist Protestant group – although it may be said in the government's defence that the attack by an Islamicist group on the World Trade Centre in 1993 had considerably inflamed the atmosphere.

The latter did not hesitate to strike at the heart of those it considered the enemy. But Islamicists were not the only ones dictating the bloody march of events, contrary to an editorial in the *International Herald Tribune* which argued that 'the Muslim fundamentalist is rapidly becoming the main threat to global peace and security',[18] or an editorial in *Le Monde* which began the year 1997 by identifying such movements as the main danger facing 'the planet, [which now] lives at the rhythm of the advances of intransigent Islamicism'.[19] A twin survey of the American public and its leaders conducted in 1998 by the Chicago Council of Foreign Relations[20] gives some idea of the impact of such messages: 84 per cent of 'ordinary' respondents but only 61 per cent of leaders thought that international terrorism was a 'serious threat' to their country, while 38 per cent of the former and 31 per cent of the latter had a special fear of Islamic fundamentalism. In a survey conducted in France in 1999, 64 per cent of respondents mentioned 'the rise of religious extremisms in the Islamic countries' when they were asked to name the main threats facing the country.[21]

As we can see, the degree of perceived danger varies not with actual disasters that radically reactionary versions of Islam cause in the respective society, but with their power to strike outside the country where they have their base. It is not the fate reserved for Afghan women that threatens to topple the Taliban regime, but rather the haven it offers to the terrorist Osama bin Laden. In the eyes of the West, radical Islamicism is dangerous for two reasons. First, it promotes the idea of a different and potentially rival universalism precisely where that of the West is unable to make itself heard, among the impoverished masses of the South. Second, in opposing the realm of justice to the realm of freedom, and in promising glorious acts of revenge to those excluded from the global feasting, it speaks a kind of paupers' Esperanto and has on its side both numbers (which already make it threatening) and a capacity to foment revolts around the world. Now, these perceptions are by no means completely false, but they do leave out a number of aspects which affect their relevance, such as the geographically limited nature of the Muslim space and the great diversity that fragments it. It is the size and international ramifications of the Islamicist galaxy which give it an air of familiarity for Western strategists, reminding them of the now defunct organization of the communist movement.

Nevertheless, just as the transnational dimension of Islam does not mean that it is a universal readily capable of globalization, the existence of an International does not give Islamicism a global dimension. The dangers of Islamicism, though real enough in societies where it has an influence or where it seeks to expand, are not directly proportional to the space that Islam occupies on the world map.

The usual interpretations of Islamicism overlook the fact that its political victories have so far been very rare, and that its main effect has been to make Muslims as a whole appear politically dangerous objects of the fear it inspires. From denunciation of movements within the social and political field, it is easy to pass to condemnation of whole cultures for public consumption – with the results that we know. The French writer Alain Finkielkraut, for instance, sees in Islam only 'a culture where corporal punishment is inflicted on children, sterile wives are repudiated and adulterous ones sentenced to death, a man's testimony is worth two women's, a sister has only half the inheritance rights enjoyed by her brother, female circumcision is practised, mixed marriages are forbidden, and polygamy is authorized.'[22] This horrifying picture fails to note that nearly all the Muslim countries have long abandoned corporal punishment, that female circumcision is also practised by Christians in every region where it exists, that sexual equality in inheritance law is only a recent acquisition in Europe, and that the treatment of women as minors goes far beyond the confines of the Muslim world.[23]

It has become a habit in the West to blame Islam for every archaic feature in societies where it is established, thereby painting the picture in even darker hues. Much use has been made of the Bengali Taslima Nasreen, who, subject to vicious attacks from fundamentalists, has made Islam responsible for nearly all the evils affecting women in Bangladesh, without distinguishing between religion and custom or appreciating that the terrible position of women throughout the subcontinent transcends religious affiliations. Her condemnation of Islam alone has earned her praise from various commentators, who are only too happy to see their views confirmed by a woman from a Muslim country.[24] It is true, of course, that the profound conservatism of most Arab–Muslim societies draws its legitimacy from religious sources, and that for a long time the Muslim world has not been the bearer of any emancipatory project. This fossilization leaves the way open for all aberrations, including that which sees Islamicism as the liberatory shock that this part of the world appears to have been awaiting for so long.

Muslims, then, inspire fear. Essentially located in Middle Asia and Africa, where population growth is the highest in the world, they also flank Europe on the south and east. Once conquering, now dominated, they are both the most familiar foreigners in the West and those considered most worthy of suspicion. A Muslim is a Turk in Germany, a North African in France, a Pakistani or Egyptian in Britain, someone with whom one rubs shoulders but of whom one must be afraid, someone close yet different. His or her presence in the landscape arouses passions that can fill whole pages of newspapers, especially in France, where since 1989 the 'Islamic scarf' issue in schools has reached proportions that indicate the touchiness of the public mood. The French conception of secularism requires a watertight separation between private space, where religion can be expressed, and the public sphere, where similar displays are theoretically forbidden. But the scarf affair, which still flares up at quite regular intervals in various parts of the country, has revealed something more than a mere wish to enforce a rule that usually admits of some bending (as in the wearing of the kippa in schools for children of religious Jews). The violence with which some teachers refuse any concession and send home scarf-wearing girls is evidence of the diffuse yet widespread fear that French society has of Islam, as if any outward display of Muslim identity indicated a survival of the conquering spirit.

This does not mean that scarf-wearing is a trivial mark of identity, any more than the veil is. But it is necessary to challenge the argument that a blanket ban is needed to protect girls at school, of whom some are forced into wearing it, while others do so voluntarily. For such a ban punishes them twice over: it removes them from the only place that might eventually liberate them from the veil and sends them back into the narrow confines of their family and community; and it punishes the female sex alone for the development of fundamentalism. As so often, the community here gives to women the task of bearing its sign of identity; boys from a fundamentalist milieu, not being identifiable in the same way, have never been denied the right to attend school because of that background.

Other European countries, which have other ways of handling the issue of secularism and the coexistence of people with different origins, find it difficult to understand this extreme and typically French example. But there are signs everywhere of hostility to the visible roots of Muslim populations; what is required of them is that they should blend into the scenery or remain shut up in the areas left deserted for them. They must try to be the same lest they become the absolute Other or, often enough, the enemy Other.

The Other in cast-off clothes

If the West's image of Islam appears to encapsulate its wayward relations with the Other, Muslims can rest assured that – contrary to a paranoid tendency common among postcolonial peoples – they are not the only ones to be trapped in this dilemma. Even supposing that other 'aliens' inspire less fear, this does not mean that Westerners feel them to be any closer.

Their otherness can be recognized in the fact that they do not belong to the analytic categories that the West has developed to speak of itself. They are expelled from the sphere of politics, on the grounds that its subtleties are inaccessible to them. And, except for small groups of researchers who battle against the old typecasting, each region of the world that ostensibly corresponds to a distinct cultural area is invested with a type of behaviour that is supposed to reflect its innermost being. Neither the evolution of society nor the multifarious changes of the last few decades are usually taken into account when the pressure of current events requires a picture to be drawn of the crises and restless wandering in the major regions of the South. No comparison is attempted with phenomena occurring in the West – indeed, these are considered *a priori* to be different in nature. A single word can sometimes suffice to sum up (and hence to erase all the complexity of) a particular situation. Just as the mechanisms of public life in the Arab-Muslim world are ontologically religious, so are those in Africa necessarily ethnic. The East, an invention whose geography varies with the myths it nurtures, remains 'oriental' – and that tautology is generally thought enough to describe the practices that take place there.

One might have thought that the implosion of Yugoslavia and its accompanying conflicts would have caused some hesitation about the idea that African wars are peculiarly ethnic. But this has not been the case. Although one comes across the term 'ethnic cleansing' in both contexts, it occurs quite rarely in the abundant literature of recent years on the Balkans, whereas it is still ubiquitous in texts describing the chaos of Africa. It is true that some of its leaders resort to a practice whose tragic dimension is well known, but Africa by no means has a monopoly on the ethnicization or tribalization of politics, whose advances have everywhere accompanied the state's loss of legitimacy. Nor can the political divisions or struggles to appropriate mineral rents which punctuate African public life be understood in the purely ethnic terms that most Western commentators use to speak of them.

In fact, since the end of the East–West confrontation and the onset of so-called civil wars, banalization of the term 'ethnic cleansing' has not prevented the West from continuing to regard Africa as the continent where ethnicity encompasses virtually the entire space of politics. The Rwandan tragedy and the chaos in Zaire are supposedly due to its ubiquitous presence, and it forms the customary grid for interpretations of the wars of rapine in the Congo or the corrupt practices of the regime in Kenya. In a sense, ethnic division is seen as consubstantial with the African personality, just as the sophistication of politics reflects the essence of the Western spirit and will be learned by others only over a period of decades or centuries. Once again, history vanishes into the received wisdom through which Westerners more than ever try to persuade themselves, not of their difference, but of their superiority.

Here again is the Other in cast-off clothes, slightly recut to conjure away the outmoded touches, but the closeness or distance depends on how great the resemblance is deemed to be. Westerners need others who are close to themselves, since it is by their resemblance that the power and seductiveness of the West can be measured. But they also need others who are remote, since this allows them to construct their own archeology by identifying incomplete versions of themselves. So we can see that the mimetic injunction – whose closure of the universal is the vital historical thread – and the culturalism that freezes identities are the two faces of Janus, that jealous guardian of the Western temple entirely occupied in measuring the humanity of the Other. Between the two extremes may also be found intermediate postures, which reflect ways of instrumentalizing the Other-directed gaze more than they do the hypothetical complexity of the Other.

At bottom, others seem to find the attributes of their own existence only once they are dead. It is only in the eternity beyond this world that they are recognized as such, by 'a society which plays out for itself the comedy of ennobling them at the moment when it finally suppresses them, but which felt for them only terror and disgust when they were its genuine adversaries'.[25] Today, Western societies can afford a certain nostalgia and use this register to evoke civilizations that have disappeared beneath their blows; they can even sometimes regret that their disappearance has impoverished humanity by making it lose a dimension of itself.

This curious deception becomes apparent in the aisles of New York's National Museum of the American Indian, whose heavy neoclassical building in the Wall Street district used to be given over to finance before housing the feathers and masks of the ancient peoples of North America. In this place, history is nowhere called upon to explain the exhibition. At most one learns that 'of course there were changes: there would have been even if non-Indians had never approached these shores'.[26] An off-guard visitor would learn nothing about the nature of contacts between the conquerors from Europe and the people they found on those coveted lands; nothing about the wars, nothing about reasons for the disappearance of the tribes whose artistic wealth is on display. On the contrary, everything is done to produce the illusion that the Indian civilizations are alive and equal in value to all others. 'All roads are good' spits out a poster encouraging us to listen to the 'native voices of life and culture'. Soothing litanies of politically correct statements, taken to the point of absurdity, are all that accompany a visit, as one is made to feel that the wisdom of the Indian peoples had no parallel, that their traditions – still alive, we keep being told – are a precious lesson, and that their art can reach extraordinary peaks. It is not cynicism that informs such statements – rather, the easy conscience of conquerors who seem to take pride in their false modesty before dead cultures.

In the autumn of 1998, a large exhibition in Venice was devoted to the Mayan Indians, that 'wonderful people which invented zero and infinity', as the catalogue tells us. But once again, beyond the fascination with pre-Columbian mysteries, Europe's homage sounds like self-absolution long after the event.[27] The living are entitled to different treatment.

The Same and its declensions

Others never come closer to perfection than when they really seek to become Western – not just modern or democratic (praiseworthy though that may be), but Western, since that is naturally what opens the way to modernity and democracy. In one of the countless articles on Algeria that have appeared in the French press since the early 1990s, the journalist Bernard Guetta welcomes such a desire with all the assurance of his convictions: a character in one of his reports 'used the term democratic Algeria to describe that whole part of the country which fully lives in European time'.[28] To have a Western 'look' may even be enough to pass as democratic, since the cowl often makes the monk in countries where most citizens are still convinced that they serve as models for the rest of humanity.

Many leaders in the South have understood this, and so they first of all groom themselves to achieve international respectability. Mahfoud Nahnah, a leader of Hamas, one of the legal Islamicist parties represented in the Algerian parliament and government, is obviously more moderate than the leader of the Islamic Salvation Front (FIS) Abassi Madani, since his three-piece suits contrast sharply with Madani's stubbornly worn *kami*s (the long white tunic that Islamicists in Arab countries have adopted as their uniform). The Western public has doubtless paid more attention to differences in dress than to political projects in sizing up these two advocates of an Islamic state. The former Turkish prime minister Tansi Ciller also knew how to play skilfully on this confusion. Resolutely modern, elegantly dressed in Parisian suits, this emblematic woman of Kemalist Turkey was credited in Western capitals with a wish she never had: to democratize the political life of her country. In fact, it was she who set the Islamic fox to mind the government geese, by agreeing to form a coalition with it, and the links she kept with the powerful local mafia are well known.

Similarly, Benazir Bhutto's strong Oxford accent long obscured the fact that she was little attracted to democracy, and made people overlook her alliances with fundamentalists and her cursory methods of defending her power and possessions. More exotic than her Turkish counterpart, this Pakistani aristocrat – who was twice prime minister – certainly had a habit of half-covering her head with a thin veil. But that kind of sartorial detail, itself more suggestive of a tourist brochure, did not necessarily damage the fascination that her general mimetism inspired. The wearing of a Marabout boubou, a sari or colourful *couvre-chefs* can even give Westerners a shiver of exotic curiosity and make them think that the Other therefore deserves recognition.

Obsessive mimetism might be almost inoffensive if it just involved a few simple mirror-effects. But there must be no mistake: true modernity, true democracy, can have only one face and can draw upon only one set of references. Any idea that its forms might vary or that several different roads might lead to it is suspected of narrowing its reach. Any attempt to trace its manifestations where they do not officially exist is considered tantamount to a wish to alter its meaning. The Other's discourse or practice is acceptable only if it returns the West to its own certainties by confirming its status as model. Consequently, that model operates as a formidable machine for shaping the Other in the West's own image – an image superimposed on reality that makes it more difficult to read.

No field remains unaffected by this setting of norms. Since it is mainly a question of an image, we can easily see why Hollywood is in the vanguard of the whole enterprise; it did, after all, excel for decades in the manufacturing of the Other, especially in the shape of the savage and threatening Indian. But the time has passed when the superiority of the white man could be simply exalted. Everyone is equal nowadays, and this advance should certainly not be taken lightly. For this equality to remain unchallenged, however, it must be possible for the Other to be recognized.

Steven Spielberg's *Amistad* – his film on the revolt and trial of newly enslaved African deportees in early-nineteenth-century America, which was released in 1998 – tried to make the Other recognizable. As Cinque, the leader of the revolt, gradually moves further away from his comic-strip Africa, as he is transformed into a tailor's dummy in accordance with the dominant aesthetic canons, enamoured of liberty, captivated by the Christian message, he becomes worthy of being a true American. The metamorphosis engineered by the film director makes it possible for him to rise to this dignity.

Spielberg's symbolism and Hollywood-style direction by no means signify that this is an isolated phenomenon; an identical tendency to produce sameness exists in the field of politics. One illustration of this is the way in which most of the French media and intelligentsia viewed the Algerian tragedy of the 1990s. In a civil war that was seen as opposing two distinct camps to each other, the cause of democracy involved not so much any real adherence to principles defining the rule of law or any strategy to break out of the impasse, as an adaptation to the kind of language that people in France expected to hear. With anti-Islamicism 'recycling all the multifarious hatreds', as one French sociologist put it,[29] the perfect Algerian democrat was a French-speaking Berber from the Kabylie region. For it was natural that Arabs, having given birth to Islam, were now producing Islamicism, whereas a rather less evident line of descent meant that modernity was a dimension of Berberhood. As to the French language, it was intrinsically a vehicle for unspecified 'republican values', which Arabic was incapable of conveying, just as it could never produce thought because there could be no Arabic-speaking intellectuals.[30]

The computer-drawn image of the Algerian democratic intellectual flows from a rudimentary syllogism: Arabs invented Islam (a religion with every archaic feature) and imposed a language that has become such an obstacle to modernity; the Kabyles, who do not like them, are therefore modern, secular and Francophile. In January 1992, shortly after the army's cancellation of legislative elections that had given victory to the Islamic Salvation Front, *Le Monde* headlined one of its articles: 'Relief in democratic Kabylie'.[31] The formula was soon doing the rounds. In an issue of *Le Nouvel Observateur* in 1998, the editorialist Jacques Julliard took his dreams for reality and made Kabylie 'the expression of that secular and democratic Algeria which was the common hope of Algerian patriots and French supporters of decolonization'.[32] Three years earlier, a report in the same weekly on a village in Kabylie that had formed one of the first self-defence militias against raids by the Armed Islamic Groups (GIA) quoted a local inhabitant as saying: 'We are experiencing aggression; we risk being robbed of our honour at any moment. The least we can do is defend ourselves.'[33] Puffed up with admiration for such courage, the author of the report immediately raised honour to the rank of a democratic virtue, without asking himself the meaning of that word in the traditions of the region. And, during the years of saturation coverage of events in France's former colony, no one went to see how the mothers, wives and sisters of Kabyle democrats lived in their villages, what rights they enjoyed, or what the real status of religion was among those heroes of secularism.

Yet journalists continued to work the seam: the Kabyle was an archetype of the good Arab. Thus, in March 1997, France Inter turned into a 'Kabyle singer' the Rai music star Khaled, who was increasingly popular in France and could not therefore decently be a native of Oran. And in July 1998, following France's victory in the football World Cup, French parliamentary deputy Jean-François Deniau expressed his joy, also on France Inter: 'France is a plural country, thanks to the overseas departments, thanks to Africa, thanks to Kabylie!' The football star Zidane had in one sentence been made an honorary native of Kabylie and stripped of any connection with Algeria.

To give more solidity to this non-Arab Algeria that supposedly recognized itself in France, numerous pens dipped into the old colonial

rhetoric in which the imported Arab culture of North Africa was opposed to a native Berberhood historically linked to the northern Mediterranean through a Christian and Latin past. 'The Maghreb is Berber',
wrote researcher Robert Jaulin in 1991, in the daily *Libération*.[34]

> The Arabs who settled there over the centuries numbered tens of thou-
> sands at the most – less than the Vandals, less even than the Romans,
> Turks and French. The mark they left behind is much more linguistic
> than cultural; it is recent, was assisted by French colonization, and really
> took off only during the last half-century.... This legacy was, and still is
> more than ever, the torchlight passion of arbitrariness; it goes together
> with artificiality.

The cause is the same as for other writers: the Maghreb did not even
become Arab–Berber, and any affirmation of its Arab dimension involves an act of usurpation. Even if something could be detected, it
would still bear – via the Islamicists – 'an obscurantism which drove
this country back to the Middle Ages of the Umayyad and Hammudid
warriors', according to the weekly *Le Point*.[35]

Yet there remains Islam, which cannot be so easily eliminated from
Maghreb identity. As it is impossible to deny the existence of a Muslim
Maghreb, attempts have been made to trace even here a dichotomy
between Arabs (more or less explicit embodied in the Islamicists) and
'real' Algerians. The Islam of the former is fanatical, intolerant and, so
to speak, totalitarian; that of the latter is a civilized religion, 'a typically
Algerian Islam, an Islam of tolerance, an Islam that is our identity,
because it is given to us with our mother's milk'.[36]

Instrumentalization of the very real Berber issue, which the Arab
nationalism and dogged Jacobinism of Algerian ruling circles caused to
explode in the 1980s, has thus conjured up an ideal Algerian, scarcely
Arab and close to France, who deserves to be defended. Similarly,
Islamicist misogyny is supposed to have made of women the emblematic
victims of a bearded barbarism, with its roots in a different planet from
the humdrum machismo of Algerian society.

On the other side of the Mediterranean, the so-called 'eradicatory'
movement has been nimbly slipping into a computer-drawn image of
Algerian intellectuals and addressing its appeals more to French public
opinion than to fellow Algerians. In this vein, a parallel between Islamicists and Nazis has been one of the key arguments. 'To negotiate with
the FIS is to collaborate with throat-slitters – like Pétain collaborated
with the Nazis in France,' thundered novelist Rachid Boudjedra in *Le
Nouvel Observateur*,[37] at a moment when several Algerian parties – in-

cluding the FIS – were meeting in Rome to try to end the violence and bring back political debate. 'The veil is our yellow star', echoed Khalida Messaoudi, feminist and leader of the Rassemblement pour la Culture et la Démocratie (RCD),[38] who commands considerable attention in France. She also overworks the theme of the alien character of the Islamicists, describing their offensives as a 'war against Algeria',[39] or claiming that 'Algeria has been fighting for a long time against women's oppression and fundamentalism.'[40] French democrats should rush to the aid of 'vast Algeria, noble Algeria, heroic Algeria, proud Algeria', now that it is threatened by dangerous invaders, Afghans, Iranians, Saudis, Sudanese and 'children of harkis'.[41] Many of these democrats heard her voice, and Jack Lang, for example, could write in 1998 on returning from a lightning trip to Algiers: 'The soul of Algeria is freedom.'[42] That Algeria is naturally secular and democratic: 'There is a real practice of secularism in our traditional society', RCD general secretary Saïd Sadi told Le Monde with a straight face. 'The head of the village assembly or the tribal chief is distinct from the sheikh, who occupies himself with religious worship.'[43]

In this irenic country, jointly pieced together by French opinion-makers and sections of the Algerian intelligentsia, true Algerians bear a miraculous resemblance to French people. The GIA underground are not the monstrous lost children of Algerian society, barbarism exists only in one camp, violence has no endogenous roots, the Family Code was not voted through the Algerian Assembly without a protest from intellectuals,[44] the Islamicist bastions of popular districts of Algiers are not partly inhabited by people from Kabylie, and there are no Kabyles in the ranks of the bearded men. According to historian Mohammed Harbi, this fiction has been internalized through compulsory references to Algeria's nationalist mystique as well as glorification of French influ- ences, but it conceals 'another, communalist Algeria, whose social ties are strongly marked by religion and whose relationship with France is unambiguous'.[45] This more problematic Algeria is a prey to the diver- sity of its constituent elements, an inheritor of contradictory influences, a prisoner to the consequences of its intricate history. It is incomparably more difficult to understand, and to accept.

The fortunes of a term

Never stray from the model, never try to break free from it, for it is the only road open to seekers after universality who have been reduced to consuming a ready-made modernity. There is no alternative; everything that is part of universality and modernity belongs only to the West. This phenomenon of appropriation – another variant of denial of the Other – can take several forms, from the most anodyne to the most elaborate. If Saint Augustine of Hippo, who was born in Tagaste (today's Souk-Ahras in Algeria), was the most famous of the early Church Fathers, then he must have been a 'pied-noir' *avant la lettre* – states a French journalist with calm assurance.[46] A theologian who so crucially influenced Christian doctrine could not have been even a Romanized native of the area. So he must have been a European, a simple émigré on African soil.

Is Turkey a secular nation? Well, then, it cannot 'quite be part of the Muslim world', opines political scientist Pierre Lellouche,[47] who is quick to annex its modern dimension to the West. Severed from the modernist transformations that may occur within it, the 'Muslim world' is here reduced to its archaic spaces and is therefore incapable of generating any advances.

These liberties taken with reality look like trivial offences alongside another instance of annexation which has been banalized to such a point that one forgets its enormity. The expression 'Judeo-Christian' appears so often, and in such a wide range of writers, that the adjectival juxtaposition seems to go without saying. But things have not always been so, and the fortunes of the term are more suspicious than one might think from its present banality. Of course, its scholarly use goes back a long way, and it owes its existence *inter alia* to the fact that both Judaism and Christianity predate Islam, the last of the monotheistic revelations. We cannot enter here into the theological and historical debate, but we should bear in mind that Europe too has been 'the daughter of the Bible and Greece' – to borrow the definition of philosopher Emmanuel Levinas. The entry of the term into ordinary language, where it has been widely used over the past twenty years or so, has given rise to a quite different political meaning.

Everything in Western civilization is now seen as Judeo-Christian, so that it can be almost totally summed up in those Siamese twins. Its values, foundations and culture entirely derive from them. Politicians lay claim to them to justify their actions. A candidate in the American presidential election in the year 2000 declared that 'being the only superpower gives the United States certain responsibilities, particularly intervening abroad to protect Judeo-Christian values'.[48] The world is divided between 'Judeo-Christian cultures' and the rest.[49] In 1998 a conference was held in France on 'the political integration of Muslim French people and their place in the Judeo-Christian world'.[50] When people write about economics they refer to it.[51] When they write about culture the reference is obligatory. And always the double adjective relates exclusively to the West: the current literature contains no trace at all of 'Judeo-Christianity' outside the frontiers that the West has given itself. The only explanation for this unparalleled success – even the myth of the 'Greek dawn' has not been worked so hard – would seem to be the threefold process of obfuscation, appropriation and exclusion that the symbolic use of this term has permitted.

First, obfuscation: the combined term has made it possible to cast a veil over nearly two millennia of anti-Jewish hate and the Catholic Church's long denial of its Abrahamic descent. After all, everyone must agree that a civilization cannot hate that which it considers part of itself. The establishment and then sanctification of a 'Judeo-Christian identity' allowed the era of Christian anti-Judaism to be closed without further ado.[52] Countries with a Christian tradition can thereby exonerate themselves for their past, and for a part of their present.

But that is not the essential point. The new collective identity that the West has officially given itself, after repudiating for so long any affinity between these two variants of Abrahamic revelation, makes it possible to incorporate the Jew into the space of the West and thus to gain exclusive property rights over the share of universality with which he is credited. In fact, the emergence of the Judeo-Christian collective subject conjures the Jew out of existence – that eternal incarnation of the Other who used to come from some other distant part of the East,[53] but who had to be recognized as the first historical formulator of monotheistic universalism. The insoluble questions of descent or heritage can now be left aside:[54] the undifferentiated Judeo-Christian makes the West appear as sole inventor of universality, with all its roots finally brought back home. When the Other cannot be plunged into total alterity, he is somehow absorbed along with all his properties.

Lastly, as the hard core of Western, and only Western, identity, the 'Judeo-Christian' functions as a machine for driving others out. Islam thus becomes the excluded third of that Abrahamic revelation whose monotheistic universalism is supposed to have heralded the profane rights of modernity. Outside a few ecumenical circles with a limited audience, it would not occur to anyone today to relate the Judeo-Christian object to Islam – or at least to establish some correspondence with it. Its religious practice and accompanying prohibitions make it closer to Judaism than either is to Christianity, it drew much of its inspiration from Judaism, and the text of the Koran is peppered with references to both of the preceding revelations:[55] none of these things matters, however, since Judeo–Christian universality, with the West as sole proprietor, locks Islam up in an alterity where it occupies the territory of specificity. The existence of an Abrahamic triptych, if recognized at all, is strictly limited to the religious sphere; it extends neither into the field of culture nor into that of politics, where the splitting of revelation strengthens the frontier between the North (homeland of the first two variants) and the South (camp of the third).

The phenomenal success of this annexation–exclusion is due to the fact that, beyond the West, all the relevant protagonists have laid hold of its object and pushed its instrumentalization to the extreme. The Arab world has systematically used it for largely nationalist purposes and the struggle against Israel; the 'Judeo-Christian plot'[56] created by the state of Israel – itself a foreign body established by force of arms at the heart of the *Dar al-Islam* – is the most scandalous illustration of this way of thinking, which has become a central element of anti-Western discourse in the region. From Iran to Morocco, all components of the Islamic galaxy have revelled in it for decades. The 'Judeo-Christian' is the enemy; its formidable power is entirely devoted to the weakening of Islam, the last prophecy, whose only mission is to become universal.

The Westernization of 'Judeo–Christianity' thus involved the demonization of Islam, as a force locked into specificity that would not recognize itself in a universality with which it could nevertheless claim affinity. But the widespread use of the same expression in the Arab world was not only reactive. Through a process opposite to that which occurred in the West, the Arab world also used it to expel the Jewish part of itself. The term 'Judeo-Christian', as an epithet reserved for Western culture, made it possible to conceal the Judeo–Arab element in that culture, to excise the historical existence of eastern Judaism, and to remove all trace of it from collective memories. Driven from Western universality by the extraordinary political fortunes of a term, the Arab world also made use of it to obfuscate and exclude.

The Jewish world, for its part, seems at first sight to have held itself aloof from that term and to have been alone in failing to sanctify it. Yet, in its way, it too helped to spread its use by breaking with its own share of the East.[57] Its main political expressions saw the West's embrace as one of the means of rooting Jewish destiny there, and of strengthening, in the face of the Arab enemy, a Eurocentric solidarity that involved the same exclusions. The state of Israel grew out of modern nationalism and the European idea of the nation-state, and it was founded and ruled for decades by Jewish representatives of the European intelligentsia. It never ceased to think of itself as Western and persistently fended off any threat of Easternization, and in pursuing this aim its elites faithfully internalized a discourse of supremacy that had been elaborated for other loci of domination.

Although Palestinians – both second-class citizens of Israel and inhabitants of the occupied West Bank – continued to bear the brunt, Jewish immigrants from the Arab world also found themselves intellectually and politically marginalized as they faced a total denial of their cultural existence. Israeli intellectuals, including those in the peace camp, had the greatest difficulty placing their country in an East from which everything, except geographical location, seemed to distance them. The danger of sinking into it could, in their view, be averted only through unambiguous tokens of belonging to the West. All such tokens, then, were to be welcomed.

This survey of the many different uses of a Western invention has not been a digression; it points ahead to an account of the complex relations that 'others' have with the models and norms elaborated in the West. In the case of the Arab world, reactive tensions compound endogenous exclusions to strengthen the identity-locking devices that are seen as a defence against the insupportable hegemony of the hereditary enemy.

The assignation to difference

But the Other is not always a more or less faithful reincarnation of the Same; it can happen that it remains other. In that case, it may be sent back into an original barbarism, generally in direct proportion to its distance from the Western world. The ever more frequent use of this term to denote paroxysms in certain regions of the South once again makes it easier to replace analysis with tautologies. Thus, since black Africa remains linked to the huge imagined world of savagery, Liberian or Sierra Leonean or another barbarism is most often attributed to the inherent characteristics of the respective population, over and above the particular circumstances that trigger conflicts in the region. Again left to themselves after a period when their 'nature' (as the eighteenth century called it) was held in check by colonialism, these peoples are supposed to have reverted to their primary instincts. Although it is not actually said, the usual implication is that the behaviour of the mad gunmen of Freetown or Monrovia forms part of a kind of African essence that eternally hands the continent back to its demons, the same not being the case in the less remote regions of the West. The present anomaly of parts of the Balkans has thrown up a profusion of historical and political analyses, ranging from the decomposition of the Ottoman Empire to the consequences of the Communist freeze. But one hears less about an essence of the Serbian or Croatian people as an explanation for the lurching aberrations.

The assignation of the Other to a supposedly essential specificity independent of history does not always stem from a reaffirmation of superiority. Indeed, a whole generation associated with the 'white man's sob'[58] rebelled against such feelings and made itself the apostle of difference; the Other had a right to remain other, and his humanity was not measured by a talent for mimicry. But this welcome recognition of genuine equality rapidly shifted into an opposite injunction to remain other without deviating from one's culture – a culture doomed to immobility.

In reality, the distance is not so great between the champions of difference (who assert the non-negotiable equivalence of all cultures but wish to mummify them by making them impermeable) and the upholders of the superiority of Western values (who see others as imperfect early versions of themselves). Whether by turning dominated cultures into sanctuaries of authenticity, or by turning the lock on an irreducible alterity, they assign the Other to the idea they construct of it and an identity that it can never change. Forbidden to produce culture – that is, to innovate – the Other is reduced to no more than a product of its culture. Between these two versions of identity assignation – consignment to unhistorical 'barbarism' or glorification of everything, acceptable or sometimes even unacceptable,[59] that can find a place for itself in tradition – there is no room for an Other in movement.

As much as the false universalism that it combats, the difference-centred approach blocks access to any universality that could be built together with others; it condemns them to repeat their history, now reduced to successive incarnations of their deepest being. In this very heterogenous current, one can find people who consciously hold all universal projects in contempt, on the grounds that they deliberately seek to destroy the Other.[60] But it goes far beyond such extremists of particularity, and feeds into a whole area of Western thought that has moved back to a more or less assertive culturalism.

For its supporters, Islamicism is the compulsory horizon of Muslim countries, and people who live there have no option but to embrace it as the latest historical form of their identity. *L'Islamisme au Maghreb: la voix du Sud*,[61] the very wording of the title of this first book by French writer on Islam François Burgat does not leave the future very open in one Muslim area that he strangely identifies with the whole of the South; the banner of political Islam will defy reality by uniting the entire hemisphere. In the late 1970s, the Muslim Middle East did indeed give birth to one of the most remarkable manifestations of the culturalist reading of contemporary events. Apart from their general fascination with the Islamic revolution in Iran, many Western intellectuals saw it as a necessary stage through which that country had to pass, and regarded its aberrations as cultural realities that it would be out of place to criticize. French philosopher Michel Foucault appeared for a while to be the head of this tendency, before taking his distance from the regime that arose out of the much-admired uprising against the Shah.[62] Others soon followed his lead. Several journalists at *Libération* displayed a curious mixture of enthusiasm for a revolution which, though taking unfamiliar paths, had destroyed the established order, and reverence for the cultural 'authenticity' of its forms.[63]

Should we be surprised at this? The fate that the new Islamic order reserved for women did not particularly disturb its Western admirers, busy as they were tracing the signs of a legitimate restoration of identity in a society threatened with acculturation. They did not really question the fact that this involved the institutionalization of sexual discrimination: indeed, the compulsory wearing of the chador was for them a symbol of the cultural revolution that they went to witness in Tehran. In the Iranian capital, wrote Serge July in 1979, 'black is everywhere. It veils ... Iranian women as a symbol of struggle, an anti-Shah statement, and a refuge from which their eyes leap out as from so many living mummies.'[64] Only a few feminists, soon consigned to their hysteria by serious analysts, stepped up their protests against the misogyny of the regime in Tehran, which lowered the minimum age of marriage for girls to nine years and introduced stoning as the punishment for female adulterers. Several years later, another journalist credited the Iranian revolution with having 'always claimed an active role for women: they work, they vote, and they participate in political life'.[65] What more could they want? What did they have to complain about? More trivially, Western experts on political Islam rarely consider the position of women to be an issue really worthy of their interest.[66]

In fact, justification of women's lot in the most conservative societies is a constant of culturalist discourse. A journalist on the weekly *L'Express* commented as follows on what might happen following a FIS seizure of power in Algeria:

> The fate for women? It is scaring only for the French-speaking minority, in their ghetto-like luxurious areas, who with ever greater difficulty lead a Western lifestyle.... It is true that there will be the question of the compulsory veil. Although the question is important in France, ... the practice seems less incongruous in Algeria. (In the early twentieth century, Frenchwomen did not walk in the street without a hat.)[67]

In the affair that has periodically flared up over the wearing of the Islamic veil, most of those who opposed sending girls home from school – rightly, because it solved nothing – did so in the name of respect for an 'identity' whose basis they never took the trouble to examine. 'To accept the wearing of the veil', declared the general secretary of the Ligue de l'enseignement in 1989, 'is to recognize a wish to asssert one's identity. Yes to the separation between churches and state, no to denial of the other's identity.'[68]

In the same register, but in a context going beyond the Muslim world, a whole current has spoken out several times in recent years against condemnation of traditional practices such as polygamy and female circumcision. 'I still do not see by which principle polygamy should be forbidden', writes sociologist Alain Touraine.[69] And ethno-psychiatrist Tobie Nathan deplores the attacks on female circumcision, a structuring practice without which

> many young African girls living in France ... would suffer from grave disturbances ... . Without that ritual, a woman is incomplete ... and seeks replacement initiations such as the first 'fix' or the first break-in. Ethno-psychiatrists are well aware that a girl who undergoes excision will never fall into such errors. She doesn't need them. Excision has ... extraordinary social benefits, which French society should urgently reconsider.[70]

The leading figure in French ethnopsychiatry has taken the logic of difference to the extreme by telling people that they must not use any register other than that of their 'original culture' and that they should condense in it all of themselves.[71] 'Tell me your ancestor, and I'll tell you who you are! That might be the key formula ... of the therapeutic systems', he explains in one of his writings.[72]

As Césaire already complained half a century ago, when he ridiculed European talk of Bantu philosophy,[73] original culture – or what is thought of as such – is more or less summarily declared to be the only paradigm to which most non-Westerners have a right to lay claim; plurality of cultural reference is not generally an option. Even quite sophisticated analysts of contemporary conflicts with a cultural dimension do not always avoid this trap. Thus, in an otherwise salutary critique of anti-Muslim prejudices, the French sociologist Jocelyne Cesari sees in mosques the 'only enclosed space to have resisted the cultural pressure of the North', and in 'the apparent return of religiosity ... a rehabilitation of the (especially political) references of local culture, which are now asked to regain the universal ambition they lost during the colonial parenthesis'.[74] Like sanctification of the communalist legacy, the fiction of a colonial parenthesis – which is also used in the South by theorists of a return to pristine 'purity' – overlooks the complex historical sedimentation that has made all societies what they are and focuses instead on dangerously petrified single affiliations.

In the kind of approaches we are discussing, there are no principles but only identities; each creates its own rules for itself alone. It is not the nature of contacts between different cultures that may be a factor of anomie, but mere contact in itself. The structuring concern is not to protect the weakest from the strongest (whose cultural imperialism is daily evident), but rather to refer everyone back to what is supposed to be their essence. In this logic, no transcultural regulation built around common acceptance of universal principles can ever take priority over cultural specificity.

The West used to ban interbreeding in order to defend the purity of its race. Today a whole way of thinking would like to rule out the mingling of cultures, so that the future of humanity becomes shut up in the fossilized past of its various components. But this closure only affects non-Westerners: those who advocate it always exempt themselves from its effects, giving themselves tools that others lack to escape from themselves and to apprehend the world in its totality. This classification of human beings into two categories – the first remaining a prisoner of local horizons, the second having the whole planet as its field of experience – should not be laid at the door only of the culturalist movement. Those who look at the Other only if he is a reflection of themselves adopt a similar view as soon as the Other ceases to send back their own image and becomes genuinely different. Yet no sooner is it enunciated than this difference has implications of its own. A captive of his origins, entirely absorbed by his identity, the Other has neither the same aspirations nor the same need for rights as those of his contemporaries who have broader horizons. This seems to be the explanation for the tolerance that people in the North can have for the manifold violations of rights that the inhabitants of the South endure.

Political opportunism plays a role in this – but it is not the only factor. When Jacques Chirac says loud and clear that a multiparty system is not suited to Africa, he at least partly voices what he takes to be an interest closer to home.[75] But when a Bernard-Henri Lévy salutes a freedom fighter in the Afghan commander Massoud[76] – a representative of feudal Islam who wishes to control the whole of social life, less severe than the Taliban towards women but highly respectful of traditional hierarchies – he does not give the same meaning to words in every latitude. According to the same logic, one could consider despotism and democracy equally as marks of identity, again barring the way to any movement.

The same or striving to become the same, a barbarian danger or bearer of a culture loaded with the weight of eternity: it is not clear where the Other is to be found among the injunctions and the prohibitions. What scope does it have to reinvent itself? The set of prescriptions to which it is exposed, the categories in which it is enclosed, reveal the inability of the West to embrace plurality thinking. In the West's schemas, others do not seem to move from the status of simple beings to that of complex realities driven by multiple demands and contradictory aspirations. Is this the blindness of power? Or is it a refusal to take others for what they are, because that would mean recognizing the new character of their presence in the world? Is the culture of supremacy once more inventing new ways of protecting itself, so that it does not have to think that the Other may be changing and forcing the West to alter the place that the Other occupies within it?

But what about those whom we have so far called the others, seeing them only through the prism of the powerful. How do they look at the world? What spaces of autonomy do they create for themselves through their reading of it? What alchemies appear between the reactive tensions or eruptions of identity that we have briefly considered, and that entry into new times which is by no means always synonymous with progress? We must now look on the other side of the mirror, to try to discover how things are on the 'southern slope of freedom'[77] where the coming future of the world will also be played out.

TWELVE

The Other Side of the Mirror

What relationship can be established between the Peruvian guerrilla movement Sendero Luminoso, the Senegalese historian Cheikh Anta Diop, the Algerian Islamicist leader Ali Benhaj, and the late president of Zaire Mobutu Sese Seko? At first sight, none. There seems to be no link between a Maoist-inspired guerrilla organization not unlike the Cambodian Khmer Rouge, a controversial but respected academic who has always defended pluralism in his country, the representative of the most radical wing of Algerian political Islam, and the ultra-rich dictator with a leopard-skin hat who was a vassal of the Western powers and an exploiter of his own people's hunger. Yet one thread, however slender, does run between them: namely, their wish to differentiate themselves from the West. This takes various forms, but one finds it in each case. A strategic alliance with his former colonial masters and unfailing support from Washington did not prevent the Zairean autocrat from swapping his baptismal forenames Joseph and Désiré for Sese and Seko, more rooted in the Lingala language. Marx and Lenin, the spiritual fathers of Abimaël Guzman and his comrades, were forced to sit beside the Inca gods on the Peruvian altiplano. Cheikh Anta Diop spent his life trying to show that Europe was in his debt. And, for Ali Benahj, the West is the evil embodying everything that must at all costs be kept at a safe distance.

They may have been trained by its thinkers, fascinated by its power, captivated by its technological prowess, attracted by its lifestyle comforts, won over to its values, but the conquered cannot love the West. All who think of themselves as wronged by history maintain a relationship with the West that is based upon a serious bone of contention. All

207

who have had a brush with one or another form of its hegemony also have a revenge to take upon it. And since its limits are those of the terrestrial globe, the whole world has a litany of reproaches to recite. In the vast and heterogeneous galaxy of today's South, there is not one movement, one collective attitude, one analysis, one political project which does not include a more or less overt anti-Western dimension.

The omnipresence and omnipotence of the West, real or exaggerated as the case may be, are measurable by the place it everywhere occupies in people's minds – even if their reactions take the most varied forms and do not always involve open hostility. Although the discourse of the South's elites may draw upon other sources and paradigms than those of the West, it always organizes itself around a relationship to what the West says and does. Even when those elites are directly addressing their fellow citizens, they are never far from its shadow – whether they hold it responsible for all the world's evils or call upon it to cure them. It is exactly as if each episode of Western expansion – or, to be more precise, the memory it has left behind – each form of its hegemony and each of its theoretical legitimations have led, in the South, to the construction of defences as so many responses to its acts of aggression.

This reading would mean that its various reactive discourses have been built as inverted doubles of the discourses of supremacy. It would mean that they are invested with an often violent charge, since their function is to answer both five or more centuries of history and contemporary forms of domination that perpetuate the relations of dependence between conquerors and conquered. With features simultaneously of a settling of accounts, a political strategy and an alternative social project, they can never occupy a realm separate from the national and global relationship of forces upon which they leave their mark. Thus, the world seems to be structured around a series of oppositions between the masters and those who contradict them. Although we cannot accept this as the whole of the truth, since each movement in the southern parts of the world is mainly the complex product of broader trends, many have been born out of a determination to limit the West's role (which they both reject and overestimate) in building the collective destiny of their peoples.

How should one live in the face of an entity that daily manifests its power and makes autonomy impossible? After independence, some did try to turn dreams of autarky into economic and sometimes political reality. We know what became of those. Another possibility is to 'exist against', to proclaim one's differences, to try to rise above want, and to offer proof of it to those who are so sure of themselves that all their decades of analysing the problems of the South have yielded no more than a list of things in short supply. Lack of money, knowledge and skilled personnel, lack of a bourgeoisie and a working class, lack of an industrial and technological infrastructure – each region has been presented with a catalogue of everything it does not have which makes the model inaccessible to it. The urge to refute such reasoning is a crucial part of the recent history of the South and of the communities that have grown out of it. They relate their anger, their frustration, their nostalgia for a time in the past – a time they have reinvented to build memories with which it is not unbearable to live. They also weave the fabric of relations between the two hemispheres, by making the West the prime mover behind the ills of the planet.

What if the West's superiority was just an illusion, its most evil weapon to convince others of their inferiority? What if it was wielded only to efface the memory of what it owes to, and has stolen from, the rest of the world? What if the civilization it has created, at the summit of a hierarchy of its own making, was the bearer of questionable values, or anyway of values less worthy of generalization than those of the societies it has attempted to destroy? What if, fearing for itself, it used all means to prevent those societies from holding their head high and regaining some of their lost splendour? Is it not in the West's passion for domination, rather than in the inadequacies of the South, that we should seek the cause of the latter's setbacks? What if there were other models than those coming from the North, other sources of inspiration to break out of the doldrums and find a path back to prosperity? What if the South's own past offered more resources than the present of others to recover its dignity? Such are the questions structuring reactive thought in the various parts of the South. The answers, context-dependent yet drawing upon a stock of similar arguments, vary to a large extent with the precise shock that threw the region into contact with one or another phase of Western imperialism. Whether they glorify a pre-colonial past more or less reassembled for the needs of the cause, or try to find in a return to primal authenticity reasons for pride that would be hard to find in the present, they all seek to construct defences against that culture of contempt which has been the mark of the conqueror, occupier or guardian from the North. The most self-assured of those who formulate these answers dispute the North's privilege of laying down the law, and counterpose their own norms to a universality in which they can see nothing but an element of the arsenal of hegemony.

From China to the Arab world, from the American Indian lands to black Africa, from India to the Caribbean, these varied discourses draw upon history and myth to invent other futures than those which the West offers them. Sometimes they sound like appeals for recognition, whereas at other times they are more like sketches for a nightmare. Increasingly, however, reactive incantations are also instrumentalized to safeguard privileges, to combat local opponents, or to enable elites to shake off their share of responsibility for their country's torment. The sanctification of traditions, especially when these are reformulated in the present, may actually serve as a barrier to any desire for new paths that might threaten the established powers.

Some are beginning to forsake the past, however, or to abandon the register of demands, as they take account of new realities thrown up by the changes of the last half-century. Others wish to put an end to the identity dictatorships in a way that does not involve breaking with themselves, so that they can try to construct syntheses where the desire for freedom is no longer equated with betrayal of an affiliation. The paradoxical, but ever more conflictual, coexistence of these contradictory attitudes reveals the complexity of the South's relationship with what is called modernity.

But although the debate that has developed in the South oversteps the limits of its confrontation with the North, the relationship to the West remains a central dimension that seems for the moment impossible to go beyond.

Revenge of the past

So, glory to the past, whose beautiful harmony succumbed to the blows of Western domination. Honour to the great ancestors whom the West despised, as it assumed all the merit for human creativity and denied its new subjects any role in history. In the regions of the South where the present is gloomy and the future uncertain, dreams can often take the colours of an ancient utopia. But it must be worth glorifying, and those who claim to inherit it must be able to feel some pride.

In accordance with the motto 'as long as lions don't have their own historians, the histories of hunting will continue to glorify the hunter', the last few decades have witnessed a number of ambitious attempts to deconstruct the former masters' view of history and to challenge the traditions of Western historiography. In overturning the old certainties, in forcing established researchers to review their dogmas, become aware of their omissions and reopen long-closed files, these recent approaches have dared to defy the Western teacher and to withhold the status of truth from historical constructs that mainly served to spread the discourse of supremacy. In this connection, however, the West is not the only one to engage in manipulation, and guests at its universities have subsequently realized the huge amount at stake in the rewriting of history. The originators of deconstructionist projects have opposed their own interpretation to the Eurocentric reading of the past, in order to give back to the vanquished their dignity as historical agents. Yet in a sense they have followed in the footsteps of the vanquishers, swapping roles without breaking with their historical schemas.

Is it because the West denied them a right to a history that Africans – and, more generally, the black world – have gone so far in attempting to rewrite it? The work of some of their researchers does, in any event, point down the path of reappropriation, from its legitimate first steps to the construction of a founding counter-myth destined to clear the continent of all its humiliations. For this myth to work, it is not enough to take apart the Western deception which, by allowing the dark continent only a prehistory, implied that it had no historical existence and that the world owed it nothing. It is also necessary to show that Africa is the source of all histories and that others therefore owe it everything. Western classical history downplayed the influence of Egypt on the rest of the ancient world, while at the same time considering it too remarkable to be recognized as African.[1] From the nineteenth century in the American black community, and from the 1950s in sub-Saharan Africa in the work of Cheikh Anta Diop that renewed the genre, historians have therefore endeavoured to bring ancient Egypt back home to its continent by advancing proofs of its African character. This veritable revolution has changed the way in which one of the oldest civilizations on earth is viewed, and today no historian would dare to obscure its Africanness.

Nevertheless, by virtue of a series of short cuts, the enterprise served as the starting point for a theory of Afrocentrism that is today firmly held among a not insignificant section of African intellectuals and their diaspora. By making Egypt 'the cradle of civilization for ten thousand years, at a time when the rest of the world was plunged into barbarism',[2] and by making Africanness strictly synonymous with membership of the Negro race, Cheikh Anta Diop forged the thesis of the 'anteriority of the Negro civilizations'.[3] Similarly, ancient Egyptian became the origin of all Negro-African languages – a role comparable to that of Sanskrit in relation to Indo-European languages, which made it possible to attach all civilizations in the subcontinent to a common pharaonic trunk.

The thesis of Cheikh Anta Diop and his followers thus appears as an exact counterpart of Eurocentrist discourse. The themes of anteriority and superiority of a single true civilization – the root of all others – are its main axes. Racial arguments also figure prominently, since race is here productive of civilization and one has to be black to call oneself African.[4]

Finally, the wish to establish lines of descent between past and present similar to those which Europe constructed for itself makes of ancient Egypt the Greece of Africa. 'For us,' wrote Cheikh Anta Diop in his last work, 'the return to Egypt in every field is the necessary condition to bring African civilizations back together with history.... In a reconceived and renewed African culture, Egypt will play the same role that Greek and Latin antiquity plays in Western culture.'[5]

This was the doctrinal trunk from which Afrocentrism spread its branches, until it became a theory explaining the most crucial events in human history. First it obsessively affirmed the Negro character of the Egyptians and, more generally, of all the great figures in African history, keeping quiet about the ultra-Greek Cleopatra, the Carthaginian Hannibal or the Numidian Saint Augustine. It also put forward the idea that Africans discovered America centuries before Columbus – an exploit variously attributed to the Egypto-Nubians (who supposedly landed there around -650 and gave birth to the Olmec civilization) or to navigators of the Mande ruler Abu Bakari in the fourteenth century, or to both, some two thousand years apart. According to Afrocentrist sources, the indisputably African character of the vestiges of many American Indian civilizations proved this thesis beyond all possible doubt.[6]

How is it that such obvious historical facts did not become part of the universal store of knowledge? How could the fraud of the Greek miracle – which owed so much to Egypt, where all branches of human thought were invented – become accepted as truth? Which ruse was used to obscure the essential contribution of black Africa to European civilization? Imprisoned in its mirror obsession, the Afrocentrist narrative could not rest content with simply showing the reality of that contribution. It also had to demonstrate its anteriority, and therefore its superiority, vis-à-vis the Western discoveries. In *Stolen Legacy*, a hugely successful work published in 1954, the American George James developed the oft-repeated theme that Greece committed the original fraud by simply stealing the Egyptian heritage.[7]

Sheltered from criticism by the theory of a white plot, Afrocentrist discourse could claim that its opponents were mere descendants of Greek copiers of Egyptian science. The Negro answer to the Western culture of supremacy did indeed present all its foibles in inverted form. To the racism of white historians, who thought it inconceivable that a great civilization could be African, it responded by constructing a myth of the civilizational superiority of a racial entity, which ignored, among other things, the extensive interbreeding that took place for millennia in the ancient Afro-Mediterranean world. To give the black race a historical visibility over and above its trials and tribulations, it did not simply give it back a place in world history but sought to 'Negrify' world history itself. Symmetry demanded no less.

Actual opponents were not the only target of this rewriting; it also, or mainly, addressed the vanquished peoples, seeking to give them reasons to believe in themselves. Grounding a reconstructed identity upon glorification of the past, it was meant to point the way to more fulfilling forms of existence in the present. This reaction was most powerful in the United States, where hopes for integration in the dominant society had for a time been strong, so that Afrocentrism became not only a counter to the arrogance of white certitudes but a veritable way of life. The roots had certainly been there since the time of slavery and then segregation, and 'Black Is Beautiful' had always been one line of defence for a black community marked down for martyrdom (before this was replaced with disparagement). But in the 1960s and 1970s, American blacks had believed that the winning of civil rights would open the door once and for all to assimilation.

As the harsh years of the 1980s and 1990s spread disenchantment among an ever more marginal black population, Afrocentrism gained a new lease of life, and considerable numbers of African Americans took refuge in it as a kind of internal exile. A whole section of the population lives today with a makeshift identity that is conceived in terms of 'Come Back Africa'. With its ideologues who have taken 'African' names, its distinctive end-of-year festivities (the Kwanzaa),[8] its styles of dress and its college courses, Afrocentrism sees itself as a real counter-culture centred on an imaginary Africa and refuses any cultural compromise with the dominant white world. But although it may serve as a theoretical support for the self-affirmation of a minority community in the United States – the only one to have gone there against its will – it obviously does not take the same forms in Africa. Though strongly implanted among intellectuals in Senegal and elsewhere, the ideas of

Cheikh Anta Diop have not given rise to cultural inventions comparable to those flourishing on the other side of the Atlantic. Africa, in Africa, is not an imaginary object, and no return to an original homeland adorned with all the virtues can serve there as an outlet for the present.

Memory cults

The past lends itself to that more readily – not only distant epochs whose eventful moments are scarcely familiar to most Africans, but a whole world stretching endlessly back 'before the whites'. Everywhere in the South, not only in Africa, the hiatus between the period before and the period after the arrival of conquerors from the West is seen as a split between an age of grandeur and happiness and an age of sub-mission and loss of self. By destroying or overturning what existed before, by opening a period of unparalleled breaks in the history of the occupied peoples, the colonial cataclysm gave an Edenic allure to the time before the conquest. Anomie-generating colonization was thus counterposed to a pre-colonial state that knew nothing of conflicts and whose traditions had the task of guaranteeing equilibrium.

And yet, in all the societies of the South and its northern marches, everyone is well aware that time does not repeat itself. Everyone knows that they have been irreversibly transformed by the innovations intro-duced since the colonial era, accepts most of them, and demands some that have not yet made their effects felt. No one is really opposed to the material gains of modernization. American indigenist movements at-tribute countless virtues to Indian cultures, the African village faces towns that are seen as the antithesis of an ever harder-to-find 'deep Africa', Arabs dwell on the lost splendours of their golden age – but everyone knows that these idealized figures will remain confined to the past. Apart from a few marginal currents with a potentially high nuisance value, which are determined to relive the past or to live in what they take to be a repetition of it, people are content to sing of bygone glories. From Afghanistan to Algeria, self-proclaimed emirs of the extreme Islamic fringe may well perfume their beards and border their eyes with a *kohl* pencil, in the manner of the Prophet, but they do not represent their own society or even a majority within the Islamicist movement.

Incantatory narratives, on the other hand, are a favoured means of banishing the trials of the present. So it is that the cult of remembrance invests the Arab world, where the yardstick of past power so constantly measures the present that it blurs people's view of the future. Nostalgia for the time when its prestigious dynasties ruled the Mediterranean basin here replaces the desire to exist in the eyes of the West. Whereas for American Indians the West is the agency of their ruin, or for the black world it is guilty of the crimes they suffered, for the Arab world it appears as a rival empire which, ever since the Crusades, has never stopped envying its influence and opposing its power. Is this, as many think, the sign of thwarted imperialist ambition? Certainly the Arab relationship to the West most often expresses itself in confrontational terms. A whole nationalist mythology has built its discourse around recollections of Umayyad and Abbasid glory or Andalusian splendour, and has promised its hearers that it will wash away the humiliation of centuries of decay – two key words in Arab political vocabulary – through a reissue of that inspiring period. It is the register of restoration, more than repetition, which Arab nationalist rhetoric has used to build its vision of revenge.[9]

Each episode in the contemporary face-off has its equivalent in bygone centuries; hopes of victory have the conscious aim of making those alive today worthy of their ancestors or of erasing the memory of past defeats. It is exactly as if time has not settled the balance, as if people still cannot be consoled over the illegitimate Spanish presence in Andalusia. During the Gulf War, Saddam Hussein drew without restraint on such imagery. While Westerners made him a second Hitler, he donned Saladin's armour and told a willing Arab audience that he was confident of repeating his exploits again. Just as that emblematic ruler once drove the Christians from the East, so would he inflict a humiliating lesson on the latter-day Crusaders.

But it is not only to bless war that the past is invoked against the present; it is also called upon to answer criticisms emanating from the West. Are today's Arabs – especially Muslims – prisoners of a religious straitjacket that makes them unreceptive to modernity? Straightaway, Ibn Rushd is offered as proof that the Arab Enlightenment preceded by several centuries the pride of Europe, without a mention of the fact that it was European universities which made the Cordoban thinker's legacy bear fruit. Does the Arab world today treat its minorities as second-class citizens and place affiliation to the state religion higher than the right to citizenship? The answer comes back that three religions happily coexisted in Al-Andaluz, or that the Ottomans were infinitely more tolerant than Christendom of religious minorities. Here the past has the function of clearing the present of suspicion, although it is never asked (except in certain minority circles) why the present bears such little resemblance to it. The discourse is symmetrical to that of the West, and it is meant to answer the West's obscuring of the contributions of the Arab golden age – in a kind of competitive points system, where others recall that they were once more powerful, more cultured, more philosophical and more open than those who claim to teach the lessons. As neither partner–adversary seems to want to stop using history in this way, no end appears to be in sight for this exhausting game.

In addition to being an instrument of legitimation for Arab nationalism and the regimes issuing from it, the rhetoric of restoration is also a central plank in Muslim discourse. In the late nineteenth century, the theme of a betrayal of origins provided many of its thinkers with an explanation for the ease with which Dar al-Islam was subjugated by the Western powers. The Nahda intellectual movement, for example – a herald of 'rebirth' that is one of the key sources of modern fundamentalism – called for the revival of original Islam and argued that its abandonment had been the signal for the decay of Muslim societies.[10]

Subsequently, modern Islamicist movements made this a central theme in their arguments, proclaiming that there could be no salvation or greatness outside the restoration of 'Islamic values' and the forms of political and social organization that they ordered. Of course, most of these discourses that sanctify the past – turning it into a 'dream of eternity' in its religious expression[11] – date the onset of decay to a time before Western penetration and indeed explain the latter as one of its consequences. But it is the West's implantation in foreign lands that threatens to make it irreversible. The struggle must therefore be waged against the West, since its ubiquitous presence is a cruel reminder that what used to exist is no longer. The only hope of reviving past grandeur, or at least of remaining as one is now, is to oppose all forms of Western hegemony, from the most visible to the most disguised.

It matters little how this 'as one is now' is defined. Both Muslim fundamentalism and those flourishing in the shadow of the other two monotheisms, as well as Hindu and other forms, see the predominance of religious norms as the surest means of preserving their integrity. But this urge to conjure up the danger of self-dissolution, this wish to regain a purity corrupted by various forms of Western preponderance (nearly all experienced as forms of aggression), is far from being a characteristic peculiar to these movements. It is found everywhere in one or another of its various forms, including the one known as identity. It has often been said that the new century is beginning with its triumph, and that praise for specificity fills the emptiness left by all the failures of our age – from the inglorious demise of the communist illusion to the endless list of frustrations bound up with the contradictions of modernity. Withdrawal into a tangible sense of belonging and easily mobilizable types of solidarity are supposed to provide an answer to the wrecking of socialist hopes, the watering down of state protection, the relative obsolescence of the nation-state, or the unfamiliarity of what is called globalization.

Both supranational identities (with religion as their commonest support) and local identities do seem to have the wind in their sails, attracting world attention because of the violent rivalry between paroxystic self-expressions. But the phenomenon predates the explosions since the end of the cold war. Modern identities in the southern part of the globe first emerged in opposition to the West and its seismic interventions: they usually come down to the fact of not being Western and wanting to build defences against any such possibility; their very definition of themselves is in terms of conflict with an Other incomparably stronger than any previous one in history. All the ambiguity of the term comes from this sense of hollowness. Is it because 'whoever fears losing his identity has already lost it'?[12] In a way, the register of identity may be seen as a long list of defensive strategies against a supremacy that is rightly feared to have already won its final victory in this respect.

The ruses of omnipotence

For the West is not content to embody omnipotence: it also has a signal determination to preserve it. Its all-encompassing hegemony procures it a panoply of means in the face of which all resistance may seem derisory. Indeed, so great is its power that it is even thought to have a capacity for action that it does not actually possess. All (or nearly all) the calamities raining down on the South appear there as so many proofs of a deliberate strategy to nip in the bud any possibility of escaping the West's control or standing in its way. No negative event can be due simply to chance, or have essentially endogenous causes. An evil genie is loose who knows both how to create deadly viruses and to ruin a whole economy.

Even the North's philanthropic actions may conceal sinister purposes and serve its goal of remaining sole master of the world. In politics, as in economics and other fields, everything coming from the North becomes an object of mistrust – sometimes even before questions are asked about the reasons behind it. There is no movement or family of ideas which has not, at one time or another in the last few decades, embraced the thesis of a Western plot to explain the failure of efforts that might supposedly have enabled the South to pick itself up again. Marxists and third-worldists of all descriptions, nearly every variant of nationalism, then the Islamicist movements in the Muslim world have succeeded, or on occasion united with, one another, to assign the West an unlimited power for harm and to do the exact opposite of what it was suggesting, for fear of falling into ready-laid traps.

When the West is in favour of population control, it must find some advantage in it. One should therefore support high birth rates and treat with utmost suspicion its eagerness to lower them. Its very readiness to fund contraceptive programmes can only mean that it is seeking to weaken the South in the guise of helping it. For a long time, the wide-spread belief that any initiative in this connection served some Machiavellian purpose obscured the seriousness of an unmanageable rate of population growth, for which no economy, however dynamic, was able to provide answers.

Until the early 1980s, and even later in some cases, most of the third-world elites – whether in power or in opposition – were united in the conviction that the West's encouragement of fertility control merely expressed its dream of ending their collective existence.[13]

> I read in a French paper a disturbing report about declining fertility rates in the Maghreb.... It presented this as good news.... Quite apart from the poisonous racism in this report, which saw our marvellous region only as home to progenitors of dangerous species ..., the news itself struck me as a terrible blow. My God, what has happened to us?

This point of view, in a daily belonging to one of the main parties of the Moroccan left,[14] is by no means an isolated case. Though weakened by growing awareness of the harm done by over-rapid population growth, these pro-birth coalitions are not exactly disappearing. They continue to express themselves in international arenas, where their voice threatens to merge with those of traditionalist movements opposed in principle to any birth-control policy.[15]

Nor are such suspicions the only ones aroused by the North's fertility-control strategies. Since these took a long time to produce results, some circles in the South grew convinced that the AIDS pandemic, a direct result of Western moral decadence, was not a chance explosion but a deliberate export to the world's most populous regions, designed to produce a high level of deaths to match their high birth rates. Having created and released the HIV virus, American laboratories were supposed to have done all they could to conceal their heinous crime by inventing the fiction of its African origin. These delusory theses, though refuted by the scientific evidence, have acquired the status of truth in many countries in the South, from India to sub-Saharan Africa, where some leaders have made public reference to them.[16]

In the view of those who hail the growth and youth of their population as so many proofs of dynamism, the South is successfully resisting such attacks. But the West is also supposedly trying to weaken it in other ways – for example, by cobbling together extremist movements in important Muslim countries to block processes of development that might be harmful to its interests. One target of these attacks is Algeria, an influential country long at the head of third-world protests, where the major Western powers have been supplying the Armed Islamic Groups, either directly or through accomplices in the Gulf. Already in 1994 Khalida Messaoudi feared that the 'war against Algeria' would plunge her country into 'the Yugoslav syndrome, … which would certainly suit those external forces who are waiting for nothing more to finish off the leaders of the third world'.[17] One historian, a fellow Algerian, later went a step further: 'These war machines', he wrote, 'are ravaging Algeria not because of some historical inevitability, but because of a ploy by a fundamentalist International, and because the rulers of the world want it that way.'[18]

But it is Iraq during the Gulf War – 'that racist war of the white Judeo-Christians against a third-world country', to quote a forthright author from Martinique[19] – which suffered the most pernicious form of destabilization. From Rabat to Amman, numerous intellectuals from every quarter convinced themselves at the time that the United States and its European vassals had deliberately encouraged Saddam Hussein to invade Kuwait, in order to have a pretext for putting an end to the construction of a genuine regional power (that would be highly dangerous to their interests) and nipping in the bud any attempt to achieve Arab unity of the kind that the Iraqi leader wished to bring about. Having naively fallen into the trap, the 'ruler of the last Arab country in the Middle East still standing upright',[20] the long-awaited Bismarck,[21] could then be crushed like a wisp of straw by the world's foremost power, and with him the dreams of revenge that he embodied. 'It is a genocide of our identity. Since Spain/Andalusia in the fourteenth and fifteenth centuries, Arabs and Muslims have never experienced such a challenge', the Jordanian crown prince summed up the war, making the West primarily responsible for the sufferings of his people.[22]

No one was safe, and the emergent nations, being the first to challenge the West's hegemony, were the most exposed to the ire of those whose aim it was to ruin the third world. Nevertheless, economics could become a formidable weapon in the hands of certain leaders in the South. In 1997, at the height of the Asian crisis, Malaysian prime minister Mahathir bin Mohamad stood out by the violence of his attacks on the alleged authors of a Jewish financiers' plot to end the prosperity of one of the world's most dynamic regions.[23] The accusation was picked up in South Korea, where a section of public opinion convinced itself that the diktats of the IMF and pressure from the Clinton administration 'on Japan not to support the South Koreans' were part of a vast plot programmed by Wall Street to destroy the country's economy.[24] The protean enemy was therefore active on all fronts and, when necessary, knew how to conceal its operations beneath a cloak of virtue.

Such are the certitudes of large sections of the population in the South. Some are indeed only exaggerated readings of the true situation, rendered credible by the West's outrageous methods of defending its supremacy. But they also fuel a paranoia that makes the world appear only in the light of the evil that others supposedly wish to inflict. The different versions of the plot thesis have all the greater impact on public opinion since many leaders try to use it to cover up their own failings. Western turpitude, real or imaginary, regularly serves to deflect popular resentment towards convenient scapegoats, thereby masking some thoroughly indigenous crimes or bolstering allegiances under strain from the harsh conditions of life. The populations of these countries are by no means always duped by the tales dished up to them, but they still feel a thrill when they hear them, especially if they play on a sense of identity, as they very often do.

Although school textbooks in Europe and North America do not really question the basis or methods of Western supremacy but glorify its various architects, their counterparts in the South tend to lapse into a nationalist exaltation as unlikely to involve any actual listening to the world as the ivory-tower superiority of their former masters. Demonization of the West and glorification of their own past are the twin refrains used for the education of younger generations. While Indian children have to think of the Vedic age as a 'marvellous epoch, clean, stable and well-organized, free of corruption or social disturbances',[25] those in Morocco are consciously brought up in hatred of others. They are taught that Islam and Muslims are the victims first of Jews, then of free-masonry (itself a 'secret association of Jewish origin'), and finally of all Westerners in general. In Algerian history books, the population of European origin in the colonial epoch consists almost exclusively of ultra-rich landowners and, during the war of independence, lackeys of the OAS. Moreover, that epoch is 'presented as if it was just a paren-thesis between an idyllic age before 1830 ... and the insurrection of 1954'.[26] Overall, textbooks in the Arab countries give a violently anti-Western reading of world history and limit schoolchildren to brooding over Arab-Islamic grandeur.

In every case, however, from the rancid hatreds of the Arab world through India's fascination with its own past to the construction of national histories under the shock of contact with outside conquerors, the West serves as the only or principal reference in the tales that are supposed to expel it from the collective memory or a newly nationalized past. It is to clean away its stain that efforts are made to transmit the mythical heritage of original purity. It is with the West's tools – those of the nation and the state – that people in the South write their own history. It is by hating it that they think they can forge an existence for themselves. And it is its presence everywhere, in all these ways, which makes it more hateful still.

Identity dictatorships

Fear of being unable to escape the West's power of attraction, of being the eternal victim of its ruses to keep others at its mercy before finally dissolving them into itself, mingles with old hatreds, fresher resent-ments and unlikely feelings of nostalgia for a lost paradise, to define the programme that the elders allocate to their descendants. Against the Western enemy it is one's identity that must be defended, even if this means shutting oneself up in it as in a would-be fortress. Tradition remains its preferred habitat, modernity one of the Trojan horses that the enemy knows so well how to build. Feeding on the specificities of a culture, identity has to banish universality as the most recent form of an incurable imperialism. Whether it thinks of itself as defending tradition, safeguarding authenticity or protecting specificity, a whole generation thus locks the future into the dead-end of a reclusive identity that is its alternative to the West's constrictive mimetic injunction. These prob-lematic forms of self-affirmation are always ill-defined, because they ceased a long time ago to exist in and through themselves. Destroyed and reconstructed in accordance with the demands of those who shape their contours, alternately fantasized and instrumentalized, they have for decades lent themselves to serving anything and almost anyone.

Tradition is indigenous, modernity Western. This postulate, tirelessly repeated since the two words became the most famous pair of opposites in contemporary sociology, implies that in order to remain oneself it is necessary to respect the former and to reject the latter. The content of the two terms, however, is by no means fixed. Whatever one might like to think, they have for a long time been developing in concert, fuelling and drawing upon each other as the one seeks to gain a new legitimacy for itself and the other tries to acquire a native look. But whereas modernity seems to advance at its own pace, using its simple power of attraction to dispel everything prior to its own scheme of things, tradition now exists mainly in opposition to it.

But who resist, and why? What do they claim as their legitimacy, and against what do they actually rise up? What meaning do they give to the modernity whose path they try to block? Do all the forms of reinventing tradition have the same motivation?[27] Since no one really envisages a return to the past, what do the upholders of tradition want to save from its legacy – and for which reasons? Today, on planet South, the reactions to modernity fall into two broad categories: one is a kind of spite; the other inhabits power systems that feel threatened by the demands of modernity and the change that it produces. The two may come together, and both have characteristically ambivalent relations with the object of their rejection.

To grasp the full depth of this ambivalence, we must go back a little in time to the two seemingly antinomic objectives of the liberation movements that put an end to foreign occupation: namely, the restoration of a pre-colonial tradition to weave again the threads of identity, and the construction of a progress-oriented future with its back turned on the past. The new leaderships often used this dual patronage to build the broadest possible unity around their movements. Serving up a discourse in praise of tradition to conservative layers in their society and to everyone for whom colonization was a long history of dispossession, they employed the other register to rally indigenous modernist elites and to attract the sympathy of the left in the core states. But they rarely kept an equal balance between these two contradictory poles around which the future was supposed to be built. Most of them disavowed the modernist questioning that had punctuated the colonial period, by equating the defence of tradition and religion with defence of the nation. Those who sought to challenge the former to begin building the latter were accused of joining the enemy camp. In reality, the modernity of the various nationalist movements boiled down to appropriation of the nation-state.[28] Whilst continuing to conflate tradition and nation, they deemed this appropriation sufficient to proclaim themselves modern, since the liberation struggles and the construction of the nation-state were indisputably following the grain of history.

The independence era did not bring an end to these confusions. Once in power, the nationalist leaderships continued to search the registers of identity and tradition for ways to strengthen their legitimacy; they swore to make a clean sweep of the colonial past and to rediscover the most ancient strata of their societies, but most of them also set about modernization in accordance with formulas supplied by their old enemies. Material and technological modernization was supposed to be ideologically neutral: it would, in the best-case scenario, satisfy the general striving for progress without instilling the Western poison into people's minds. In the southern parts of the world, then, modernization took place without the achievement of modernity.

Monsters were born of this hiatus. Authoritarian modernization drives relied on it to repudiate every political aspect of modernity as alien and illegitimate. Making the construction of industrial cathedrals and more or less totalitarian state apparatuses the alpha and omega of progress, they treated any demands for individual liberty or a redefinition of gender roles as deadly threats to the very foundations of identity. Thus, in the Muslim world as many mosques as factories were built, and the teaching of philosophy was often replaced with 'Islamic sciences'.[29] Africans were called upon to consider their leader's discretionary powers and personality cult as perfect expressions of a respect for tradition, while authoritarian rulers in the Far East denounced the treachery of supporters of political liberalization in daring to challenge the legitimacy of Asian values. As they praised traditions reinvented for the sake of their cause,[30] the more or less populist regimes of the South used the techniques of democracy as additional instruments of legitimation – elections as plebiscites, parliaments as rubber-stamping chambers. To an ever greater extent, local authoritarianism came to overlap with imported modes of legitimation in the fields of post-colonial politics. Reduced to its material dimension, that which was called modernity also helped to ensure the survival of regimes on the point of exhaustion.

For want of liberty, they promised at least a degree of prosperity to their peoples. But, as material progress was confined in many countries to small layers of the population, it often aggravated the split between well-off minorities and a majority who experienced modernization only through its destabilizing effects. In paternalist states that opened wider layers to its benefits, the inadequacy of the material gains – and their increasing insecurity under the pressure of population growth and political systems based on the exploitation of mineral rents – generated frustrations that eventually became impossible to calm. In the social as well as the political field, therefore, inhabitants of the South knew only caricatures of modernity. These were the prism through which they saw the West – a West already hated for its domination and condemned in the name of the longing for identity that mushroomed within its shadow.

For many of the modernizing elites of the newly sovereign states, the driving force was a fear of not being sufficiently nationalist, or a competitive raising of the identity stakes, or a wish to mark their distance from the West (guilty of too many crimes to be claimed as a source of inspiration), or a desire to draw closer to the heart of a country from which they felt in many ways too remote. In any event, they accepted the dissociation of tools and meaning and even produced its leading theorists. Refraining from a head-on challenge to tradition or the dogma of identity, they constantly submitted their questioning to the judgement of these other guardians of the temple, thereby legitimating the splits that had developed in the name of the nationalist or religious paradigm.

In the Arab world, modernizing nationalists followed in the footsteps of religious reformists by presenting 'rebirth' as a reconquest of identity around the pivot of Islam. But whereas the latter made religion the norm to which everything should conform, nationalist intellectuals saw it as the most solid guarantee of self-affirmation, since Islam had provided 'a framework for historical continuity over thirteen centuries, in the face of Western imperial attempts to denigrate it, and an acceptable form of mediation between sectors of the Arab world whose language directly stems from the Koran and a kind of "implicit ideology" in relation to contemporary technological civilization'.[31] It was thus by the yardstick of an inescapable Islamic identity that a whole generation confronted the variants of modernity, from Marxism to liberalism, and measured the legitimacy of their local offshoots. The application of similar standards meant that, at least in their early years, many dictators in sub-Saharan Africa – including the most grotesque and bloody, such as

Idi Amin Dada – benefited from the embarrassed indulgence of intellectuals who saw them as unchallengeable restorers of African authenticity. Jonas Savimbi, the unscrupulous Angolan war-maker, also received support from such circles, on the grounds that he personified the just native struggle against the 'mixed-race' regime in Luanda.

As they offer sacrifices to totalitarianism, many intellectuals in the South still feel constrained to give immediate assurances that they respect the norm of identity whenever they might be suspected of transgressing it: that is, whenever they proclaim principles supposedly deriving from an alien modernity, such as democracy or human rights. If, in the Muslim world, for example, they have some sympathy for the separation of the religious and temporal spheres, they are suspected of the sin of secularism and must immediately declare themselves more Muslim than anyone else. Some invoke their Marabout origins, real or imaginary, while others recall the serene religiosity of a childhood that taught them to distinguish good from evil. In 1994, *Le Nouvel Observateur* published a dossier on 'resistance to fundamentalism' in the Muslim countries and asked a dozen intellectuals for their view of Islamicism. Before launching into the usual condemnations, most expressed their reverence for the unattainable 'true' Islam that had been tragically deformed by fanaticism. The Moroccan writer Tahar Ben Jelloun maintained that 'the best way of fighting this aberration is to strengthen the spirit of Islam, that is, its real foundation and not the superficial interpretations that are made of it.' The Egyptian legal expert M. Saïd Al-Ashmawy defined himself, in opposition to extremists, as a 'true Muslim'. The Tunisian film-maker Moufida Tlatli stated: 'My husband and myself are Muslims deeply attached to our rites and traditions', while the Algerian novelist Rachid Mimouni informed readers that all his children 'are brought up in the Muslim religion'.[32]

In 1999, the Lebanese singer Marcel Khalifé was prosecuted for setting to music a passage from a Koranic sura. Intellectuals immediately took up his defence and condemned 'all violations of human rights', but before doing so they expressed their 'amazement at the charges brought against Marcel Khalifé, a man well known for his patriotism, his sense of democracy, and the positions he has taken in defence of the great Arab causes'[33] – as if the real scandal was not the content of the charge but its use against someone with impeccably patriotic credentials. Since no one is allowed to infringe the norm of identity, but at most to discuss its interpretation, it is hardly surprising that modernity has been whittled down to versions whose effects are there for all to see.

It is sometimes thought possible to escape the impasse by separating modernity from its Western cradle and seeking inspiration in other experiences. Many intellectuals in the South have for a long time looked towards Japan, an ancient eastern kingdom which, in the space of just a few decades, caught up with the world's most advanced civilization yet did not lose its own identity. Perhaps this great modern power, industrial and more or less democratic, showed a way forward. 'To catch up the West without losing oneself' – this programme, which every region in the South has so often echoed, gives the measure both of the power of the dominant model and of the desire to shake off its influence. The pendulum has never ceased swinging between fascination and repulsion vis-à-vis this obligatory focus; it has never really stopped at either of the two positions.

The nationalist uncoupling of modernization and modernity has certainly had a remarkably long life, since most of the reactive movements that have emerged in the South in the last few decades have been willing to reassert it. To borrow from the West its 'formidable modern machinery' while rejecting its 'debauchery and depravity': this is how Tunisian Islamicist leader Rached Ghannouchi spurns nearly everything in the West save its technological achievements. Of the rest, he has kept only 'rather negative impressions'. As he put it: 'What I saw in the night clubs deeply shocked me. I was not religious, but the spectacle of unchained sexuality made me indignant. No restraint, no sense of modesty!' This was to be explained by 'the respective places of moral values and natural instincts. In the West, the instincts tend to dominate to the detriment of morality, whereas in a Muslim society it is morality which governs, regulates and educates the instincts.'[34] Ever present in the propaganda of Islamicist movements, this horrifying vision is not peculiar to them:[35] it is one of the reactive discourses that have tried to respond in kind to Western attitudes of contempt. Many of these inverted Eurocentrisms are built around the theme of Western decadence, their repulsive colours not unlike those featuring in old accounts of primitive savages ruled by their instincts. The old antinomy between nature and culture, once used to mark the frontiers of civilization, is now employed to cast the West into spheres where it for so long consigned others.

Many researchers have sought to provide a key to the Islamicist enigma by arguing that these reactive symptoms, in which modernity often finds paradoxical self-expression, are themselves signs of a thwarted modernity. This view would seem to be supported by analysis of practices within societies, or counter-societies, where the dominant discourse is one of reverence towards tradition or political projects seeking to restore particular traditions. The fact that women in the Arab world unreservedly adopt methods of contraception where they are made available,[36] the massive demand for education (of both boys and girls) among urban petty bourgeoisies recently arrived from the country, the innovative compromises between traditional types of family organization and the conjugal family: these, without a doubt, are all paths to modernity. The way in which it is formulated, and the contents with which it is invested, are still too ambiguous to be clearly accepted. But it is in command of decisive trends that are more and more acquiring endogenous contours.

Making use of traditions

It would be too easy, however, to read the South's resistance to trends within it simply by the light of reactive theories whose aim it is to answer the Western discourse of supremacy. Assignation of identity and reinvention of tradition are also matchless instruments of power, not only in the hands of authoritarian rulers but for much broader layers who have everything to lose from a breakup of the normative framework structuring the control they exercise over society.

These groups, whose size varies from region to region, have excluded from what is on offer educationally any critical discourse capable of questioning the structuring framework and its points of reference. Designating Western preponderance and unjust global relations as alone responsible for misdevelopment in their country, continuing to exert the authority of a communalist or religious magisterium, they see the demonization of modernity as a condition for the survival of their power. For this to succeed, then, modernity must continue to be perceived as alien: the greatest danger is that it should become indigenous and thereby remove a central plank from the dominant discourse. Politics is, of course, an immediate target of these protective strategies, but it is not the only one; the social dimension of modernity is rightly viewed as the most serious threat now taking shape against the established orders. These brandish the weapon of specificity to combat the discourse of universality and what they present as its inherent danger of dissolution into the West. At the same time, however, they must conform to the present-day codes governing international relations: they cannot simply opt out of them or challenge them head-on if they want their voice to be heard; or, rather, they must adopt the language and formal avenues for resistance contained in these codes if they are to have any prospect of influencing their content.

In this context of social and political conservatism dominating most of the Arab-Muslim world, attempts are made to insert the specificity of religious norms into new frameworks. Thus, in 1990 the Organization of the Islamic Conference, grouping most countries in the world with a mainly Muslim population, adopted a 'declaration on human rights in Islam' which, though using the vocabulary of human rights, appeared to be an actual negation of them. The signatories, including all the Arab countries (even those the West persists in classifying as secular states), stated their conviction that 'in Islam, basic rights and public liberties are an integral part of the Islamic faith, and that no one has in principle the right to fetter, violate or ignore them'. This commendable *petitio principii* is immediately followed by a series of articles justifying, among other things, the death penalty and inequality between the sexes, all stemming from the most conservative interpretation of sharia law ('the only reference for the explanation or interpretation of any of the articles contained in the present Declaration').[37] The Muslim world was called upon to recognize its essence in these prescriptions, which, though supposedly embodying specificity, were to serve as an alternative universal for those living under sharia.

Specificity was also sovereign when it came to justifying opposition to any real progress in relations between the sexes. In many countries, amid the widespread indifference of modern elites and the cautiousness of political leaders,[38] a heterogeneous alliance of conservative circles, rural milieux and first-generation city-dwellers enforced respect for so-called traditional values and fiercely opposed any challenge to the sexual division of labour. With power the key issue, the whole arsenal of identity was usually mobilized to thwart women's aspirations to a better status in life. At every official gathering – from national parliaments to international conferences – the danger that the very soul of nations might disintegrate was brandished as soon as the position of women came up for debate.[39]

Furthermore, by demonizing feminism as a purely Western anti-male ideology productive of grave social disturbances, the dominant discourses managed to instil guilt in women who heeded its arguments. On all continents, with the exception of the long-Westernized Southern Cone of Latin America, women who chose to fight for emancipation felt compelled, before presenting their demands, to deny any affinity with the imported poison. A critique of the means and ends of women's struggles in the West formed nearly everywhere the obligatory preamble to any commitment on the issue.[40] In this and other cases, the spectre of 'contamination' by Western values – a term frequently used – serves to hold up thoroughly indigenous demands to social opprobrium.

In the identity schema, to remain oneself means to reject, as mere expressions of Western civilization, any universals that might transcend one's own cultural specificity. The West abuses its position of dominance to pass off values inherent in its own culture as a set of principles valid in all places; it is thus largely responsible for reductionist aberrations, since over the last few centuries it has constantly instrumentalized universality in accordance with its own beliefs and interests. But today, others use culturalist theories as a weapon to keep from bowing to rules and associated principles that they accuse the mighty of wishing to impose on them. Since the attributes of political modernity – from individual liberties to a democratic system – are never any more than particular characteristics of a given culture, other particularisms from other cultures may well stand opposed to them.

This line of argument has been the foundation for an 'Asianist' current that has sought to dismiss so-called universal values in the name of values specific to the Asian spirit – a spirit in no need of foreign borrowings for its forms of political and social organization. Popularized by Singapore premier Lee Kuan Yew, who counterposes Confucian traditions based on discipline and the family to Western libertarian individualism, Asianism has met with considerable success among other political leaders in East Asia. After the death of communist universalism, Asian socialist regimes soon rallied to this ideology as a new way of legitimating their absolute control over society. From Malaysia to China, most states in the region have developed their own variant of this authoritarian neo-nationalism to protect themselves from democratic contagion.[41]

Like most reactive discourses, Asianism fans out in several dimensions. Although it should be read as a defensive strategy against universalization of the democratic system, it also sees itself as a response to the West's monopoly claim on the elaboration of universality, and hence a quest for a new modernity rooted in the civilizations of the Far East. Ideas about a way beyond Western modernity are sometimes presented, mainly in Japan, as 'an enrichment of the West's civilizing message'[42] rather than a challenge to the universality of its principles, but authoritarian regimes in the area, whose methods are increasingly contested, have reduced Asianism to the role of a shield. In the 1990s, under attack especially for their human rights record, they systematically asserted the primacy of the group over the individual and the benefits of collective efficiency over individual liberty, and countered calls for greater democracy by pointing to the regulatory virtues of authoritarian paternalism.

Poles apart from any attempt to expand the field of universality by de-Westernizing its sources, this totally politicized Asianism of withdrawal has found its main contradictors among sections of the intelligentsia within Asia itself. In the name of universality, human rights organizations and political dissidents have refused to be trapped by the identity injunction and objected to its assignation of cultures to the realm of specificity. Thus, Far Eastern associations mobilized against the Asianist argument as early as 1993, on the margins of the international human rights conference in Vienna, and soon came to view it as a new weapon in the arsenal of established powers. In 1998 their principal leaders met in Geneva to issue a joint protest against 'the supposedly Asian values that are in fact an insult to Asians'.[43] 'Torture is always torture, wherever it is practised', argued the director of the Tibetan Centre for Human Rights and Democracy. And the Timorese leader José Ramos Horta added: 'So-called Asian values are just a demagogic slogan used by certain authoritarian leaders to divert the debate on human rights', and he singled out 'such admirers of so-called Asian values as the prime minister of Malaysia or the people in charge in Singapore and Beijing'. All the participants at the Vienna event argued that Asian values did exist, but that it was better to look for them in the Buddhist message of tolerance.

Thus, although voices were raised in the West to criticize the instrumentalization of Asian cultural values, the debate remained primarily Asian. This is a fact of capital importance, and its pertinence stretches well beyond the Far East. Everywhere in the fragmented lands of the South, minorities of the population – and not always insignificant minorities – set out to loosen the principles of modernity from their moorings in the West. Eager to clear up misunderstandings, they managed in a few short years to introduce the debate on universality into their own societies, instead of reducing it to a mere variant of the North–South confrontation. In opposition to the identity totalitarianism in which others wished to imprison them, a new generation of intellectuals have sought to go beyond the reactive anti-Westernism of their elders and are now inaugurating what we might call the era of post-nationalism.

This does not at all mean that traditional norms, or the identity refuges and reactive explosions that serve as such, now belong only in the museums of the South. They everywhere still command majority allegiance and shape the processes of involution that affect huge areas of the world – from religious conflicts to the communalist wars in which the return of barbarism wreaks its well-known ravages. Their hold is all the stronger since very many of these discourses respond to the anxieties of proletarian and middle classes hit hard by rapid changes that they undergo more than they originate. Yet, in among the ambivalent hatred that the former masters continue to provoke, the fear that their supremacy will persist, the refusal to aim only at becoming their doubles, the awareness that withdrawal identities open prospects which are, to say the least, limited, the hour may have sounded for syntheses, or perhaps for radical new departures.

Towards new modernities?

'Our aim is not to copy the West,' writes Iranian reformist Kazem Kardavani, 'but to appropriate the gain for the world that democracy represents.'[44] This programme now seems to be shared by a section of the elites in the South. Nor is it any longer a generational issue. The generation which grew up with the liberation struggles, aged with the twentieth century and gradually handed over to the twenty-first is also one of the objects of present questioning. The generation of lost illusions, which saw all its idols collapse and all its dreams melt into air, has become in recent years the official receiver for the socialist utopias and nationalist projects in which it once believed. The devisers of a challenge to the dogmas that fossilized their societies for decades are recruited from its ranks, as well as from a younger generation that never stops asking it for the accounts.

From Asia to Africa, reactive postures and identity proclamations no longer occupy all the terrain of ideas. To escape their hold, new circles of thinkers are seeking to participate in a reformulation of universality that disconnects it from geography. How can one recognize the West's decisive part in the elaboration of modern universality while also making it one's own? Although it is right to challenge those who wish to continue in the role of masters, how can legitimation be found in one's own country for the principles that they enunciate, so that these become established at the core of collective consciousness? How can the threads

of history be woven again, without falling into the trap of reactive interpretations that block all independent thought? How is it possible to
escape the dictatorship of ancestors – who seem in these uncertain times
to be 'twice as fierce as before'[45] – without becoming that Other who
claims to be the model and a kind of terminus of human evolution?

Questions such as these have ceased to be taboo and are beginning to
structure new thinking in the South. They vary greatly, of course, according to the context in which they are posed. Against the reduction
to specificity that is the hallmark of their dominant ideologies, many
Arab intellectuals claim a place of their own within universality and
wish to be among the architects of its new constructions. In black Africa,
on the other hand, new generations of intellectuals are mainly rising up
against the obstacles of tradition, or what stands in its stead.

The new questioning has not spared the field of politics – indeed, it
is often the explicit focus. The post-colonial page that is now being
turned was one of totalitarian or authoritarian systems in most parts of
the South. Sponsored by the 'free world' or by socialism, the various
dictatorships blocked any evolutionary path towards local forms of political modernity. Competing totalitarian constructs, based on sanctification
of the past and embroidering on themes of authenticity, were meant to
serve as alternatives to the failed series of authoritarian modernization
projects, while still shaking off the yoke of Western supremacy. But
today, in a South worn down by endless constraints, the promise of
freedom is becoming more seductive than that of the helmsmen and
prophets of exhausted systems. Their arbitrary rule and cruel methods,
involving systematic elimination of anyone suspected of challenging them,
have finally run out of steam. The struggle for physical integrity of the
person and for defence of elementary rights has gradually acquired priority status, in place of false utopias that came to look like nightmares
and in which, as the years went by, no one even pretended to believe.

In each continent, human rights movements have appeared and people
have gradually come round to the view that none of the pretexts invented during the decades of fear could justify continued violation of
those rights. Everywhere, such associations have rejected 'any attempt
to use civilizational or religious specificity to contest the universality of
human rights' and have called upon the Arab world 'to consider those
rights provided by international human rights law as a minimum to
build upon and not to seek to reduce or call for their violation in the
name of specificity or any other pretext'.[46] As the competing universals

elaborated within the bosom of socialism breathed their last, the end of the cold war made it easier for that other universalism of human rights to return to centre stage. The democratic idea now began to make some sense in the South. Beyond the numerous caricatures designed to satisfy the West's new requirements, the negotiated political compromises of the 1990s, from Taiwan to South Korea or Senegal, began to express themselves in peaceful alternation of governments and to give real local roots to rules of democracy that were no longer seen merely as imports from the West.

As it emerged from its long gestation, the questioning approach did not remain confined to the political sphere. Many intellectuals probed whole new areas as they took stock of endogenous factors that might have ensured the longevity of now-rejected systems. Some made use of tradition themselves, not to seek justification for authoritarian lurches but to derive arguments in support of their new objectives. Whether in Africa or the Andean altiplano, the ancestral legacy ceased to embody itself in the cult of a leader, and the old village organization gave glimpses of a proto-democracy that might allow people living today to draw upon it without betraying the instruments of a modernity that still had to be built.

In the Arab world, alongside the rare movements openly embracing secularism, a different current has been seeking for a number of years to reconcile Islam with the spirit of the age, as if, after decades of trying to 'Islamicize modernity', thinkers there again felt an urgent need to modernize Islam. Heterodox readings of sacred texts are becoming more and more common, although those who venture into them know that they risk the wrath of conservative circles and, more threatening still, of extremist emirs. The Egyptian Nasser Hamed Abouzeid, having incurred the fatwa of theologians in his own country, is continuing in Europe his iconoclastic historical researches into the text of the Koran. Others, who either moved first or have followed his lead, are also trying to bring Islam back into history. Since the mid-1990s, the Moroccan review *Prologues* has been engaged in a project to 'renew contemporary Arab-Islamic thought', gathering around it intellectuals who wish to see 'Muslim religious thought establish a living internal relationship with the modern ethic of democracy and human rights'.[47]

Publishing houses propose to reconcile 'Islam and humanism',[48] by bringing out texts that again raise questions after the age of certainties, or to renew contact with others after the long seclusion.

Others wish to go further. Still in the Arab world, those struggling for secularization of their societies or of the rights of the individual are making themselves ever more widely heard, even if the religious fixations that stir crowds or the reluctance of governments to challenge sacred norms all too often make them inaudible. Newspapers open their columns to views that would have caused uproar a few decades ago.[49] Women's movements launch ever stronger attacks on traditional hierarchies and associated systems of discrimination.

The time seems to have come publicly to shake off the straitjacket. Already in 1989, commenting on Ayatollah Khomeini's fatwa against Salman Rushdie, the Palestinian writer Abdel Kader Yassine stated that 'only the struggle for freedom will give Arabs the means to resume their forward march'.[50] In 1993, a hundred intellectuals from the Arab and Muslim world published a collection of texts dissociating themselves from the Iranian anathema.[51] Not all broke with the obligatory reverence for tokens of identity, but most considered, like the Algerian Rabah Belamri, that 'a society which refuses to question itself, which denies its artists and thinkers the right to create doubt, ... has no chance of flourishing. It will continue to slumber ... amid its ossified ancestral values.' For many, there was no shame in wishing to take the long-closed paths to freedom.

Africa, too, is riven by such questioning. 'Does it need a policy of cultural adjustment?' asked Daniel Etounga Manguelle from Cameroun,[52] while his compatriot Axelle Kabou wondered why her continent persisted in 'refusing development' and sternly recalled that 'each people ... is responsible for all of its history'.[53] The profusion of the literature indicates the scale of disenchantment and expectation, and layers long denied speech are now trying their hand at it – even in the depths of the countryside. The South is moving, even if the North is not generally very attentive to its tremors.

It is still a timid blossom, however, and we would be mad to think that it will come on fast. On all sides there is so much resistance that it may seem doomed to remain a set of isolated phenomena. Its thinkers and spokespersons themselves give out contradictory signals, so difficult is it to distance oneself from the norms without being seen as a traitor, and to invent other discourses than those which served for so long as truths. Besides, even if this movement is charting the future, it cannot do it in a linear way and may be halted or slowed down for long periods at a time. At present, most people seem to want one thing as well as its opposite. They revolt, when they can, against the oppressive weight of the existing authorities, but they do not risk abandoning the familiar points of reference, which they see as protection against threats from elsewhere and the adversities that undoubtedly lie ahead.

May we nevertheless consider these discourses, and the slowly rising strength of the groups that bear them, as the beginning of a new moment in the history of the South? Can we detect the gradual emergence of ideas and attitudes which will no longer need to produce reactive identities or to sanctify existing affiliations in order to affirm their existence, and which will seek out new ways of being in the world? Once all the caricatures of Western modernity, as well as the thousand ways of challenging its legitimacy, have finally exhausted themselves, will new syntheses be invented in which universality finds local languages to construct modernities that gain widespread acceptance? There can be no doubt that these are already clearing a path for themselves, in the diverse regions of the South that have not given up looking for them. If they are not always visible, it is because they pause now and then before resuming their march and often find unusual idioms in which to express themselves. The language of the West is not the only one that forges modernity, as it may not be the only one that articulates universality.

The emergence of post-reactive identities and the quest for post-identity modes of collective expression are necessary conditions for the globalization of the idea of universality. But if this is not to be seen as the latest form of Westernization of the world, the West must stop regarding itself as the only model for the future of humanity. Its deeply entrenched culture of supremacy, its will to hegemony still displayed in all circumstances, its obsidian desire to play the central role in all things: these have hitherto provided fertile ground for the reactive passions whose violent effects repeatedly leave the South struggling to pick itself up again. But it is only if Westerners abandon their certainties and non-Westerners their nervous reactions that new beginnings might make a real impression.

Will the West allow universality to escape its grip and finally become what it is supposed to be: a body of ideas and a discourse in which the whole of humanity can recognize itself? As Indian historian Dipesh Chakrabarty puts it: can 'Europe be provincialized' in such a way that 'other tales of human convergence can be written ..., drawing strength from imagined pasts and futures in which collectives are defined neither by rituals of citizenship nor by the nightmare of "tradition" created by "modernity".'[54] The new questioning in the South, the determination to be part of a world that has not been conceived only in other latitudes, certainly enter into this process of rewriting. Yet, on both sides of the mirror, the immortal guardians of the temple are still alive and kicking; they have not finished pronouncing what the world should be like, or trying to find refuge from it.

Conclusion

What can be read of the future in the worldwide recompositions taking place before our very eyes? What will be the content of the chapter of history that they are opening? Instead of an 'end of history' completing the Westernization of the world, do they not herald a new epoch in which the West will be forced to reach a compromise with everyone else?

Some see the new configurations as initiating an unprecedented relationship between the Norths and the Souths, yet these forms still obey a logic that allows the West to prolong the hegemony it gradually built over the course of five centuries. It has the strength, the wealth and the technology to achieve this, as well as a belief in its 'manifest destiny'. Everything still seems to point to it as the only model, which the rest of humanity must set itself the task of copying. The model is challenged, of course, but its success is due to the absence of attractive and credible alternatives to the view of the world that it offers.

Although it is not certain that the West's supremacy is on the wane, the forms in which it is exercised are changing as other forces, having gradually emerged from the shadows over fifty years, acquire greater visibility. The real novelty of recent history is probably that the West can no longer afford to ignore altogether their massive presence and the long list of their demands. If it held power over the world for so long and still believes that this should remain beyond dispute, it is partly because the societies that fell under its sway were, as Lévi-Strauss put it, 'struck down by that monstrous and incomprehensible cataclysm which was ... the development of Western civilization'. Those which survived are today settling accounts with the former master, and as they call on the West to respect its own principles they deny its right to build without them a future of which it aims to be the sole beneficiary. Initially dazed by the violence of the onslaught, then confined to the pictures that others painted of them, they now want to take back possession of the world and to make the West take account of their existence.

These new encounters give rise to new conflicts. Since the modes of domination are not the same as they used to be, the resistance too takes different forms. It may accentuate the divisions of the world, without really challenging the systemic structures. The fact that Westernization marginalizes the majority of the population, while procuring dividends for its beneficiaries, might result in a growing number of revolts against Western hegemony. Carried along by rival discourses of legitimation, such movements may disturb the operation of the dominant machinery without having the capacity to halt it.

Yet, despite the vast power of the West, the resurgence of other forces creates a context in which it is no longer so sure of itself, as the negative fallout from a model that claimed to embody the truth makes itself felt at its core, and the globalization driven by its elites can be achieved only with the help of the rest of the planet. The terminal phase of an evolutionary process with ancient roots is shaking what once seemed to be a rock-solid organization of global relations, one in which the masters behaved as if they were almost alone on earth. Paradoxically, the unification of the planet now taking place under the aegis of the West demands the invention of new languages and new relationships with others; or, rather, it demands that the West should stop inventing these by itself and allow others to play a role.

There is no sign for the moment that the West is convinced of the need for this, or that it is capable of making it a reality. But it is being pushed in that direction by a no longer marginal, though still unclear and hesitant, global quest for universals that finally deserve the name. Is this unintended yet inevitable accompaniment of globalization capable of opening different perspectives from those laid down in the dominant schemas? 'Nothing is settled', Lévi-Strauss wrote. 'We can still take everything back. What was done and botched can still be redone.' Even if one does not entirely share that faith, it is possible that current changes are bringing to an end the very long period in which a single actor shaped the destiny of humanity.

Notes

Chapter 1

1. Speech by Jules Ferry to the Chamber of Deputies, 28 July 1885.
2. In fact, we should speak of a Berber–Arab–Jewish–Muslim entity, so as not to pass over the origin of the Almoravid and Almohad dynasties that ruled North Africa and Spain.
3. On the contribution of the Muslim world to medieval philosophy, see Alain de Libera, *Penser au Moyen Âge* (Paris: Seuil, 1991); and *La Philosophie médiévale* (Paris: PUF, 1993).
4. 'Averois che'l gran comento feo' (*Inferno*, IV, 144). In his preface to the new edition of Ernest Renan's classic *Averroès et l'averroïsme* (Paris: Maisonneuve et Larose, 1997), Alain de Libera maintains that Averroès brought to a conclusion a 'centuries-long history of the transmission and renewal of ancient philosophy and science, begun in the ninth-century Baghdad of the Abbassids, developed in the twelfth-century Cordoba of the Almohads, and continued in the lands of Christendom.... Ibn Rushd is the cornerstone of the intellectual structure that enabled European thought to construct its philosophical identity. His physics, his psychology and his metaphysics outlined for Europe the highest form of that rationality which is today called Western or Greek.'
5. I am far from swallowing the Arab myth of Andalusia as a lost paradise of perfect toleration that was able to flourish in the shadow of the minarets. The period of Almohad rule, among others, was hardly auspicious for either minorities or freethinkers. Nevertheless, for centuries Muslim Spain was one of the most important cultural centres in the European continent, and was less harsh than Christian Europe towards its minorities.
6. Rodrigo de Zayas, *Les Morisques et le racisme d'État* (Paris: La Différence, 1992.
7. Total estimate for the Caribbean and mainland population. The calculations for Mexico and Peru are those of researchers at Berkeley. See Sylvie

Brunel, ed., *Tiers mondes, controverses et réalités* (Paris: Economica/Libertés sans frontières, 1987). On the conquest and colonization of so-called Latin America see, among others, Eduardo Galeano, *Open Veins of Latin America: Five Centuries of the Pillage of a Continent* (New York: Monthly Review Press, 1973); Carmen Bernard and Serge Gruzinski, *Histoire du Nouveau Monde. De la découverte à la conquête* (Paris: Fayard, 1991); Ignace Berten and René Luneau, eds, *Les Rendez-vous de Saint-Domingue. Les enjeux d'un anniversaire, 1492–1992* (Paris: Centurion, 1991).

8. Already in sixteenth-century Spain it was becoming more and more difficult to explain the barbaric acts of the conquistadors. In his *First Lesson on the Indians*, Francisco de Vitoria (1486–1546) recognized that 'it would be inadmissible to withhold from those who have never committed an injustice what we accord to the Saracens and the Jews, those perpetual enemies of the Christian religion; for we recognize that they have real power over their goods.' Quoted in Ruggiero Romano, *Les Mécanismes de la conquête coloniale: les conquistadores* (Paris: Flammarion, 1972).

9. Juan de Sepúlveda, *Dialogum de justis belli causis*, quoted in Romano, *Les Mécanismes de la conquête coloniale*.

10. Ibid.

11. Bartolomé de Las Casas, *Apologetica Historia*, quoted in Romano, *Les Mécanismes de la conquête coloniale*.

12. Elikia M'Bokolo, *Afrique noire, histoire et civilisations*, vol. 1 (Paris: Hatier-AUPELF-UREF, 1995).

13. It is so difficult to establish precise figures for the population transfer to various destinations that the statistical dispute will never be settled. Dozens of historians, often influenced by their political and ideological affiliations, have made a number of calculations. For the Atlantic trade, the number of slaves who actually made it to America is variously set between a low of just under 10 million (Curtin's estimate in 1969) and a high of nearly 16 million – to which should added another 10 to 20 per cent for the numbers lost in the sea crossing. Over a much longer period of time, 6 to 9 million people are thought to have been deported by the trans-Saharan route, and some 5 million Africans across the Indian Ocean (mainly by Arab–Bantu traders as well as Europeans, Portuguese and French). For greater precision, the reader may reliably consult M'Bokolo, *Afrique noire*.

14. According to legend, Bilal was the first black man to convert to Islam. And before the Hegira to Medina (AD 622), a group of persecuted Muslims from Mecca found refuge with the Negus in Ethiopia.

15. From the tenth century, depreciation of the Negro became a recurrent theme of Arab literature. In Al Masudi, for instance (896–956), blacks are characterized by 'the imperfect organization of their brain, resulting in feeble intelligence' (Al Masudi, *Les Prairies d'Or*, quoted in M'Bokolo, *Afrique noire*).

16. Aimé Césaire, *Discours sur le colonialisme* (Paris: Présence africaine, 1955); *Discourse on Colonialism* (New York: Monthly Review Press, 2000).

Chapter 2

1. I shall return to the term 'human rights', which was never neutral and which soon became an instrument for limitation of the very universality whose emergence it had initially proclaimed.
2. Quoted in Carl N. Degler et al., *The Democratic Experience*, vol. 1 (Glenville, IL: Scott, Foresman, 1963).
3. Ibid. Another useful work on this subject is Joëlle Rostowski and Nelcya Delanoe, *Les Indiens dans l'histoire américaine* (Paris: Armand Colin, 1996).
4. The expression was popularized by feminist literature of the 1970s and 1980s, which provided major contributions to the analysis of Euro-American universality.
5. On these questions, see Yves Benot, *La Révolution française et la fin des colonies* (Paris: La Découverte, 1987); and Jean-Pierre Biondi and François Zuccarelli, *16 pluviose an II, les colonies de la Révolution* (Paris: Denoël, 1989).
6. Speech to the Chamber of Deputies, 28 July 1885.
7. Ernest Renan, *Oeuvres complètes* (Paris: Calmann-Lévy, 1947).
8. Saint-Just, *Essai de Constitution pour la France* (Paris: Gallimard, 1968).

Chapter 3

1. This definition continues to be criticized, on the pretext that hatred of the Other is a feature characteristic of nearly all human societies – which is true. But xenophobia should be distinguished from racism: the latter seeks more elaborate theoretical foundations than the former, which is generally content to reject that which is nearby, or far away. It has also been objected that racism is not peculiarly Western, since its arguments can be found elsewhere than in Europe or America, and in the most remote times. It has had a strong presence among the Arabs, for instance, whose discourse in this regard is often close to that of Europeans. We could also mention – as an example of the imputed inferiority of vanquished peoples – the contempt in which Pygmies are held by Bantu peoples from east to west of central Africa. Refusal to accept the complete humanity of people living in lands that one has occupied is therefore not peculiar to the West. Yet it remains true that the West has gone much further than other dominant civilizations in theorizing a hierarchy of races and in translating its theories into action.
2. This is what Louis Harmand, a French historian of the Roman world, was still writing in the late 1950s: 'The population of North Africa, nearly always lagging behind prehistoric Europe, evolved in a more original way than one used to think.... The human type of the prehistoric Dordogne has its pendant in Meshta man (south of Châteaudun-du-Rhumel in Algeria), a pale replica, but a replica all the same, of the Homo sapiens of our caves. The presence of fair-skinned types among these primitive

populations of North Africa would seem to indicate a northern origin.' And further on: 'After a certain point, these lands ... were home to two population groups which cannot, of course, be regarded as consanguine ..., but whose habits and customs display parallels that it would be hard to deny ...: we would speak of the great Celtic family and of its pendant on the opposite shores of the Mediterranean: the Berber family.' Louis Harmand, *L'Occident romain* (Paris: Payot, 1960). Observe the contradiction between Harmand's wish to ascribe a European origin to the Berbers (to distance them from the Arabs) and his concern to maintain a strict hierarchy between the populations on the northern and southern shores of the Mediterranean.

3. Ernest Renan, *Oeuvres complètes* (Paris: Calmann-Lévy, 1947).

4. George Wilhelm Friedrich Hegel, *The Philosophy of History* (New York: Dover Publications, 1956).

5. Jean-François Champollion was one exception. He did not hesitate to write: 'With all due respect to scholars who make a religion of believing in the spontaneous generation of the arts in Greece, it is evident to me, as it is to anyone who looks closely at Egypt, that the arts began in Greece through slavish imitation of the arts of Egypt (which were much more advanced than is commonly supposed), at a time when the first Egyptian settlements were in contact with the savage inhabitants of Attica and the Peloponnese.' Quoted in Jean-Claude Simoën, *Le Voyage en Egypte* (Paris: J.-C. Lattès, 1989).

6. This racialization of differences often more imaginary than real served a number of times to legitimate through science xenophobic fantasies or the positions of a ruling group. Two cases may illustrate this phenomenon: the hysteria that raged in France against immigrants from Italy in the early twentieth century; and the unflagging contempt of Ashkenazim in Israel for Jews coming from the East. Like Spaniards, southern Italians in particular were suspected until recent times of being too close to Africa to be truly European. In the Israeli case, the 'racial' justification is even more transparent, as eastern Jews were considered in the 1950s to be half-primitive (like the population of the countries of origin) by an originally European intelligentsia imbued with the Western culture of supremacy.

7. Here it is not only a question of North America, since the Iberian elites of central and southern America – which in the first third of the nineteenth century led their respective colonies to independence in the name of Enlightenment principles – based their power upon a strict hierarchy of races and continued both to marginalize the Indian peoples and to keep the blacks in slavery. Slavery was abolished in Peru only in 1860, and in Brazil only in 1888.

8. Karl Pearson, *National Life from the Standpoint of Science* (London: Cambridge University Press, 1905).

9. Francis Galton, *Inquiries into Human Faculty and Its Development* (London: Dent, 1907).

10. Quotations from an article by Jean-Denis Bredin, in *Le Monde*, 1 March 1997.

11. Alexis de Tocqueville, *Travail sur l'Algérie* (Paris, 1841).
12. Pearson, *National Life from the Standpoint of Science*.
13. François Maspero (in *L'Honneur de Saint-Arnaud* [Paris: Plon, 1993]) accepts the estimate that the Algerian population fell from 3 million in 1830 to 2.3 million in 1856.
14. On the violence in the Congo, see *inter alia* Jules Marchal, *E.D. Morel contre Léopold II. L'histoire du Congo 1900–1910* (Paris: L'Harmattan, 1996); and Adam Hochschild, *Les Fantômes du roi Léopold. Un holocauste oublié* (Paris: Belfond, 1998); *King Leopold's Ghost: A Story of Greed, Terror, and Heroism in Colonial Africa* (New York: Houghton Mifflin, 1998). Hochschild's well-documented book, which deals in impassioned tones with the bloody methods of the Leopold era, has given rise in the French press to criticisms that it dwells too much on the misdeeds of colonization. 'Is it right', asks journalist Josyane Savigneau in *Le Monde des Livres*, 10 December 1998, 'to accuse colonizers of murder when speaking of epidemics or even of lower fertility rates? The picture of a sovereign who had the Congo occupied purely for the sake of profit ... is plausible, but it would need to properly supported.'
15. Helmut Bley, *South-West Africa under German Rule* (London: Heinemann, 1971).
16. Ibid.
17. In June 1845, the Ouled Riah tribe in the Dahra gathered their herds and took refuge in caves to escape from French troops. Colonel Pélissier then had huge bonfires lit at the entrance to the caves, causing the death by asphyxiation of a thousand or so people.
18. Quoted in Maspero, *L'Honneur de Saint-Arnaud*.
19. Catherine Coquery-Vidrovitch, *Le Congo au temps des grandes compagnies concessionnaires, 1898–1930* (Paris: Mouton, 1972).
20. Jean Suret-Canale, *Centenaire de la conférence de Berlin*, documents of the international colloquium held in Brazzaville, April 1985 (Paris: Présence africaine, 1987).
21. *Mr Chamberlain's Speeches*, 2 vols., ed. Charles W. Boyd (London: Constable, 1914), quoted in French in Malet-Isaac, *Histoire contemporaine 1852–1939, classes terminales* (Paris: Hachette, 1953).
22. The inverted commas do not imply that I doubt they were civilized, but merely that they thought of themselves alone as civilized.
23. All these figures are taken from Sophie Bessis, *La Dernière Frontière. Les tiers mondes et la tentation de l'Occident* (Paris: J.-C. Lattès, 1983).
24. Régence de Tunis, Protectorat français, Direction de l'Agriculture, du commerce et de la colonisation, *Notice sur la Tunisie*, 6th edn, 1909.
25. Malet-Isaac, *Histoire contemporaine 1852–1939*.
26. Quoted in Maspero, *L'Honneur de Saint-Arnaud*.
27. At the beginning of the twentieth century, a high-ranking official in the French colonial ministry protested as follows at the moral gloss that was being placed on the colonial enterprise: 'What lies at the basis of any colonial policy is force.... We understand that the African races "yield" the most. What have science, justice, goodness and especially progress got

to do with it?' Charles Régismanet, *Questions coloniales* (Paris: Larose, 1912), quoted in Suret-Canale, *Centenaire de la conférence de Berlin*.

28. See Jacques Couland, 'L'Égypte de Muhammad Ali, transition et développement', in Catherine Coquery-Vidrovitch/Daniel Hémery/Jean Piels, ed., *Pour une histoire du développement* (Paris: L'Harmattan, 1988); and, within a wider framework, Maxime Rodinson, *Islam and Capitalism* (London: Allen Lane, 1974).

Chapter 4

1. P. Hallnyck and M. Brunet, *L'Antiquité* (Paris: Masson, 1950).
2. Ibid.
3. Malet-Isaac, *Histoire contemporaine 1852–1939, classes terminales* (Paris: Hachette, 1953).
4. The quotations from Spanish textbooks are taken from Gema Martín Muñoz, Begoña Valle Simón and Maria Ángeles López Plaza, *El Islam y el mundo árabe, guía didáctica para profesores y formadores* (Madrid: Ediciones mundo árabe e islam, 1998).
5. Numerous textbooks thus describe that part of the history of the United States. See, among others, Samuel E. Morrison, Henry S. Commager and William E. Leuchtenburg, *The Growth of the American Republic* (New York: Oxford University Press, 7th edn, 1980) – a book intended for high-school use which is representative of the changed tone of official discourse and of the ambiguities that it has been unable to clear up. Without using the word, it reports the genocide of Californian Indians between 1850 and 1860 (when their numbers fell from 100,000 to 35,000), but in a way it absolves white America by insisting that many politicians of the time were disgusted by the brutality of the conquest.
6. See, among others, Oscar and Lilian Handlin, *Liberty in America, 1600 to the Present*, vol. 2, *Liberty in Expansion, 1760–1850* (New York: Harper & Row, 1987).
7. *Second Congress of the Communist International: Minutes of the Proceedings*, vol. 2 (London: New Park Publications, 1977).
8. On the communist parties of the Maghreb, see Juliette Bessis, *Maghreb, la traversée du siècle* (Paris: L'Harmattan, 1997).
9. These peaks did not arrive on the same dates for all the parties of Western Europe. The Italian Communist Party entered a period of decline in the 1920s from which it would emerge only during the wartime resistance. The German party began its descent into hell in 1933, while the French had its hour of glory under the Popular Front. In this section the French Communist Party, the PCF, will serve as a guiding thread for our analysis of the attitudes of metropolitan communist formations on colonial issues. In fact, France was the only imperial power to have a strong Communist Party.
10. Quoted in Jacob Moneta, *Le PCF et la question coloniale* (Paris: Maspero, 1971).

11. Karl Marx, 'The Future Results of the British Rule in India' (1853), in *Surveys from Exile* (Harmondsworth: Penguin/New Left Review, 1973).

12. Ibid.

13. Quoted in Moneta, *Le PCF et la question coloniale*.

14. 'Le communisme dans l'Afrique du Nord, projet de programme d'action présenté au congrès fédéral d'Alger du 14 janvier 1923', quoted in ibid.

15. Aimé Césaire, *Lettre à Maurice Thorez du 24 octobre 1956* (Paris: Présence africaine, 1956).

16. In 1945 Éditions sociales, the publishing house associated with the PCF, brought out a collection of Maurice Thorez's reports to the 8th, 9th and 10th Party congresses, plus a report to the session of the Central Committee meeting at Ivry on 19 May 1939, under the title *Une politique de grandeur française*. As far as the interests of France are concerned, they are mentioned in the PCF statement of 8 November 1954 on the situation in Algeria and in several other texts.

17. Immigration in France, which goes further back than in other West European countries, began with the arrival en masse of Italians and Poles between the two world wars. In the 1950s these progressively Frenchified immigrants were succeeded by a new influx from the Iberian peninsula, and around the same time France, Britain, West Germany and the Benelux countries all received large numbers of workers from the colonies or the underdeveloped periphery of the European continent (Yugoslavia and Turkey, for example).

18. 'People are amazed and grow indignant. They say: "It's really strange! Ah, well! It's Nazism: it will pass!" And they hush up the truth even to themselves: that it is barbarism, but the ultimate barbarism, which crowns and sums up the everyday barbarisms; that, yes, it is Nazism, but that before being its victim they have been its accomplice; that they tolerated this Nazism before being subject to it, exonerated it, closed their eyes to it, legitimated it, because until then it had been applied only to non-European peoples; that they cultivated this Nazism, are responsible for it. Yes, it would be worthwhile ... to show the very distinguished, very humanist, very Christian bourgeois of the twentieth century ... that in the end what he does not forgive Hitler is not crime against man as such – but crime against the white man.' Aimé Césaire, *Discours sur le colonialisme* (Paris: Présence africaine, 1955).

19. My aim here is not to discuss the validity of the Frankfurt School's critique of Enlightenment reason, but to point out that the question of the genealogy of Nazism was posed at the time, that a minority of thinkers were investigating the founding myths of Western modernity in an attempt to explain its aberrant forms.

20. Again I do not wish to confuse massacres and genocide. But it seems impossible to refuse the term 'genocide', as many Western intellectuals still do, to describe such events as the extermination of the American Indians. The official version of United States history has itself recognized, in a summary used for educational purposes that any American or tourist can read on Ellis Island, that 'the native American population

NOTES TO PAGES 53-61

declined from some five million in 1500 to less than 250,000 in 1900'. Since most of this 'decline' took place in little more than a century, and since the conquerors' drive to eliminate a population in their way was its primary cause, we need to ask why there is still so much resistance to use of the term 'genocide'. The French philosopher Christian Delacampagne is here following many others when he accepts it only for the massacres of Armenians by Turkey during the First World War, the extermination of the Jews during the Second World War, and the attempt to eliminate the Tutsis in Rwanda in in 1994. See Christian Delacampagne, *Essai sur la banalisation du mal* (Paris: Odile Jacob, 1998).

21. Ernest Renan, lecture at the Sorbonne in 1882, in *Oeuvres complètes* (Paris: Calmann-Lévy, 1947). The American historian Scott Ellsworth, who has studied the anti-black pogrom in Tulsa in 1921, describes this attitude as 'the segregation of memory' (*The Economist*, 24 April 1999).

22. Alain Corbin, 'L'âge d'or de l'agressivité', *Le Monde des livres*, 13 November 1998.

23. See Yves Benot, *Massacres coloniaux, 1944–1950. La IVe République et la mise au pas des colonies françaises* (Paris: La Découverte, 1994).

24. Vincent Auriol, *Journal du septennat*, vol. 1 (Paris: Armand Colin, 1970).

25. Speech of 23 October 1947, in Charles de Gaulle, *Discours et messages*, vol. 2 (Paris: Plon, 1970).

26. Quoted in Benot, *Massacres coloniaux*.

27. At the height of a polemic about poetry with Louis Aragon, Césaire wrote in a poem entitled 'Réponse à Depestre poète haïtien': 'Leave them/ the minuet hum of their blood the tasteless water trickling/ down pink steps.../ let us turn them chestnut-brown Depestre/ as we used to brown our masters with the whip/ get away Depestre get away let Aragon talk' (*Présence africaine*, new series, 1–2, April–July 1955).

28. Frantz Fanon, *Les Damnés de la terre* (Paris: Maspero, 1961); *The Wretched of the Earth* (London: Macgibbon & Kee, 1965).

29. *Avant les blancs* is the title of the French translation of Basil Davidson's *Old Africa Rediscovered* (London: Victor Gollanz, 1959).

30. See the episode dealing with the Negro from Surinam in Voltaire's *Candide*.

31. I have not mentioned Japan before now. The evolution of the only rich and developed non-Western country has, of course, been interpreted in many ways. Its omission here is due to the fact that it does not belong to the West and is not part of its history; indeed, its own history has to some extent been forged against the West. The memory and collective consciousness of the Japanese have drawn upon other sources and constructed other epics. As to the country's imperialist designs, they were deployed within the limits of East Asia and never entertained global dreams. Asiatic expansionism has always spawned regional imperialisms. The fact that, in the 1960s and 1970s, Japan had some of the most radical far-left groups of the developed world is mainly to be explained by a number of local causes. As in Europe and America, however, young people in Japan rebelled against the dreamless future inscribed in the market project of a consumer

society, and they were convinced that it was possible 'to unite in the same struggle those rebelling against wealth and those fighting against poverty', to quote the terms used by Chris Marker in his film *Sans soleil* (Paris, 1982).

32. Drawing some of their arguments from the third worldist messianism that was then all the rage, and their inspiration from a hardline version of Marxism-Leninism developed outside Europe and completely out of sync with the reality in their own countries, the Maoist movements represented the consummate expression of Western revolutionary fantasies. Their very brief lifespan is proof of a total lack of roots in the Western countries themselves.

33. Carlos Fuentes, 'Révolution: Annonciation', in *L'Amérique latine et la Révolution française* (Paris: La Découverte/Le Monde, 1989).

34. Ibid.

35. Ibid.

36. Walt Whitman Rostow, *The Stages of Economic Growth: A Non-Communist Manifesto* (Cambridge: Cambridge University Press, 1960).

37. Arthur Lewis, 'Economic Development with Unlimited Supplies of Labour', *The Manchester School of Economic and Social Studies*, vol. 22, no. 2, 1954, pp. 139–91.

Chapter 5

1. Thus, in *The Bell Curve* (New York: Free Press, 1994) the American researchers Richard Herrstein and Charles Murray sought to prove that blacks were hereditarily less intelligent than whites. The book sold in hundreds of thousands of copies.

2. Georges Liver and Roland Mousnier, *Histoire générale de l'Europe*, vol. 3 (Paris: PUF, 1980).

3. This term, which is also the title of a book by Pierre Moussa (*Les Nations prolétaires* [Paris: PUF, 1959]), summed up a shift in the communist paradigm of class struggle to the field of North–South relations.

4. Pascal Bruckner, *Le Sanglot de l'homme blanc. Tiers monde, culpabilité, haine de soi* (Paris: Seuil, 1983).

5. Interview with Sophie Bessis, *Jeune Afrique* 29, September 1986.

6. One journalist, for example, wrote in a major American daily that 'the old tribal quarrels, which were eliminated by European armies in the colonial era, resurfaced with all their old savagery, now strengthened with automatic weapons' (*Los Angeles Times*, 25 January 1985).

7. This is the argument of David S. Landes (*The Wealth and Poverty of Nations: Why Some Are Rich and Some So Poor* [New York: Norton, 1997]), who places side by side the cruelty of the pre-Columbian empires and the brutality of the conquistadors.

8. 'Géopolitiques internes en Afrique', *Hérodote* 46, July–September 1987 (Paris: La Découverte).

9. In France, the six-volume *Aventure coloniale de la France* published by

Éditions Denoël is an example of such history. The first volume, *L'Empire triomphant (1871–1936)*, makes an emphatic apology for empire. And in a review of the latest volume in *Le Monde* (18 July 1997), the journalist Bertrand Legendre adopts the same reading when he evokes 'that glorious history not without shadows'.

10. Alexandre Adler, *Courrier international* 338, 24–30 April 1997.

11. Jean-Pierre Cot, *À l'épreuve du pouvoir. Le tiers-mondisme pour quoi faire?* (Paris: Seuil, 1984).

12. *Le Point*, June 1997, quoted in *Jeune Afrique* 1906, 16 July 1997.

13. A play performed in Paris in 1997 illustrates this return to old imagery. Arnaud Bédouet, the author of *Kinkali* (January–March 1997, National Theatre of La Colline), was described in the publicity as having 'spent all his childhood in Africa' (which, being a single area, does not need to have a location in a specific country). In an Africa destined for uniformity 'this *huis clos* drama, which brings together three generations of European émigrés living in Africa – a female tourist, an old man and a young woman – tells us more than many reports about Africa.' These words of the director make things clear: the imagination describes this land of strangeness better than an account of reality would. As to the European characters, they require us to ask 'about the true nature … of the colonizer's original aim: humanitarian mission or blind passion?' The author himself, who was born in 1958, is not an old colonial. But it was exactly as if the simple choice of scenery, Africa, required him to turn to the most archaic figures of a fantasy-memory, and that it was right to invest the colonizer with a heroic charge of whatever kind.

14. Stephen Smith, 'Le rêve fracassé de Freetown', *Libération*, January 1999.

15. An analogous tendency might be the 'cold war against women' that followed the great emancipatory movement of the 1970s. See Susan Faludi, *Backlash: The Undeclared War on American Women* (New York: Crown, 1991).

16. Denise Bouche, *Histoire de la colonisation française*, vol. 2 (Paris: Fayard, 1991).

17. I have intentionally left out of my research the whole of the far-right press in Europe and North America. It is ordinary opinion in the West that interests me here, not that of its extremists.

18. 'Histoires d'Europe de Jules César à l'euro', *L'Européen* 19–20–21, 29 July–23 August 1998.

19. The process stretched from the decree of 16 Pluviôse, Year II (1794) and its repeal in 1802 by the Consulate to the abolition of slavery in Brazil in 1888.

20. Speech of the overseas secretary of state Jean-Jacques Queyranne (quoted in Lydie Ho-Fong-Choy Choucoutou, 'Du bon usage d'une commémoration', *Dérades* 3, 1999, Petit-Bourg, Guadeloupe).

21. Among the most recent works in French are: Claude Fohlen, *Histoire de l'esclavage aux États-Unis* (Paris: Perrin, 1998); 'Routes et traces d'esclaves', special issue of the journal *Diogène* 179 (Paris: Gallimard, July–September 1997); and 'De l'esclavage', special issue of *L'Homme* (Paris: EHSS, January–March 1998).

22. *Washington Post*, August 1997.
23. Jean Suret-Canale, 'La politique coloniale', in Jean Suret-Canale, *Centenaire de la conférence de Berlin*, documents of the international colloquium held in Brazzaville, April 1985 (Paris: Présence africaine, 1987).
24. This figure excludes the traditional Koranic schools. See A. Jenaistar, 'École, famille et société au Maroc', *Lamalif* 116, May 1980 (Casablanca).
25. Brahim Benmoussa, *Femmes et éducation en Algérie*, report prepared for the '95 Maghreb Égalité collective but not published, Algiers 1994.
26. WHO figures reprinted in World Bank, *World Development Report 1978* (Washington, DC: World Bank, 1978).
27. Jacques Marseille, *Empire colonial et capitalisme français, histoire d'un divorce* (Paris: Albin Michel, 1984).
28. Paul Bairoch, *Mythes et paradoxes de l'histoire économique* (Paris: La Découverte, 1994); *Economics and World History: Myths and Paradoxes* (New York and London: Harvester Wheatsheaf, 1993).
29. Bairoch notes, however, that 'at the dawn of the twentieth century 79 per cent of British cotton fabric was exported, and more than half of these exports were to the third world' (*Economics and World History*).

Part II Introduction

1. Until 1991 the World Bank did not concern itself with the USSR and the European countries of the socialist bloc, but since then it has created a new region to take in the countries of Eastern Europe and Central Asia, which it generally defines as developing even if it does not favour them all with the same treatment.
2. The multiplicity of terms reflects both the South's evolving perceptions of itself – which have been successively or simultaneously political, geographical and economic – and the perceptions that the North has of it, as well as the difficulty that specialists have in giving a meaning to the word 'development'. The group of countries forming the North has never been subject to the same terminological profusion.
3. World Bank, *World Development Indicators*, published annually (Washington, DC: World Bank). The World Bank divides the world into six 'regions' (only four of which deserve the name on geographical grounds): East Asia and the Pacific, Europe and Central Asia, Latin America and the Caribbean, the Middle East and North Africa, South Asia and sub-Saharan Africa, high-revenue OECD countries and 'others with high incomes'.
4. UNDP, *Human Development Report*, published annually (New York: Oxford University Press).
5. I could also have mentioned Spain and Portugal as atypical. But their cases are less convincing in that, since their admission to the European Union in 1986, the growth and structure of their economies and the routinization of their democratic life have erased most of the differences that used to separate them from the rest of Europe. This is not true of

Greece and Ireland: the former stands out because of its chaotic and clientelist economic management and the archaic character of its political practices, while the latter reminds one, in economics, of an Asian assembly-shop country.

6. Works in French in this vein include: Christian Sautter, *Les dents du géant. Le Japon à la conquête du monde* (Paris: Orban, 1987); Karel von Wolferen, *L'Énigme de la puissance japonaise* (Paris: Robert Laffont, 1990); Dominique Nora, *L'Étreinte du samouraï. Le défi japonais* (Paris: Calmann-Lévy, 1991); and Pierre-Antoine Donnet, *Japon achète le monde* (Paris: Seuil, 1991).

7. In 1956, at the Twentieth Congress of the CPSU, Khrushchev and other Soviet leaders repeated Lenin's phrase about 'catching up and overtaking the most developed capitalist countries'. And *Le Monde* commented on the sixth five-year plan: 'It is true that the USSR can be proud of the figures it has made public today.... It must be recognized that the rate of industrial development in the USSR has been impressive and faster than in Western capitalist countries' (*Le Monde*, 17 January 1956). In its issue dated 27 September 1957, one could read: 'The balance sheet of the five-year plans from 1928 to 1955 ... has been clearly positive, and it has radically changed the predominantly peasant economic and social structure of old Russia.' As we can see, the idolization of industry transcends the ideological frontiers of the West.

8. Opinion in Russia has endorsed this divide, which for a long time was masked by communist ecumenism. Hostility to the Caucasian population, together with a drift in political discourse and the press associated with the bloody troubles since 1996, have shown how deep it is. See, among others, 'Russie, la "tiers-mondisation" des esprits gagne du terrain', article in the Moscow journal *Novoye Vremya*, reprinted in *Courrier international* 470, 4–9 November 1999.

9. In his preface to Fanon's *Les Damnés de la terre* (Paris: Maspero, 1961); *Wretched of the Earth* (London: McGibbon & Kee, 1965).

Chapter 6

1. This was the dominant climate, but in some regions the situation was beginning to worsen. In the Sahel, for example, a grave drought in the first half of the 1970s speeded up the bankruptcy that was already on the cards as a result of aberrant development options.

2. According to the theory developed by Rostow (see above, Chapter 5) and other American economists such as Rosenstein-Rodan and Nurske, only a massive input of capital could give the 'big push' required for 'take-off'.

3. The optimism was such that the United Nations named the 1960s the 'development decade', implying that the countries of the South would be nearly developed by the next decade. It was only in the 1970s, when the early illusions began to fade, that the UN started counting the decades: the 1970s thus became 'the second development decade', and the 1980s the

'third'. This did not continue, however, as disappointments had reduced the value of the Coué method of which the UN had made a speciality.

4. 'La politique commerciale des États-Unis', *Africa Wireless File*, 1 October 1985. This figure represented in 1983 barely 4 per cent of total US imports of goods ($259 billion). But such opportunities gave a boost to exports from a number of countries that had chosen in the early 1970s to base their development strategy on the export of manufactured goods.

5. In 1986 thirty voluntary export limitation agreements covered 10 per cent of world trade (*Le Monde*, 20 April 1999). And in 1992, according to UNCTAD, 23.5 per cent of imports from developing countries were impeded upon arrival in the rich countries: International Coalition for Development Action, *An Alternative Report on Trade* (Brussels, 1995).

6. Let us just note that, since its early institutionalization in the 1960s, the public development aid of the major donor countries has been 'linked': that is to say, part of this aid (more than half the bilateral aid of the OECD's Development Assistance Committee until the early 1990s and a little over a quarter since then) has to be used by the recipient to purchase goods or services from the donor country.

7. See Gilbert Rist, *The History of Development: From Western Origins to Global Faith* (London: Zed Books, 1997); and the collective work *Critical Development Theory: Contribution to a New Paradigm* (London: Zed Books, 1999).

8. In the 1980s, when public opinion in the West began to call on governments to justify their support for dictatorships in the South, the US ambassador to the United Nations, Jeane Kirkpatrick, argued that there was a difference in kind between authoritarian regimes and totalitarian systems; she defended American support for the former, on the grounds that they had a capacity to evolve.

9. Rostow's theory was also at the origin of the idea of a trickle-down effect, which meant that development did not have to concern itself with distribution of the growth dividend because it would naturally trickle down from the rich to the poor as soon as it reached significant proportions. Only in the mid-1970s did this thesis give way to a more qualitative approach to development, based on the satisfaction of 'basic needs'. The economic dimension of containment theory found its best illustration in the tireless promotion by the United States of the 'green revolution'. A revolutionary technical means of permitting sizeable output growth for the world's three main cereals – wheat, maize and rice – was thus supposed to avert any danger of social revolution by satisfying the food needs of the world's most populous countries and enriching the peasant classes that were still a majority there. See, among others, Sophie Bessis, *L'Arme alimentaire* (Paris: Maspero, 1979).

10. Among the most important of these study groups have been: Sweden's Dag Hammarskjöld Foundation and its journal *Development Dialogue*, which echoed the positions of the South in debates on the new world order; the Brandt Commission (an independent commission on international development issues created in 1978 on the initiative of the World

Bank and chaired by the former West German chancellor), which in 1980 published its first report, *North–South: A Programme for Survival* (London: Pan), and in 1983 its second report *Common Crisis: North–South: Cooperation for World Recovery* (London: Pan); and the Swiss-based International Foundation for Development Alternatives, whose booklets have hosted the writings of third-worldist thinkers and third-world political leaders. To these should be added the countless suggestion boxes created in all the major international agencies attached to the United Nations.

11. See Sophie Bessis, 'Banque mondiale et FMI en Tunisie, une évolution sur trente ans', in *État et développement dans le monde arabe* (Paris: Éditions du CNRS, 1990).

12. This fascination has always been the source of ambivalent feelings. The first generations of modernized elites in the South were tempted by mimetism but also pursued the dream of 'remaining themselves', without knowing too well what that meant. 'Before donning the stoker's overalls,' wrote the Senegalese novelist Cheikh Hamidou Kane, 'we shall put our soul in a safe place' – a warning more to his own people against the copycat danger than to whites about their capacity for cultural resistance. Cheikh Hamidou Kane, *L'Aventure ambiguë* (Paris: Julliard, 1961).

13. Nearly all the countries of Africa and the Arab world succumbed to the single-party form, as did a great majority in Asia. But not every state in the South adopted it. Some regions found local authoritarian equivalents better suited to assertion of the power of dominant layers. Thus, during the 1960s and 1970s, Latin America toppled into military dictatorships which, by silencing all opposition, were able to lead a profoundly inegalitarian modernization of the economy. In India, which remained at least formally a pluralist democracy throughout this period, the hegemonic Congress Party adopted the mystique of development and led it for the profit of the urban and rural bourgeoisies that were its social base.

Chapter 7

1. In 1973, on the eve of the first oil price shock, the United States produced 520 million tons of oil a year and imported 280 million tons. In 1978, on the eve of the second shock, it produced 490 million tons and imported more than 400 million (OECD statistics). Since then, its consumption of oil has been divided more or less equally between national production (472 million tons in 1997) and imports (445 million tons). Its proven recoverable oil reserves are the eleventh highest in the world, and those of natural gas the sixth highest (United States Energy Information Administration for the 1997 figures and the reserves).

2. In 1979 ten oil corporations were among the fifteen worldwide that had made the highest annual profits. Of these, six were American (Exxon, Standard Oil of California, Texaco, Standard Oil of Indiana, Gulf Oil and Standard Oil of Ohio), the first was Anglo-Dutch (Shell), one was British (British Petroleum), one Venezuelan (Petróleos de Venezuela) and one

French (Elf–Aquitaine) (*Le Monde*, 19 July 1980). In 1973 several of these companies had defended the principle of raising oil prices (*Le Monde*, 25 October 1993: 'La fin du pétrole à bon marché'). Recent mergers in the sector have further increased the size and reduced the number of the giant corporations.

3. Many of these countries tried to convert their wealth into military and geostrategic power, allocating a disproportionate amount of their petro-dollars to arms purchases. Apart from the well-known case of the Gulf monarchies, countries such as Iran, Iraq and Algeria used their oil resources to make a bid for regional power.

4. The international organization of the Muslim Brotherhood has long been linked to the Wahhabi kingdom. Its leaders, on the wanted list in their respective countries, took refuge there and received sizeable subsidies. Through the intermediary of the World Islamic League, among others, Riyadh provided financial and logistical assistance to all the Islamicist movements that (to a greater or lesser extent) gave it their allegiance. Some sources estimate at $50 million the aid given between 1988 and 1991 to the Algerian Islamicists. Saudi Arabia massively funded the war of the Afghan mujahidin against the Soviet 'atheistic communists', and until the Gulf War Kuwait was also an important source of finance for the international organization of the Muslim Brotherhood. See, among others, *Jeune Afrique* 1627 and 1628, March 1992; and Antoine Sfeir, *L'Argent des Arabes* (Paris: Hermé, 1992).

5. The successive oil shocks came at a time when the Bretton Woods system was falling apart, both because of the sudden rise in the global stock of footloose capital (to which they in turn contributed) and because of the Jamaica Accord of 1976 ratifying abandonment of the system of fixed exchange-rates.

6. Statistics on official development finance are taken from the annual reports of the OECD's Development Assistance Committee: *Development Cooperation Report* (Paris: OECD).

7. UNDP, *Human Development Report 1993* (New York: Oxford University Press, 1993).

8. At that time, 12 to 13 per cent of total official assistance was made up of food aid, and we know the role that has played in increasing the food dependence of many countries in the South (OECD, *Development Co-operation Report*).

9. The real GNP of G7 countries increased at an annual rate of 3.3 per cent between 1974 and 1980. For the OECD as a whole, yearly growth averaged 3.2 per cent for the same period, compared with 4.6 per cent between 1966 and 1973. World Bank, *Global Economic Prospects and the Developing Countries 1994* (Washington, DC: World Bank, 1994).

10. The debt figures are taken from: OECD, *Finances and External Debt of Developing Countries*, annual report (Paris: OECD, 1977); World Bank, *World Debt Tables*, annual (Washington, DC: World Bank); and IMF, *World Economic Outlook*, semi-annual (Washington, DC: International Monetary Fund).

11. World Bank, *World Development Report 1981*.

12. The copious literature on the subject is divided between critical analyses and rather more favourable studies, the latter often produced by the organizations (or associated economists) responsible for implementation of the programmes. On the critical side, we might mention: Jacques Adda, *L'Amérique latine face à la dette, 1982–1989* (Paris: La Documentation française, 1990); Jacques Adda and Elsa Assidon, ed., *Dette ou financement du développement* (Paris: L'Harmattan, 1991); Gilles Duruflé, *L'Ajustement structurel en Afrique (Sénégal, Côte d'Ivoire, Madagascar)* (Paris: Karthala, 1988); Louis Emmerij, *Nord–Sud, la grenade dégoupillée* (Paris: First, 1992); Susan George, *A Fate Worse than Debt: A Radical New Analysis of the Third World Debt Crisis* (London: Penguin, 1988). And, on the other side: Christian Morrison, *Adjustment and Equity* (Paris: OECD, 1992); World Bank, *Adjustment in Africa: Reforms, Results and the Road Ahead* (Washington, DC: World Bank, 1994), and *The Social Impact of Adjustment Operations* (Washington, DC: World Bank, 1996); World Bank and UNDP, *Africa's Adjustment and Growth in the 1980s* (Washington, DC: World Bank, 1989).

13. Philippe Norel, 'L'évolution conflictuelle des politiques de développement', *Le Monde diplomatique*, May 1987.

14. Report of the Commissariat général au Plan, quoted in *Le Monde*, 8 April 1978.

15. Between 1967 and 1977, Algeria is estimated to have spent the equivalent of $25 billion on more than three hundred industrial projects. Pierre Judet, 'Conséquences sociales de l'industrialisation dans les pays du tiers monde', *Dossiers FIPAD* 20, November–December 1980, Noyon, Switzerland.

16. The Middle East absorbed nearly half of the exports, followed by Africa (including the Maghreb). Latin America took third place and South Asia fourth. Michael Brzoska and Thomas Ohlson, *Arms Transfers to the Third World 1971–1985* (Oxford: SIPRI/Oxford University Press, 1987).

17. World Bank, *Global Economic Prospects*. At the end of the 1970s, when the hour of reckoning sounded, official agencies began to criticize the enthusiasm with which donors had supported the 'white elephants' that ruined the finances of certain states. In the Sahel, then already a disaster area, 'there are cases where donors yielded to pressure from their own officialdom, or even from some of their national groups, and pushed for operations on a scale quite out of keeping with the state of knowledge about costs and benefits' (Comité inter-États de lutte contre la sécheresse au Sahel, *Les Dépenses récurrentes des programmes de développement des pays du Sahel* (Paris: Club du Sahel–OECD, August 1980). In the 1980s, official criticism of the loan policy practised during the previous decade became more frequent, even on the part of those who had encouraged it at the time. The OECD concluded in 1982 that some of the loans had served 'to fund consumption expenditure and dubious investment' (*Development Cooperation Report*).

18. See Pierre Péan, *Affaires africaines* (Paris: Fayard, 1983), and *L'Argent noir. Corruption et sous-développement* (Paris: Fayard, 1988). Also of inter-

est are the revelations concerning corrupt judicial practices in the case of French oil giant Elf, one of the main French companies active economically and politically on the African continent.

19. This expenditure is legal and figures in company balance sheets as 'external commercial costs'. In many Western countries, bribes to foreign officials for the acquisition of markets were until very recently tax-deductible.

20. World Bank, *Global Economic Prospects.* According to the IMF *Annual Report 1982* (Washington, DC: IMF, 1982), GNP in the industrial countries grew by 1.1 per cent in 1981, the worst year of the crisis.

21. Average yearly growth for the period 1980–88: World Bank, *Poverty, World Development Indicators: World Development Report 1990* (Washington, DC: World Bank, 1990).

22. Per capita GNP should not be confused with average income, but it does give some idea of money income per head of the population and allows us to draw comparisons among different countries. Real GDP per head permits more sophisticated analysis, since it builds in purchasing power parity, but it did not come into widespread use until the 1990s.

23. UNDP, *Human Development Report 1993.* Rising per capita GNP in the industrial countries appears here in constant dollars – which, given the inflation raging until the early 1980s, plays down the rate of advance – but it was still everywhere significant. The continuation of the trend is confirmed by other calculations: from 1985 to 1995, per capita GDP calculated in constant 1995 French francs as well as in purchasing power parities rose from 90,000 to 107,000 francs for the whole of Western Europe/ United States/Japan (*Alternatives économiques*, special issue no. 30, 1996).

24. UNDP, *Human Development Report 1993.* On a scale in which the North is 100, real per capita GDP moved from 15 to 14 in China, and from 11 to 7 in India.

25. UNDP, *Human Development Report 1998.*

26. It is still difficult to draw comparisons between North and South. In 1997 the UNDP set the threshold of money poverty at $1 or $2 a day (depending on the country) for the developing world, and $14.40 a day for the industrial countries. But even if this huge difference is taken into account, the poor made up a far larger percentage in the South. In the early 1990s, the proportion of people living on less than $14.40 a day was estimated at 14 per cent in the United States (in 1994), 13 per cent in Britain (in 1991), and 4 per cent in Japan (in 1992). For 1993, the UNDP calculated at 24 per cent the numbers living on less than $2 a day in Latin America and the Caribbean, and at 43 per cent and 39 per cent the numbers living on less than $1 a day in South Asia and sub-Saharan Africa, respectively. *Human Development Report 1997.*

27. The Baker Plan of 1985 and the Brady Plan of 1989 (named after two US secretaries of state) sought to reduce the nominal debt and to guarantee repayment of the remaining sums, with the aim of kick-starting growth in the more developed regions of the South where the prolonged recession had adversely affected the American economy. Partial debt cancellation then began to be applied to the poorest countries, from the Toronto

initiative in 1988 to the recent scheme targeted at the most heavily endebted countries, which since 1996 has gradually lifted the dogma of non-negotiability on sums outstanding to the international financial organizations. Such cancellation, however, always with drastic conditions, has not yet produced more than marginal debt relief for the countries in question. In 1996 the total debt of the poorest countries – China and India excluded – rose to $318.3 billion (compared with $81.2 billion in 1980), and that of sub-Saharan Africa to $227.2 billion (compared with $84.1 billion in 1980). World Bank, *World Development Indicators 1998* (Washington, DC: World Bank, 1998). Moreover, the inclusion of these cancellations under the category of development aid reduces by an equivalent amount the total level of ODA.

28. This does not include the northward repatriation of dividends on capital invested in the South. OECD, *Finances and External Debt of Developing Countries*.

29. World Bank, *World Debt Tables*. The statistics may differ according to which debts are taken into account and which methods of calculation are used by the source in question – OECD, IMF, World Bank, or Bank for International Settlements.

30. Unlike the financial institutions, I do not include in the South the countries of the former USSR or Eastern Europe; this makes it possible to compare the same entities in the 1970s and today.

31. In a real sense all conditions were political, since they profoundly modified the state structures, the forms of government, the composition of the ruling apparatuses and the local relationship of forces, as well as limiting the areas in which the state in question was sovereign. As the providers of bilateral funds, the Bretton Woods institutions anyway constantly played at politics by directly steering the reforms they advocated. But they still kept up the ancient refrain: economics, being an objective science based on indisputable laws, lies outside the field of politics. So it was that the World Bank and IMF were able to present their adjustment programmes as a set of purely technical measures and to defend the fiction of their own political neutrality.

32. See, in this connection, World Bank, *Governance and Development*, Washington, 1992.

33. World Bank, *Adjustment in Africa* (Washington, DC: World Bank, 1994).

34. OECD press communiqué, 26 January 1999. This convention came into force in February 1999.

Chapter 8

1. In 1998 it accounted for 43.6 per cent of world imports and 44.7 per cent of world exports. In the same year Asia, which also has a surplus, accounted for 20.1 per cent and 24.7 per cent respectively. But the weakness of Asian imports is a temporary phenomenon, due to the crisis that hit the region, and the corresponding figures for 1996 (25.03 per cent of world

imports and 25.59 per cent of exports, or a positive difference of 0.56 per cent compared with the EU's 1.1 per cent) are more in keeping with the realities. As to North America, its global deficit is expressed in the fact that it accounts for 21.3 per cent of world imports and 17.1 per cent of exports. Sources: IMF, WTO, CEPII, taken from *Le Monde*, 26 May 1998 and 23 November 1999.

2. *Bulletin économique Euler-Sfac* 1037, November 1999.

3. *Le Monde*, 9 December 1997.

4. Apart from the fact that until recently customs duties made up the bulk of state revenue in many countries of the South, various types of import control guaranteed sizeable income for ruling layers and industrial monopolies, to the detriment of consumers. On the other hand, the industrial countries of the South were able to build up their productive apparatus only by giving it solid protection against the full force of foreign competition.

5. *Le Monde*, 23 November 1999.

6. See Sophie Bessis, *L'Arme alimentaire* (Paris: Maspero, 1979).

7. Address by Ronald Reagan on the occasion of 'Food for Peace Day', 10 July 1984, in *Africa Wireless File*, 7 October 1984.

8. OCDE, *Les Échanges mondiaux de céréales, quel rôle pour les pays en développement?* (Paris: OECD, 1993); and *Courrier de la Planète* 22, April–May 1994.

9. *OECD Agricultural Outlook 1999–2004* (Paris: OECD, 1999); and *Agricultural Policies in OECD Countries 1999: Monitoring and Evaluation* (Paris: OECD, 1999).

10. *Le Monde*, 20 December 1992.

11. See Sophie Bessis, *La Faim dans le monde* (Paris: La Découverte, 1991). These subsidies were reduced after several European NGOs waged a campaign against them in 1993. The devaluation of the CFA franc in January 1994 increased the prices of imports in the franc area, the main destination for African imports of European meat.

12. Kevin Watkins, *Trade Liberalisation as a Threat to Livelihoods* (London: Oxfam, 1996).

13. The group includes Australia, New Zealand, Canada and Hungary from the North, and Brazil, Chile, Colombia, Uruguay, Malaysia, the Philippines and Thailand from the South.

14. A category that no longer includes Hong Kong, Singapore, South Korea and Taiwan, nor the oil-rich emirates of Brunei, Qatar and the United Arab Emirates. The information in this paragraph is taken from World Bank, *Global Economic Prospects and the Developing Countries 1997* (Washington, DC: World Bank, 1997).

15. Canada, France, Germany, Italy, Japan, United Kingdom, United States.

16. CO_2 alone accounts for half of the greenhouse-effect gases discharged into the atmosphere. All these figures are taken from UNDP, *Human Development Report*, various years (New York: Oxford University Press); World Bank, *Poverty, World Development Indicators: World Development Report 1990* (Washington, DC: World Bank, 1990); World Bank, *World*

Development Indicators 1998; OECD, *Statistical Compendium 1997* (Paris: OECD, 1997); Jacques Valier and Pierre Salama, *Pauvretés et inégalités dans le tiers monde* (Paris: La Découverte, 1994); Sophie Bessis, 'De la pauvreté des États à celle des individus', in Claire Brisset, ed., *Pauvretés* (Paris: Hachette, 1996).

17. Report at the World Water Conference, Paris, March 1998.

18. Noting that the financial crisis of 1997 had a devastating impact on nearly all the countries of Southeast Asia, and that Latin America also saw its social indicators worsen from 1997, the World Bank concludes that no significant reduction in poverty should be expected in the South over the next twenty years. World Bank, *Global Economic Prospects and the Developing Countries, 2000* (Washington, DC: World Bank, December 1999).

19. It might be objected that the United States has almost returned to full employment. But, without denying the dynamism of the American economy, there are at least three reasons to consider its full employment partly fictitious: the size of its prison population, which grew by an annual average of 8 per cent during the 1990s and currently keeps nearly 2 million adults out of the labour market (Loïc Wacquant, 'L'emprisonnement des classes dangereuses aux États-Unis', *Le Monde diplomatique*, July 1998); the splitting of jobs, which artificially reduces unemployment by raising the number of part-timers; and the fact that more than 7 million unemployed do not appear in the statistics and 4.5 million Americans working part-time would prefer to be working full-time. Lester Thurow, 'Le capitalisme a-t-il un avenir?', *Politique internationale* 81, Autumn 1998.

20. Between 1990 and 1995, the waste discharged in Brazil increased by 20 per cent, in China and India by 30 per cent, and in Indonesia by 40 per cent. In the last few years, however, China has agreed to make a major effort by closing its most highly polluting coal-fired power stations and by adopting clean technologies instead.

21. Deploring the fact that, with its 4 per cent of the world's population, the United States was responsible for 20 per cent of greenhouse gas emissions, Clinton promised to consider bolder measures with a view to planetary stabilization.

22. The terminology of the preamble to the international climate convention.

23. Central Europe and Russia owe it to the socialist period that their type of growth has been the most heavily polluting and the most destructive of natural resources, and that their energy output has been the lowest in the industrial world per unit of production. The recession that hit them in the 1980s did, however, reduce their atmospheric emissions.

24. According to the experts, only a cut in emissions greater than 20 per cent would halt the tendency to global warming.

25. Quoted by *Le Monde*, 26, 27, 28 November 1997. The views of the IPCC serve as the basis for international negotiations.

26. With *sub rosa* support from Japan, one of the world's main consumers of tropical wood, which is hostile to any regulation of the use made of tropical forests.

27. Thus, between 1980 and 1995, South Korea recorded an 18 per cent fall

in the GDP-weighted intensity of its emissions – an effort equivalent to that of more developed countries in the region (21 per cent in Japan and 16 per cent in Australia – see OECD, *Statistical Compendium 1997*). Provided that it is given some meaningful content, the notion of sustainable development could reconcile the demand for a better life with the minimum growth necessary to achieve it. The countries of the South would have everything to gain in the long term if they spurned the dominant model and struck out along different (less socially and ecologically destructive) paths. We know the huge ecological cost that the countries of Southeast Asia paid to achieve growth rates that the rest of the world envied for two decades: near-total destruction of Thailand's forest cover, soil exhaustion resulting from intensively produced export crops such as manioc in Thailand, and serious urban pollution due to adoption of the Western models of transport and urban spatial organization. It would also be necessary for others not to stand in the way. For although the countries of the North offer words of encouragement, of course they do not change any of the criteria that force the South to pursue its exhausting race to copy and catch up.

28. Of course I am speaking here only of voluntary migration; the reasons are different in the case of forced movements of population resulting from war or other disasters.

29. This all-too-famous formulation comes from the lips of Michel Rocard, former prime minister of France. He did, it is true, add that France should take its share – a qualification that people usually do him the injustice of forgetting.

30. The Turkish presence in Germany is similarly part of that country's history. Of course Germany never colonized Turkey, but its close links with the Porte at the time of the alliance of the Central Powers, and the importance of German economic interests in post-Ottoman Turkey, explain why it has been the main destination for Turkish migrants.

31. This expression is borrowed from an open letter that a reader sent a few years ago to the Algerian daily *El Watan* (9 May 1994). She had wanted to spend her holidays with a *pied noir* girl-friend, but her request for a French visa was inexplicably turned down. She therefore politely recalled that, although each nation had the right to choose whom it wished to receive, the French had 'a visa-free presence in her own nation for more than a hundred and thirty years'.

32. Lomé 2000, 'Première contribution française au débat UE/ACP', March 1997, official document.

33. Gildas Simon, 'Les mouvements de populations aujourd'hui', in Philippe Dewitte, ed., *Immigration et intégration, l'état des savoirs* (Paris: La Découverte, 1999).

34. Michèle Tribalat, 'Les immigrés et les populations liées à leur installation en France au recensement de 1990', *Population* 6 (Paris: INED, 1993).

35. According to official INSEE statistics based on the 1990 census, 55 per cent of immigrants in France were of European origin at the beginning of the 1990s. INSEE understands by immigrant 'any person, even French,

born a foreigner in a foreign country and now living in France'. According to an interior ministry report on 'residence permits for foreigners in 1998' (cited in *Le Monde*, 17 December 1999), 38 per cent of holders of a residence permit at that time were nationals of an EU country, 36 per cent were from North Africa, 7 per cent from Asia and 6 per cent from sub-Saharan Africa.

36. OECD, *International Trends in Migration*, annual report, 1997 (Paris: OECD, 1998); United Nations Population Division, *Trends in Total Migrant Stock* (New York: UN, 1998). The figures may vary slightly from source to source, but this does not affect the orders of magnitude. Europeans and Canadians represent 22 per cent of the total foreign population resident in the United States.

37. OECD, *International Trends in Migration*, 1997, 1998 and 1999 reports.

38. In France the official number of new residents fell from 135,000 in 1992 (including 90,000 non-Europeans) to 68,000 in 1995 (including 52,000 non-Europeans) – according to figures of the Population and Migration Directorate of the Ministry for Social Affairs.

39. OECD, *International Trends in Migration*.

40. Through their declarations and resulting effects, which track the electoral performance of the far right, European leaders tend to legitimate its xenophobic discourse. The left occupies a frontline position in this respect. In Denmark, for example, where (mainly European) foreigners make up all of 5 per cent of the total population, the social-democratic party has repeatedly hardened its legislation on immigration in order to woo electors receptive to xenophobic ideas. As to France, in 1979 the Communist Party leadership adopted a resolution in support of immigration curbs; in the mid-1980s former Socialist prime minister Laurent Fabius argued that the Front National asked 'good questions'; in 1990 François Mitterrand legitimated the concept of a 'threshold of tolerance'; in the 1990s, during her term as Socialist prime minister, Édith Cresson backed the idea of 'charter flights' for immigrants; and in 1998 Socialist interior minister Jean-Pierre Chevènement accused those who defended the cause of undocumented immigrants of being 'a godsend for the Front National'. Actually, all in their different ways made the FN's arguments seem perfectly normal, and the rejection of foreigners justifiable to a large section of the public.

41. The first Immigration Act, adopted in 1884, drastically curtailed Catholic immigration and virtually ended new arrivals of Chinese. In 1921 the Quota Act also favoured Anglo-Saxon immigration. After 1948 the system of ethnic quotas was relaxed, but today it is gaining a new lease of life.

42. *Le Monde*, 5 April 1996 and 21 February 1997. The number climbed back up around 150,000 in 1999, after the French government had realized the negative impact of this form of temporary residence control on its economic relations with Algeria.

43. Lebon Report of the Direction de la population et des migrations au ministère des Affaires sociales, *Immigration et présence étrangère en France 1995–1996* (Paris: La Documentation française, 1996).

44. 'We should no longer be so timid with foreign criminals that we catch', he said in 1997. 'There is only one solution for anyone who abuses our hospitality: out, and out fast' (*Le Monde*, 28 January 1999).
45. 'L'Amérique immigrée', *Le Monde*, 23 May 1994.
46. Figures of the French Office for Refugees and Stateless Persons (OFPRA).
47. *Le Monde*, 27 February 1996.

Chapter 9

1. The emergent countries rank higher than developing countries in the hierarchy that is supposed to lead to 'developed' status. It is the development of their trade, that noble art of economics, which has given them international recognition, if not actual acceptance.
2. World Bank, *The Asian Miracle: Economic Growth and Public Policy, World Bank Policy Research Report* (New York: Oxford University Press, 1993).
3. Singapore, Hong Kong, South Korea and Taiwan.
4. The figures in this paragraph are taken from World Bank, *Global Economic Prospects and the Developing Countries 1997* (Washington, DC: World Bank, 1997).
5. In the 1990s the IMF, World Bank and UNDP adopted this very different way of comparing the performance of countries around the world. The above forecasts, like those of the World Bank, obviously predate the crisis that plunged the Asian economies, bar China, into recession in the final years of the century. But overall, according to the dominant criteria that systematically underestimate the social impact of such crises, these economies look set to resume the path of growth in the early twenty-first century. The World Bank (*Global Economic Prospects*) estimates that the five most seriously affected countries – Indonesia, Malaysia, Philippines, South Korea and Thailand – should experience growth of 5.2 per cent a year between 1999 and 2008.
6. According to IMF and OECD projections, tomorrow's major powers will be the United States, the European Union, Japan, China, India, Russia and Brazil. But already in 1992, the hierarchy of world powers based on purchasing power parity placed China second and India fifth, ahead of France in sixth place. See Angus Maddison, *Monitoring the World Economy, 1820–1992* (Paris: OECD, 1995).
7. Ibid.
8. The number of patent applications per 10,000 inhabitants measures this inventiveness coefficient. South Korea comes immediately after Japan, with 13.2 applications per 10,000 inhabitants in 1995 (World Intellectual Property Organization figures, quoted from *L'Expansion* 548, 30 April–14 May 1997).
9. The term widely used for subcontracting factories set up along the Mexican side of the border by US corporations, which are thus able to profit from Mexico's cheap labour and less strict social and environmental policies.
10. China is now the world's number one producer of toys.

11. Or two-thirds according to older exchange-rate calculations.

12. World Bank, *World Development Indicators 1999* (Washington, DC: World Bank, 1999).

13. World Bank, *World Development Report 1995: Workers in an Integrating World* (Washington, DC: World Bank, 1995).

14. *Fortune Global 500*, quoted in Michel Beaud, *Le Basculement du monde* (Paris: La Découverte, 1997).

15. *Le Monde*, 21 October 1999. The mergers currently reshaping this sector mean that the number of biotechnology giants is rapidly declining.

16. In the case of the United States, the rates of return on investment in the South rose to 14 per cent in 1997, compared with an average of 12.3 per cent for American overseas investments as a whole. The regional breakdown was 25.3 per cent in Africa (not including South Africa), 16.2 per cent in Asia and the Pacific, and 12.5 per cent in Latin America and the Caribbean. UNCTAD, *Foreign Direct Investment in Africa: Performance and Potential* (New York/Geneva: UNCTAD, 1999).

17. In current European and American parlance, competition from the South is always 'unfair'. On the other hand, the North's own competitive thrust always appears as a just response to this unfairness or as legitimate defence of national interests, whatever these may be.

18. See Jean Arthuis, *Les Délocalisations et l'Emploi* (Paris: Éditions d'Organisation, 1993). In 1994 another parliamentary report, drafted by the deputy Willy Dimeglio, was much less critical of relocation and advocated faster integration of the Maghreb and the ECECs into the European economy. But this study did not have the same resonance as the Arthuis report.

19. World Bank, *World Development Indicators 1999*.

20. World Bank, *World Development Report 1995*.

21. Paul Krugman, *Pop Internationalism* (Cambridge, MA: MIT Press, 1996). This figure may be set beside the six million jobs created by the United States in the service sector between 1970 and 1990 (World Bank, *Human Development Report 1995*).

22. L'Observatoire européen du textile et de l'habillement, quoted in *Le Monde*, 31 August 1999.

23. OECD, *Economic Prospects 1997* (Paris: OECD, 1997).

24. WTO statistics.

25. Morgan Stanley bank, quoted in *Jeune Afrique* 2021, 5 October 1999.

26. The percentages refer to purchasing power parity (World Bank, *World Development Indicators* 1997 and 1999).

27. It is well known that for twenty years Western Europe has had the highest unemployment rates in the developed world, while Japan joined the cycle of recession and unemployment somewhat later, and the United States has had since the early 1990s the OECD's highest rate of employment of the active population.

28. It has been estimated that, from 1971 to 1994, industrial production grew by an annual average of 2.5 per cent in the most advanced economies and by 3.1 per cent per wage-earner. 'La mondialisation est-elle inévitable?', *Le Monde diplomatique*, June 1997.

29. In the United States, according to an opinion survey carried out in 1999, only 16 per cent of decision-makers thought that economic competition from the low-wage countries posed a threat to their country – as opposed to 40 per cent of the public at large. The disparity between these two figures gives some idea of the way in which public opinion has been conditioned on this issue, but it also reveals the gap between the elite that profits from such changes and the section of the population that sees itself as their victim. Chicago Council of Foreign Relations, quoted in *Jeune Afrique* 2008, 6–12 July 1999.

30. Jean-Louis Margolin, 'Mondialisation et histoire: une esquisse', in GEMDEV (Groupement d'Intérêt Scientifique Economie mondiale, Tiers-Monde, Développement), *Mondialisation, les mots et les choses* (Paris: Karthala, 1999).

31. *Le Monde diplomatique*, June 1997.

32. Ibid.

33. *La otra bolsa de valores* (Mexico City) 37, September 1996.

34. *Le Monde*, 17 December 1999.

35. Like his colleagues in other developed countries, he was not short of pretexts. The public authorities in France continue to wave on the development of agricultural sectors responsible for the greatest pollution, such as industrial pig-breeding, and to shoulder the financial costs of the resulting damage to the environment. In January 2000, they refused to impose speed controls on motor vehicles as part of the fight against the greenhouse effect. In both cases, it is hard to see that the forces of globalization were issuing them with any diktat.

36. *Le Monde*, 21 November 1999.

37. World Bank, *World Development Indicators*.

38. *La Chronique d'Amnesty*, monthly bulletin of the French section of Amnesty International, July–August 1999.

39. Ibid.

40. See his *Le Basculement du monde*.

41. Brazil, for example, has effective legal instruments to combat the pillage of the Amazonian forest by timber multinationals. But, while the authorities make plentiful use of ecologically correct language, none of the 2,500 sawmills operating in Amazonia is officially recognized, and almost none respects the legal norms for felling trees. See FAO, *State of the World's Forests* (Rome: FAO, 1997); and Association Agir Ici, *Du bois et des forêts* (Paris, 1998).

42. The World Bank made itself the spokesman for this trend when it devoted the whole of its 1997 *Human Development Report* to the role of the state in meeting the challenges of globalization.

43. This term has certainly been overused in recent years. Civil societies are also heterogeneous, and their constituent organizations represent various social layers and interests. Associations grouped under this name do, however, affirm a power of speech that was long monopolized by official institutions.

44. In June 1999, at an international conference in Paris involving civil move-

ments from eighty countries – organized by the International Movement for Democratic Control of Financial Markets and Their Institutions (also known as ATTAC, from the initials of its French component) – a Cuban representative received an ovation when his condemnation of the United States struck the audience as more legitimate than condemnation of the Castro regime. In part of what is still called the far left, the demand for international egalitarian democracy does not prevent sympathy for authoritarian regimes, provided that these can be described as anti-imperialist. This brings it closer to many leaders in the South, who also campaign for a kind of democracy of nations yet seek to maintain their own authoritarian constructions.

45. Both currents reject the very existence of the WTO, without pausing to contest the criteria upon which its arbitrating role is based. It matters little to them that this institution defends a multilateralism which is less crushing for the weak than the unilateralism of the rich and powerful (especially its clear-cut American form); or that the WTO's agency for the settlement of disputes has several times found against the United States, especially in connection with fiscal subsidies for exports. There is now an important divide between those who simply write off the WTO and those who advocate a radical change in its regulatory approach.

46. After a period of 'jobless growth' in the United States in the early 1990s, the 'new economy' is now producing in both Europe and North America large numbers of 'working poor' whose job insecurity and very low wages deny them what is considered a decent standard of living in their own country. It is not only, or no longer only, unemployment which is extending the frontiers of poverty; another factor is the low pay given to ever broader categories of employees.

47. These ad hoc alliances showed how effective they could be in December 1999, when the combined pressure of governments in the South and NGOs based in both North and South helped to scupper the WTO conference in Seattle. But, whereas the official representatives of the South are waging a vigorous offensive to exclude any social or environmental clauses from the regulation of world trade, the NGOs campaign for a less unbearable world and for rules that will limit the exploitation of popular layers in the South as well as the North. In the euphoria of victory, no one wished to highlight the ambiguity of an actually rather fragile solidarity. Exposure of this ambiguity has gradually come from part of the associative movement in the South, which must at one and the same time combat both the global injustices that aggravate local inequality and the local inequalities themselves, whose causes are by no means only external.

48. The expression is borrowed from Susan George, *Debt Boomerang* (London: Pluto Press, 1992).

49. An 'alternative globalization' would not be incompatible with a heightened emphasis on territorial space, which might indeed reverse the trend to marginalization of whole regions of the globe that the present economic system casts outside the 'useful' world. The local economy and regional trade are today endangered, if not already ruined, by the rapid fall in

transport costs over the past twenty years. Between 1984 and 1992, the cost of air freight fell by 20 per cent and that of sea cargo by 30 per cent, while the price of an air ticket declined by 50 per cent. This essential aspect of globalization is never mentioned by some of its most virulent opponents. Of course they attack Boeing, as one emblem of multinational capitalism, but they are happy to be able to travel cheaply to the four corners of the earth. A rise in transport prices, involving, among other things, internalization of environmental costs, would breathe fresh life into local trade by revealing the artificially constructed character of the competitiveness of many goods imported over a long distance.

Part III Introduction

1. At the UN population conference in 1994 in Cairo and the conference on women in 1995 in Beijing, a veritable holy alliance was constituted between the Holy See and the Islamic states (Saudi Arabia, Iran, Pakistan and Sudan – although Riyadh did not think it useful to travel to Beijing), in order to block any significant advance in the social and legal status of women and to gain international recognition of the legitimacy of a religious presence in the social field. The NGO forums that were held in parallel saw the formation of a kind of International of Islamicist and fundamentalist Protestant and Catholic associations, with considerable resources at its disposal. Far from being merely ad hoc convergences, these *rapprochements* correspond to a new strategic conception. See Sophie Bessis, 'Les nouveaux enjeux et les nouveaux acteurs des débats internationaux dans les années quatre-vingt-dix', *Revue Tiers Monde* 151, July–September 1997 (Paris: PUF).

Chapter 10

1. During a visit to France by Chinese premier Zhu Rongji, his French counterpart Lionel Jospin publicly welcomed the 'open attitude' of the Chinese government and 'its unquestionable determination to promote the rule of law in China' (*Le Monde*, 8 April 1998). The United States, for its part, never hesitates for long before the periodical renewal of the most favoured nation clause governing its trade with China.

2. In 1993 I myself had occasion to witness a grotesque display of double standards. The UN secretary-general had invited to a world conference on human rights in Vienna a list of Nobel peace prizewinners that included the Dalai Lama and the Guatemalan Rigoberta Menchú, defender of the rights of Central American Indians. When the Chinese and Guatemalan governments then protested with equal energy against this presumptuous honouring of sworn enemies of their respective states, UN officials sheepishly barred the Dalai Lama from attending, while Rigoberta Menchú was able to give her scheduled speech to delegates.

3. The reader will, I hope, forgive here a major oversimplification of the play of interests. Let us simply add, for indicative purposes, that the Western states do not always present a united front and that their rivalries can even lead them to adopt distinct positions. Thus, Washington exposes Castro's Cuba to public contempt, whereas countries such as France or Spain treat it much more gently. According to time and place, discordant notes can be heard on both sides of the Atlantic, but not in relation to the essential point: the use of double standards as a systematic policy.

4. Between 1980 and 1989, total arms sales to Iraq exceeded $25 billion (in 1985 values). A third of these came from Western countries, France being the country's second supplier after the USSR (SIPRI, Solna, Sweden, 1990). The United States gave Baghdad important technical assistance and a good deal of military information, and from 1985 to 1989 sold it electronic equipment to the value of more than $1.5 billion. See Alain Gresh and Dominique Vidal, *Golfe. Clefs pour une guerre annoncée* (Paris: Le Monde Éditions, 1991).

5. In France Jean-Pierre Chevènement, who never loses an opportunity to proclaim the secular character of Arab nationalism, is an eager propagator of this fiction. Nor is he the only one. The Ligue française de l'enseigne-ment, a popular education movement noted for its secularism, included Iraq and Syria among the family of 'republics that are secular but not democratic', as opposed to 'genuine democracies that have not chosen secularism' (Germany). See the League's monthly *Les Idées en mouvement*, supplement to no. 58, April 1998.

6. In 1989, to increase his popularity in the most conservative sections of Iraqi society at a moment when Iran was scoring successive victories, the man seen in the West as an Arab champion of secular modernity had a law passed which removed penal sanctions for the 'crime of honour': that is, the murder of a female relative suspected of adultery or even of improper attitudes.

7. See, for example, Amnesty International, *Torture and Executions in Iraq: Summary of Amnesty International's Concerns* (London, June 1986).

8. To strengthen this analogy, the chancelleries of the West spread (and the media amplified) the story that the Iraqi army was 'fourth in the world'; the sequel showed how much truth there was in that. In 1998, attempts by UN secretary-general Kofi Annan to prevent another military intervention against an Iraq already bled dry by a seven-year embargo reminded US senator Jesse Helms of 'Neville Chamberlain's capitulation to Hitler at Munich in 1938' (quoted in *Le Monde*, 6 March 1998). Saddam Hussein was not the first Arab leader to be compared to the Nazi Führer: in 1956 British and French leaders spoke of Nasser in the same way. On the American tradition of demonizing the enemy, see Michael Rogin's essay collection *Ronald Reagan the Movie, and Other Episodes in Political Demon-ology* (Berkeley: University of California Press, 1987).

9. The list of unpunished violations of international law is not limited to the Middle East. The United States has a long record of doing the same, especially in its American and Caribbean backyard – witness its armed

interventions in Grenada in 1983 and Panama in 1989, neither with a UN mandate. Actual annexation is rather rarer, though, Israel's territorial conquests and Iraq's occupation of Kuwait being two examples. During the Gulf crisis, Saddam Hussein constantly pointed up the analogy and was well aware that Arab public opinion highly appreciated any denunciation of the indulgent international attitude to Israel.

10. Most of the Islamicist movements in Arab countries with a Sunni majority were under no illusion. Having previously shown allegiance to Saudi Arabia – which gave them generous hand-outs and saw them as the best antidote to Shiite radicalism – they changed their position at the beginning of the Gulf crisis and sided with Iraq. Anxious not to cut themselves off from their popular base, the Islamic Salvation Front (FIS) in Algeria and the Ennahda party in Tunisia, among others, became enthusiastic proponents of the Iraqi position as early as August 1990.

11. Western, and especially American, motives in the Gulf War were certainly more complex than this binary opposition would suggest. One might also include the wish of the United States to find another Satan after the collapse of the Soviet Union, or to inaugurate in a spectacular way the world imperium that it now intended to exercise. But law and war were still the key issues, as American leaders confirmed on a number of occasions. See Lawrence Freedman and Efraim Karsh, *The Gulf Conflict, 1990–1991* (Princeton: Princeton University Press, 1993).

12. At the time, the Moroccan poet Abdellatif Laabi refused to choose 'between the plague of Western power interests and supposedly virtuous warmongering, and the cholera of Iraqi leadership interests clothed in a false messianism of emancipation and justice'. *Jeune Afrique* 1561, 28 November 1990.

13. The gradual shift from defence of 'principles' to defence of 'values' was not insignificant: the former refer to laws with a general application, whereas the latter are more tied to particular contexts. By championing values, even universal ones, the Western democracies seemed to imply that it was their own values which they wished to see prevail.

14. The dangers of humanitarian instrumentalization have been the object of numerous analyses, especially in France, where the 'without frontiers' ideology has had much success. See, for example, Jean-Christophe Rufin, *Le Piège humanitaire* (Paris: Hachette Pluriel, 1993); and Rony Brauman, *Humanitaire, le dilemme* (Paris: Textuel, 1996).

15. 'A Good Idea, But Not For Americans', *International Herald Tribune*, 20 July 1998. American objections to the treaty, it concluded, were based on 'the idea that American troops always do what is right'.

16. This idea is so customary that it triggers a kind of automatic verbal reflex. In 1998, when the self-satisfied Republic managed to commemorate the 150th anniversary of the abolition of slavery almost without mentioning the centuries during which France had permitted it, the commonplace observations on this score were especially plentiful. As a matter of fact, colonial memories are never far from the motivations of the new missionaries for Good, even when they seek to distance themselves from the past.

Thus, in the late 1980s Bernard Kouchner called upon young people in Europe to spend a period doing voluntary work in the third world, not only out of solidarity but because their 'continent was lacking in adventure and dreams'. He continued: 'We prefer to work and live for a while beside and with the world's poorest, far from the official aid agencies; to discover a place where there is not yet a Social Security to take over the weight of risk and the taste for dream.' Bernard Kouchner, *Charité Business* (Paris: Le Pré-aux-Clercs, 1986). Still, from the foreign legionary to the voluntary worker, there is some progress…

17. Daniel Cohn-Bendit, 'L'Europe imite l'Amérique? Inventons le contraire!', *Le Monde*, 6–7 June 1999.

18. The dismantling of the Soviet Union and its European buffer zone has brought this chaos closer to the West, as the wars in the former Yugoslavia since the early 1990s have repeatedly shown. If I have not mentioned these before, it is because of the ambivalent status of the Balkans, in Europe but not fully of it, which is illustrated by the EU's special treatment of immigrants from that region. Its geographical proximity to the 'real' Europe and its position at a geopolitical crossroads mean that Western governments cannot entirely ignore it, while the European public is more sensitive to the horrors committed among its neighbours. At once Catholic, Orthodox and Muslim, protodemocratic and dictatorial, extremely nationalist and an Eastern pendant to the myth of Andalusia, it is at one and the same time in the South, the North and the East. This unclassifiable quality partly explains the inconsistencies of Western Europe's Balkan policy since the end of the cold war.

19. Western governments allowed Tanzania to invade Uganda in 1979 to end the bloody rule of Idi Amin Dada. But the United States never accepted the Vietnamese action in 1978 to drive the Khmer Rouge from power in Cambodia, and continued to back them until the end of the cold war. Since the early 1990s, Europeans and Americans have been trying to regionalize political intervention in parts of the world where they have no direct interests; they have urged the Organization of African Unity, for example, to establish a force capable of handling conflicts in the continent.

Chapter 11

1. Quoted in Benjamin Stora, *Histoire de l'Algérie coloniale 1830–1954* (Paris: La Découverte, 1991).

2. Ibid.

3. The 1998 edition of the Haut Conseil à l'Intégration noted: 'Coloured French people, especially those from overseas or of non-European origin, are victims of discrimination in conditions almost comparable to those which affect foreigners.' In this connection, one is struck by the political blindness of the parties of the left, none of which has ever presented a candidate with immigrant origins in any elections where there was a reasonable chance of winning – the only exception being the Franco-

Togolese Socialist Kofi Yamgnane. Though always ready to give lessons in civic spirit to marginalized groups of African–Maghreb origin, these parties have shown themselves incapable of translating their integration rhetoric into action, so that some 5 per cent of the French population is left without representation.

4. Cornélius Castoriadis, 'Les racines psychiques et sociales de la haine', in *Figures du pensable* (Paris: Seuil, 1999). For Castoriadis, this non-convertibility is the 'decisive hallmark of racism'.

5. Whereas, in 1950, the 732 million inhabitants of Europe, North America and developed Oceania made up nearly 30 per cent of the total world population, the figure (at 1,064 million) was already down to 18 per cent by 1998 and is expected to be around 11.9 per cent by 2050 (with a total 1,066 million, almost unchanged over half a century). *World Population Estimates and Projections, 1998 Revision* (New York: United Nations Population Division, 1998).

6. Christine Inglis, *Multiculturalism: New Policy Responses to Diversity*, Most/Unesco policy paper 4 (Paris: Unesco, 1996).

7. This is the object of lively debate within the European Union. Some refuse to accept the idea of Turkish membership, on the justifiable grounds that it should first give proof of its democratic transformation by ceasing to trample on the rights of individuals and minorities; while others motivate their refusal more by cultural and religious considerations, ruling out any Muslim transplant into an area marked by its Christian culture. The German Christian Democrats, in particular, have become firm defenders of this latter thesis.

8. One example among so many others is a pair of contrasting images found in a recent edition of a historical atlas, where European conquests are surrounded with a highly positive aura, while others are said to have been impelled by the basest instincts. The chapter on 'the Arab Empire' starts by telling us: 'When Muhammad died in 632, the conquests began. There were many reasons for this: bellicose customs, the Prophet's teachings, also plain cupidity.' The chapter on 'the great discoveries and the fifteenth-century colonial empires', however, opens as follows: 'Intellectual progress and technical inventions, sometimes due to the East …, partly explain the momentum behind the discoveries. But the crusading, geographical curiosity, commercial ambition and chance should also be taken into account.' *Grand Atlas Bordas* (Paris: Bordas, 1991). These two judgements show the degree of bias in the way that Westerners – in this case, French – perceive others.

9. Huntington's original article appeared in Foreign Affairs in summer 1993 and was followed by his book *The Clash of Civilizations and the Remaking of World Order* (New York: Simon & Schuster, 1995).

10. Fukuyama's famous article 'The End of History?' appeared in the Summer 1989 issue of *The National Interest*, and was followed by the book-length *The End of History and the Last Man* (New York: Free Press, 1992). In this caricatural version of the Western culture of supremacy, only the adventures of the West are supposed to give a meaning to world history.

Once victory over the communist dragon has, as in a fairy-tale, rounded off the adventures, history too comes to the end of its course – just as one closes a book after the end of the story. The world itself has no place in the tale.

11. In Huntington's view, Islam and Confucianism also have in common the fact that they are religion-philosophies less receptive to democracy than is Catholicism or (its chosen soil) Protestantism.

12. Achour Ouamara, *Oublier la France, confession d'un algérien* (La Tour d'Aigues: L'Aube, 1997).

13. In an editorial in the French weekly *Le Point* (31 January 1998), rather abruptly entitled 'Algiers: absolute evil', its director Claude Imbert maintained that 'the fundamentalist disease is part of Islam, let us say of its "family album".' But although he mentions a few of the massacres committed in the name of church and civilization, he does not say whether they are similarly inseparable from the deep core of Christianity or the West.

14. Several typologies of Islamicist movements have been attempted since researchers began to take a close interest in them. Here I borrow the one used by Jean Leca, who distinguishes between conservative and radical Islamicists and further divides the latter into two groups: 'Islamic democrats', who in principle favour pluralism, and 'revolutionary Islamicists', who are against it. See Jean Leca, 'La démocratisation dans le monde arabe: incertitude, vulnérabilité et légitimité', in Ghassan Salamé, ed., *Démocraties sans démocrates. Politiques d'ouverture dans le monde arabe et islamique* (Paris: Fayard, 1994).

15. This is not the case with other fundamentalisms, such as Hindu radicalism, which, though raised in the same mould, belongs exclusively to one cultural area and limits its harmful actions to the subcontinent alone.

16. And as it still is there today. In the new great game in relation to Central Asia, which has oil as one of its main stakes, the Taliban can still be useful to the United States, even if they continue to house the number one enemy of the day, Osama bin Laden. Trained in the school of the Saudi secret services, whose links with their American counterparts are well known, this Islamicist long served Washington's designs before becoming the chief orchestrator of the anti-Western jihad.

17. The complex question of the links between terrorist movements and groups pursuing a legal road to power has aroused intense passions since the emergence of Muslim radicalism in the late 1970s and the Algerian slide into violence in the 1990s. Originating in the same ideological matrix, fighting with the same conviction for an Islamic state, they have often constituted two sides of the same Islamicist coin, the former serving more than once as the armed wing of the latter. Strategic and political divergences have not ceased to exist, however, between these two aspects of a radical Islamicism whose vicissitudes have to be placed within a long-term context. Blanket criminalization of Islamicism has delayed a further deepening of this split, which is partly shaping the political future of many Arab and Muslim countries. For, paradoxically, acceptance of

consciously Islamic groups into the field of legal politics is one of the conditions for democratization and for an evolution in the status of religion in those countries.

18. Article by C. Hollingworth, in *International Herald Tribune* (9 September 1993), which compared the Islamicist danger to inter-war fascism and Nazism and to communism in the 1950s.

19. Jean-Marie Colombani, 'L'année de la mondialisation', *Le Monde*, 11 January 1997. This four-column article used the word 'Islamicist' or 'Islamicism' eight times, but did not so much as mention for the record such major issues as the world rise of fundamentalist movements or the worsening of global inequalities. Such obsessive repetition illustrates the role given to a phenomenon which, though certainly very important, is far from monopolizing the world geopolitical arena.

20. Ibid.

21. SOFRES survey conducted in December 1999 at the request of the defence committee of the National Assembly; quoted from *Le Figaro*, 12 February 2000. In 1994 an IFOP survey showed that, for 37 per cent of respondents, the word 'fanaticism' best corresponded to their image of Islam, and that 67 per cent thought it one of the three terms (along with 'submission' and 'rejection of Western values') that best described Islam. *Le Monde*, 13 October 1994.

22. Alain Finkielkraut, *The Defeat of the Mind* (New York: Columbia University Press, 1996).

23. In France, the Napoleonic Code was one of the monuments of modern misogyny and paternal omnipotence, whose last traces did not disappear until the 1970s. It is also well known that until the 1960s a Mediterranean country such as Catholic Italy recognized extenuating circumstances for men who committed 'crimes of honour' against female members of their family.

24. This overloading of the boat is not peculiar to Westerners. In an essay on the expansion of Islam (*Beyond Belief: Islamic Excursions among the Converted Peoples* [London: Little, Brown, 1998]), the Indian–Trinidadian–British writer V.S. Naipaul makes it the only factor in the brutality of feudal customs in Pakistan, the archaism of its social structures, and the terrible fate reserved for women. Although his work seeks out everywhere traces of a long history, Naipaul does not in this case consider social and economic traditions prior to the country's creation, and makes no comparison with the situation in India. Only Islam is held responsible for the undoubtedly real evils in Pakistan.

25. Claude Lévi-Strauss, *Tristes Tropiques* (Paris: Plon, 1973); *Tristes Tropiques* (Harmondsworth: Penguin, 1976).

26. Quotation from Helen Perterson, who is presented in one of the museum brochures as a member of the Oglala Lakota tribe.

27. Because it is self-absolution, this semi-recognition has no trouble coexisting with denial of the other. Thus, the history told today of so-called Latin America continues to exclude the Indians; its recognized actors are descendants of the conquistadors, who are alone supposed to represent

the fate of the sub-continent. Examples of this expulsion are legion. In the same vein, it is useful to read the pitiless denunciation of indigenist literature by the Peruvian writer Mario Vargas Llosa: *La Utopía arcaica. José María Arguedas y las ficciones del indigenismo* (Mexico City: Fondo de Cultura Económica, 1996).

28. Bernard Guetta, 'Les islamistes et la démocratie', *Le Monde*, 14 September 1999.

29. Véronique Nahoum-Grappe, 'Algérie: sang et brouillard', *Chimères*, 1997.

30. Refusal to recognize Arabic-speaking members of the Islamicist movement as intellectuals prevented a whole section of the French intelligentsia from understanding the genesis of Algerian Islamicism, and therefore from combating it with arguments less primitive than the ones it used itself.

31. 'Le soulagement de la Kabylie démocrate', *Le Monde*, 19 January 1992.

32. *Le Nouvel Observateur*, 2–8 July 1998.

33. *Le Nouvel Observateur*, 19–25 January 1995.

34. *Libération*, 1 March 1991.

35. *Le Point*, 2 April 1994. It seems surprising that, as an example of obscurantism, this journalist chose the dazzling era of the Umayyad dynasty that historians see as the beginning of the Arab golden age. If he had wanted to remain with the Maghreb, he could have chosen the Berber dynasty of the Almohads that distinguished itself in the twelfth to thirteenth centuries by its religious intolerance. But, assuming he knew of its existence, it is clear that fanaticism must always be Arab rather than Berber.

36. *Courrier international* 179, 7–15 April 1994 (reprinted in the weekly *Algérie Actualité*).

37. *Le Nouvel Observateur*, 19–25 January 1995.

38. In several statements and interviews, including on the French radio station RTL in 1994.

39. *Courrier international* 179, 7–15 April 1994 (interview with Khalida Messaoudi by Malika Boussouf, reprinted in *Le Soir d'Algérie*).

40. *Elle*, 5 December 1994.

41. *Courrier international* 179, 7–15 April 1994.

42. *Le Monde*, 5 March 1998.

43. *Le Monde*, 27 October 1994.

44. Men were almost completely absent from the expressions of protest against the code that women organized in the early 1980s. Between 1980 and 1984 women fought alone against the regime to defend their rights, and they lost. See Sophie Bessis (with Souhayr Belhassen), *Femmes du Maghreb, l'enjeu* (Paris: J.-C. Lattès, 1992).

45. *Le Monde*, 20 April 1994.

46. Henri Tincq, no. 3 in the series 'Les génies du christianisme', *Le Monde*, 15 July 1999.

47. Pierre Lellouche, *Le Nouveau Monde. De l'ordre de Yalta au désordre des nations* (Paris: Grasset, 1992).

48. Statement made by Senator McCain, quoted in *Le Monde*, 17 February 2000.

49. Summary of the fourth consultative meeting for the organization of the Alliance for a Responsible and Solidaristic World (Charles Léopold Meyer Foundation for Human Progress, Paris 1998).

50. *Libération*, 20 April 1998.

51. See, among others, Michel Beaud, *Le Basculement du monde* (Paris: La Découverte, 1997); and GEMDEV (Groupement d'Intérêt Scientifique Economie mondiale, Tiers-Monde, Développement), *Mondialisation, les mots et les choses* (Paris: Karthala, 1999).

52. This anti-Judaism did not spare the Protestant denominations, although they are much closer than Catholicism to the biblical sources of Christianity. Until recently, the Catholic line stemming from the Saint-Sulpice congregation of the seventeenth century expurgated any trace of Judaism from itself. But it is not easy to forget the vicious anti-Judaism of Martin Luther, founder of the Reformation.

53. In all Western literature until recent times, the Jew is one of the incarnations of the Oriental, both in his dress and in his eating habits, and the ghetto is most often described as Eastern flotsam introduced into the heart of the European city. Nearly all anti-Semitic writings propose sending the Jews 'back to Asia' (in Proudhon's words) – when they do not aim at their extermination.

54. On the concept of heritage, the reader may refer to the analysis by the Israeli philosopher Yeshayahu Leibovitz. The old sage has recalled that 'Christianity presents itself ... as inheritor of Judaism – and you can't inherit from someone who isn't dead.' *Le Monde*, 13 October 1992.

55. On the elements of closeness and distance among the three religions, see the different approaches in Roger Arnaldez, *Trois messagers pour un seul Dieu* (Paris: Albin Michel, 1991); Abdesselem Cheddadi, 'L'universel dans les chroniques arabes', in Ali Benmakhlouf, ed., *Routes et déroutes de l'universel* (Casablanca: Éditions Le Fennec, 1997); and Fethi Benslama, 'La répudiation originaire', *Cahiers Intersignes* 13, Autumn 1998 (Paris).

56. The expression began its modern career in the 1920s, when the ultra-conservative ulema of the dying Ottoman Empire saw the marks of a Judeo-Christian plot in the suppression of the caliphate. See Gema Martín Muñoz, *El estado árabe. Crisis de legitimidad y contestación islamista* (Madrid: Bellaterra, 1999).

57. Of course, it was helped in this by the anti-Jewish policy adopted by the Arab countries after the creation of Israel. But that was not the only factor. The general Westernization of the Jewish world was a parallel trend to the gradual emigration of its diasporas to the Western democracies, which – if one includes the state of Israel – then sheltered the great majority of the world Jewish population.

58. To use again the title of Pascal Bruckner's book.

59. The debate on female circumcision is an example of such closure. Some see societies that practise it as illustrations of barbarism, while others defend it in the name of protecting traditions or safeguarding identity. But the symmetry of cultural invariability makes both positions inadmissible. Neither of the two Western camps in question has attempted the

kind of dynamic analysis that would place it in proper perspective, by comparing it with other traditional systems and procedures for the control of female sexuality, and perhaps concluding that every tradition contains unacceptable elements and is condemned to change. Instead, the fight against female circumcision is hijacked by the identity problematic, which precisely excludes any idea of movement. Many African women have for a long time wrongly defended the practice, as a reaction to just such attacks on their society as barbarian.

60. The staunchest supporters of cultural relativism explicitly invite others to protect themselves from the temptation of universality and the tools that it conveys, arguing that these might cause them to lose their purity. The ethnopsychiatrist Françoise Sironi, for instance, accuses 'the concept of "human rights" of serving as a veritable tool of cultural infiltration' and of having 'deculturating effects'. 'L'universalité est-elle une torture?', *Nouvelle Revue d'ethnopsychiatrie* 34, 1994.

61. François Burgat, *L'Islamisme au Maghreb. La voix du Sud* (Paris: Karthala, 1988). The same rhetoric recurs in another work: François Burgat, *L'Islamisme en face* (Paris: La Découverte, 1995), where the author describes Islamicism as 'an ideological repositioning in the South'.

62. In one of the articles justifying his point of view ('Inutile de se soulever?', *Le Monde*, 11 May 1979), Foucault explains this admiration 'for a movement strong enough to overthrow what seemed to be the best-armed of regimes, while remaining close to old dreams that the West once had of writing the figures of spirituality into the ground of politics'.

63. Ten years later, Marc Kravetz recalled 'that revolution which sections of the Western intelligentsia celebrated, sometimes naively, as heralding a new era when spirituality and faith would take their revenge for the ideological bankruptcy of the East and the West.' *Libération*, 11-12 February 1989.

64. Serge July, *Dis maman, c'est quoi l'avant-guerre?* (Paris: Alain Moreau, 1980).

65. Alain Gresh, 'Quand l'islamisme menace le monde', *Le Monde diplomatique*, December 1993.

66. This is true not just in France but also in the USA and Britain, where the literature on political Islam is nevertheless very rich and varied.

67. Jacques Girardon, 'La fin inéluctable d'un régime détesté', *Les Cahiers de L'Express* 29: 'Algérie, de la révolution à l'intégrisme', September 1994.

68. Quoted in *Les Idées en mouvement* 58, April 1998. The motives for veil-wearing are rather more complex, however, and many researchers have attempted to understand what drove so many girls and women to practise it. Social and religious pressure certainly does not explain everything. Its adoption may also signify strategies to find a way out of tradition that are acceptable to the family circle. See Nilüfer Gole, *Musulmanes et modernes* (Paris: La Découverte, 1993); Gema Martín Muñoz, ed., *Mújeres, democracia y desarrollo en el Maghreb* (Madrid: Ed. Pablo Iglesias, 1995); Djedjiga Imache and Inès Nour, *Algériennes entre islam et islamisme* (Aix-en-Provence: Edisud, 1994); Sophie Bessis (with S. Belhassen), *Femmes du*

Maghreb. But Western commentators have never wanted to recognize that the collective identity they glorify is thoroughly sexed.

69. In Michel Wieviorka, ed., *Une société fragmentée?* (Paris: La Découverte, 1996).

70. *Science et Nature*, February 1995. Faced with an outcry, Tobie Nathan said that the journalist who had interviewed him had slightly exaggerated his position, but he did not go back on his views.

71. Seeing psychoanalysis only as a Western science, he pokes fun not only at 'white psychoanalysts' (whom he accuses of wanting to treat 'others' with their culturally specific methods) but, 'more seriously, African psycho-analysts "whitened" in Western universities and institutes who have not received even rudimentary training in traditional therapeutic techniques.' Tobie Nathan, 'L'Afrique n'est pas une terre à conquérir', *Le Monde diplomatique*, October 1989.

72. Tobie Nathan, 'La psychanalyse: nouvel avatar de l'hérésie chrétienne', *Pardès, revue européenne d'études et de culture juive* 27, 1999–2000.

73. In his *Discours sur le colonialisme* (Paris: Présence africaine, 1955), Césaire makes a thorough critique of Father Tempels's *La Philosophie bantoue*, a well-known work of the 1950s: 'Are you going to the Congo? You should respect – I won't say native property (the big Belgian companies might take that personally), I won't say native liberty (the Belgian settlers might think that subversive), and I won't say the Congolese fatherland (the Belgian government might take that seriously amiss) – I'll say, if you are going to the Congo, respect Bantu philosophy!'

74. Jocelyne Cesari, *Faut-il avoir peur de l'Islam?* (Paris: Presses de Sciences Po, 1997).

75. In 1990 the future head of state declared that 'one cannot judge a country's democracy by whether it does or does not have a multiparty system.... There are single-party regimes where democracy is perfectly respected: I am thinking of the Ivory Coast' – where, as a matter of fact, any dissidence was harshly repressed at the time (*Le Monde*, 24 July 1997).

76. Bernard-Henri Lévy, 'Avec Massoud', *Le Monde*, 13 October 1998. This report is a veritable paean to Massoud, compared by turns to Che Guevara and General de Gaulle.

77. To borrow the title of the work by Mahmoud Hussein, *Versant sud de la liberté* (Paris: La Découverte, 1989).

Chapter 12

1. See chapter 3 above.

2. Cheikh Anta Diop, *Nations nègres et culture* (Paris: Présence africaine, 1954). *The African Origin of Civilization: Myth or Reality?* (New York: Lawrence Hill, 1991) is a one-volume translation of major sections of this, Diop's first book, and of his last, *Antériorité des civilisations nègres* (see note 3 below).

3. The title of one of Cheikh Anta Diop's principal works: *Antériorité des*

civilisations nègres: mythe ou vérité historique? (Paris: Présence africaine, 1967).

4. Cheikh Anta Diop, *Civilisation ou barbarie* (Paris: Présence africaine, 1981); *Civilization or Barbarism: An Authentic Anthropology* (New York: Lawrence Hill, 1990). Diop's 'chronological table of the evolution of humanity in general and the black world in particular' illustrates to the point of caricature his commitment to a racial reading of history. The chronology makes 'Cro-Magnon, the prototype of the leucodermic [white] races', appear in –20,000, and 'mesocephaly and brachycephaly' in –10,000. We also learn that in –5,000 'the Semites did not yet exist', and that the period from –4,326 to –750 was marked by 'the supremacy of blacks'. This is a long way from Frantz Fanon, who wrote in the late 1950s: 'I as a man of colour do not have the right to seek to know in what respect my race is superior or inferior to another race.... There is no Negro mission; there is no white burden.... Both must turn their backs on the inhuman voices which were those of their respective ancestors in order that authentic communication be possible' *Black Skin, White Masks* (London: MacGibbon & Kee, 1967).

5. *Civilisation ou barbarie.*

6. One of the main sources of the thesis that Africans discovered America is Ivan Van Sertima, *They Came before Columbus* (New York: Random House, 1976). On the case for a fourteenth-century Mande voyage of discovery, based on a reading of Arab chroniclers, see Muhammad Hamidullah, 'L'Afrique découvre l'Amérique avant Christophe Colomb', *Présence africaine* 17–18, February–May 1958; and Pathé Diagne, 'Du centenaire de la découverte du Nouveau Monde par Bakari II en 1312 et Christoph Colomb en 1492', November 1990, preparatory text for the seminar at the C.A. Diop University in Dakar.

7. One claim is that Aristotle, among others, filched the material for his principal works from the library in Alexandria. Other tales illustrate this theory of theft. On its origins, which have a Masonic inspiration, see Mary R. Lefkowitz and Guy M. Rogers, *Black Athena Revisited* (Chapel Hill: Univerity of North Carolina Press, 1996). A collective work in French – François-Xavier Fauvelle-Aymard, Jean-Pierre Chrétien and Claude-Hélène Perrot, eds, *Afrocentrismes* (Paris: Karthala, 2000) – has the defect of giving no space to any African writer critical of Afrocentrist positions.

8. The Kwanzaa, a kind of African-American New Year, was invented in 1966 by Maulana Karenga, one of the founders of Afrocentrism, and is today observed by more than a million people. The main contemporary theoretician of Afrocentrism is Molefi Asanta, whose work *The Afrocentric Idea* first appeared in 1987 (Philadelphia: Temple University Press). Afrocentrist courses have been introduced in many schools and several universities in the United States.

9. Not all national liberation movements have drawn on this register, and some of their leaders – such as Bourguiba in Tunisia – continually condemned its sterility.

10. Its two main ideologues – Jamal ad-Din al-Afghani and Muhammad Abduh – created the Salafiya (or 'back to the foundations') movement that

fed into the whole of modern Arab–Muslim thought. Not only were its theoreticians the mentors of the Muslim Brotherhood (born in Egypt some forty years after Abduh's death); they exerted a decisive influence throughout the twentieth century upon a large number of nationalist leaders and intellectuals.

11. This term is borrowed from Monique Schneider, *Généalogie du masculin* (Paris: Aubier, 2000).

12. As the Indian–Spanish theologian Raimon Panikkar put it, in *Le Monde*, 2 April 1996.

13. A few countries, such as Tunisia, did not follow the majority and introduced birth-control programmes in the 1960s. In East Asia and the Southern Cone, the transition to a calmer demography also began quite early, unlike in black Africa and the Middle East, where it is only just beginning.

14. 'Une chute effrayante', *Al Ittihad al-Ichtiraki*, 17 March 1991 (quoted in *Panoramiques* 3, 1st quarter, 1992). This diatribe was in reponse to an article in *Le Monde*, which reported fertility rates in the Maghreb in a neutral tone devoid of any 'poisonous racism'.

15. The UN's ten-yearly conferences on world population (Bucharest 1974, Mexico City 1984, Cairo 1994) have long been a theatre for such suspicions that the West is guilty of the worst ulterior motives in its promotion of birth control.

16. In the late 1980s, Kenyan president Daniel Arap Moi advised women not to feed their new-born babies on powdered milk from the North, which, he claimed, contained substances that could make women sterile or even infect with AIDS those who ingested them.

17. Interview with Khalida Messaoudi, in *Courrier international* 179.

18. Souleimane Salah Eddine, 'Hichem Djaït n'a rien compris à l'Algérie', *Jeune Afrique* 1937, 24 February 1998. This researcher was responding to an article by the Tunisian historian Hichem Djaït, who had argued that internal causes were decisive in the emergence of Algerian Islamicism.

19. Raphaël Constant, quoted in Edwy Plenel, 'Voyage avec Colomb', *Le Monde*, 23 August 1991. The Judeo-Christian seam has certainly been worked for all it is worth in connection with the Gulf War. For the Moroccan Mehdi El-Mandjra, it was a 'conflict between the will to hegemony inherent in Judeo-Christian civilization and all other civilizations'. *Première guerre civilisationnelle* (Casablanca: Toubkal, 1992).

20. An editorial written by Béchir Ben Yahmed, in *Jeune Afrique* 1547, 22–28 August 1990.

21. Many intellectuals susceptible to Arab nationalist ideas placed their hopes in the Iraqi dictator. The Tunisian Hichem Djaït, president of a 'national committee in support of Saddam Hussein', kept quiet at the time about his democratic convictions and shouted aloud his admiration for Saddam.

22. Interview with Prince Hassan, in *Jeune Afrique* 1571, 6–12 February 1991.

23. The principal author of this plot was supposed to have been the American financier of Hungarian–Jewish origin, George Soros.

24. An article in the South Korean paper *Chugan Chosun* (quoted in *Courrier international* 476, 16 December 1999).

25. 'À livres ouverts', *Croissance* 396, September 1996.

26. Gilles Manceron and Hassan Remaoun, *D'une rive à l'autre. La guerre d'Algérie de la mémoire à l'histoire* (Paris: Syros, 1993).

27. The concept of the invention of tradition, explored in recent years especially by political sociology, has afforded a better understanding of its metamorphoses, its relationship with a shifting environment, and the external influences that determine its contents. In the field of African studies, one might mention: Jean-Loup Amselle and Elikia M'Bokolo, *Au cœur de l'ethnie* (Paris: La Découverte, 1999); Jean-François Bayart et al., *Le Politique par le bas en Afrique noire* (Paris: Karthala, 1992); Jean-François Bayart, *L'État en Afrique* (Paris: Fayard, 1993).

28. The Indian historian Dipesh Chakrabarty makes European imperialism and third-world nationalism joint architects of the 'universalization of the nation-state as the most desirable form of political community'. 'Post-colonialité et artifice de l'histoire. Qui parle au nom du passé "indien"?', in Mamadou Diouf et al., *L'Historiographie indienne en débat. Colonialisme, nationalisme et sociétés postcoloniales* (Paris–Amsterdam: Karthala–Sepis, 1999).

29. This was not only true in conservative countries such as Morocco. In modernist Tunisia, for example, both the language and the content of the teaching of philosophy were Arabized in the early 1970s, in the hope that this would dry up the soil on which Marxist movements had thrived. A decade or so later, the Islamicists had taken their place in the universities.

30. In the early 1970s, Abdallah Laroui noted in relation to Morocco: 'It is not tradition which expresses itself in this policy, but this policy which recreates a tradition.... Had there been a tradition that the current regime simply unveiled, there would certainly not be three different formulations of that tradition [those of the nineteenth century, of nationalism under the protectorate, and of the present day] from which it is necessary to choose the one closest to tradition.' *Crise des intellectuels arabes. Traditionalisme ou historicisme?* (Paris: Maspero, 1974).

31. Anouar Abdelmalek, *La Dialectique sociale* (Paris: Seuil, 1972). From the Egyptian Abdelmalek to the Moroccan Abdallah Laroui, the Tunisian Hichem Djaït or the Lebanese Georges Corm, many post-colonial modernist intellectuals legitimated the reference to Islam as the foundation of Arab identity.

32. *Le Nouvel Observateur*, 8–14 December 1994. In this dossier, only the two Egyptians who write under the name of Mahmoud Hussein (Adel Rifat and Bahgat Elnadi), the Tunisian Khédija Cherif and the Frenchman of Moroccan origin Adil Jazouli did not feel a need to foreground their Islamic identity or to invoke 'true Islam' against its extremist aberrations.

33. A leaflet distributed by the Lebanese Cultural Forum during the trial of Khalifé.

34. Interview with Rached Ghannouchi, in *Jeune Afrique Plus* 4, January–February 1990.

35. At the international human rights conference in Vienna in June 1993, the head of the Iranian delegation publicly deplored 'the increasing crime and

violence in advanced industrial societies ..., the prostitution and especially child prostitution, the pornography ..., the vulgarity and other disorders so present in those societies'. Address by M.J. Zarif, vice-minister of foreign affairs of the Islamic Republic of Iran, 18 June 1993.

36. The intensity of the demands placed upon modernity distinguishes conservative societies from societies riven by reactive movements (which resemble them on many points). In the former, full-time education, especially for girls, and contraception are still the preserve of a minority or of marginal groups. Similarly, whereas polygamy is no longer an ideological issue in the Arab world – it is now a marginal phenomenon, although its supporters reject its elimination for fear of toppling the normative edifice built upon religious references – it remains widely practised nearly everywhere in sub-Saharan Africa, where social conservatism is still considered a strategy of protection and defence in what were, until very recently, agrarian societies in which any outside intervention was synonymous with disaster.

37. Article 25 of the Déclaration sur les droits de l'homme en Islam (Organization of the Islamic Conference, appendix to Resolution No. 49/19P, 5 August 1990).

38. We may distinguish three categories in this respect: the fairly rare regimes, such as Bourguiba's Tunisia or early Communist China, which tried to shake up their society; a much larger group frozen into conservative postures; and a sizeable middle ground split among various attitudes but sharing a common pusillanimity. Some officially prohibited the most scandalous customs, such as the dowry in India or female circumcision in many African countries, but turned a blind eye to violations and avoided any measures that might ensure respect for the law. Others admitted that they did not dare attack the guardians of tradition head-on, and said they were banking on a change in customs to bring about the slow disappearance of such practices.

39. Of the many countries that expressed reservations about the International Convention on the Elimination of All Forms of Discrimination against Women, and the resolutions of the UN conference on the issue held in Beijing in 1995, most used the identity argument to withhold ratification of certain provisions. In late 1999, Kuwaiti legislators invoked a supposed danger of social dissolution to deny women the right to vote.

40. It would have been naive to think that the constellation of women's groups could escape North–South divisions. A feminist commitment does not prevent many Western women from being active vehicles of the culture of supremacy, through their proposal of themselves as a model for women all around the world and their refusal to imagine that there might be other paths to change in relations between the sexes. Conversely, the determination of many women in the South to fight the patriarchal dimension in their society does not mean that they are exempt from the influence of nationalist or identity-centred discourse.

41. Burmese strongman General Khin Nyunt drew on the same arguments to discredit the democratic opposition around Aung San Suu Kyi: 'She was

not brought up in normal conditions, according to our religious precepts, our customs and our traditions.... For most of her life, Aung San Suu Kyi has lived abroad ... She married an Englishman ... and became even more remote from the land of her birth.... If she had come back here to work and married a citizen of Myanmar, she might have become a national leader.' Interview in *Politique internationale* 76, Summer 1997.

42. Philippe Pons, 'Japon, vers un nouvel asiatisme', *Le Monde*, 3 December 1994.

43. See the debate on 'human rights and Asian values' organized by the International Federation of Human Rights Leagues in Geneva, on 14 April 1998. Quotations are taken from the Federation's summary document and the report in *Le Monde*, 16 April 1998.

44. *Courrier international* 497, 11–17 May 2000.

45. Their growls were already heard a long time ago, in 1959, in Kateb Yacine's play *Les ancêtres redoublent de férocité*.

46. Casablanca Declaration, adopted by the first conference of the Arab Human Rights Movement, Casablanca, 23–25 April 1999.

47. *Prologues* 10, 3rd quarter, 1997.

48. The title of a series of books published by Le Fennec in Morocco.

49. The Arabic daily *El Hayet*, published in London, has for some years played a significant role in the critique of contemporary Arab despotism and the broad reflection of Arab–Israeli (and, more generally, Arab–Jewish) relations.

50. Abdel Kader Yassine, 'La forme extrême de la censure', *Libération*, 17 March 1992.

51. Eglal Errera and Nadia Tazi, eds, *Pour Rushdie. Cent intellectuels arabes et musulmans pour la liberté d'expression* (Paris: La Découverte/Carrefour des littératures/Colibri, 1993). An English version later appeared as Anouar Abdallah et al., *For Rushdie: A Collection of Essays by 100 Arabic and Muslim Writers* (New York: G. Braziller, 1994).

52. Daniel Etounga Manguelle, *L'Afrique a-t-elle besoin d'un programme d'ajustement culturel?* (Paris: Nouvelles du Sud, 1993).

53. Axelle Kabou, *Et si l'Afrique refusait le développement?* (Paris: L'Harmattan, 1991).

54. Dipesh Chakrabarty, 'Postcolonialité et artifice de l'histoire'.

Index

Abbas, Ferhat, 56, 181
Abd El-Krim, Mohammed, 47
Abouzeid, Nasser Hamed, 233
Abrahamic revelation, 199
Abu Bakari, 212
Adler, Alexandre, 71
Adorno, Theodor, 53
Afghanistan, 172, 186
AFL–CIO, 150
Afrocentrism, theory of, 211–14
ageing of the population, 164
agribusiness, inroads in the South, 162
agriculture: function of, 95; surpluses of, 117
aid, reduction of, 102
AIDS, 185, 218–19
Algeria, 40, 49, 50, 55, 56, 57, 62, 63, 67, 70, 76, 90, 119, 181, 193, 195, 204, 219; colonialism in, 52; military spending in, 104; pacification of, 33; use of terror in, 35
Algerian Communist Party, 47–8
Allende, Salvador, 64
Alliance for Progress, 93
Alsace-Lorraine issue, 35
Amazonia, 163
America: and slavery, 23–5; depopulation of, 17; discovery of, 11; genocide in, 33 *see also* United States of
Americanization of the world, 157, 183
Amerindians, 192, 215; defence of, 16–17; genocide of, 14–15, 19, 24, 33; property rights of, 24; seen as barbarians, 37

amnesia, about European migrations, 130–35
Andalus, 12, 44, 45, 74, 219; expulsion of Jews from, 14
Anglo-Iranian Oil Company, 45
anthropology, physical, 43
anti-Americanism, 86
anti-black discourse, 19
anti-colonialism, 129
anti-dumping measures, 116
anti-Semitism, 36, 74, 199
AOL company, 148
Arabic language, 195
Arabs, seen as unreceptive to modernity, 215
Arendt, Hannah, 52
Argentina, 104
Armed Islamic Groups (GIA) (Algeria), 195, 197, 219
Aryans, 43
Al-Ashmawy, Saïd, 225
Asia, high-tech poles of development in, 146
Asian economies, advance of, 144
Asianism, 229–30
asylum, right to, 138–40
Augustine, Saint, of Hippo, 198, 212
Auriol, Vincent, 56
Australia, 131, 183; as pole of immigration, 135

backward nations, idea of, 56
Bairoch, Paul, *Economics and World History*, 78
Bandung Conference (1955), 96

281

Jospin, Lionel, 156
Judeo-Christian, use of term, 198–200
Judeo-Christianity: racism of, 219;
  Westernization of, 200
Julliard, Jacques, 195
July, Serge, 203

Kabila, Laurent-Désiré, 172
Kabou, Axelle, 234
Kabyle peoples, 195
kamis, wearing of, 193
Kant, Immanuel, 30
Kardavani, Kazem, 231
Kennedy, John F., 93
Kenya, 191
Keynesianism, 95, 158, 159
Khaled, a rai star, 195
Khalifé, Marcel, 225
Khomeini, Ayatollah Ruhollah, 173, 234
Khrushchev, Nikita, 85
Kipling, Rudyard, 38
Kitchener, Lord, 44
knowledge, control of, 146
knowledge-based industries, 152
Koran, 200
Korea, South, 83, 107, 131, 144, 146
Kurds, in Iraq, 177
Kuwait, 175; Iraqi invasion of, 174, 175
Kwanzaa festivities, 213
Kyoto conference, 127

L'Ouverture, Toussaint, 60
La Moricière, Colonel, 33
Lacoste, Yves, 70
Bin Laden, Osama, 187
Lafargue, Paul, 35
Lang, Jack, 197
de Las Casas, Bartolomé, 16, 17
Latin America, 'Westernness' of, 64
law: new geography of, 170–73; respect
  for, 177
leaders, cult of, 233
Lebanon, invasion of, 175
Lee Kuan Yew, 229
Lellouche, Pierre, 198
Lenin, V.I., 50, 57
Leopold II, King, 34
Lévi-Strauss, Claude, 237, 238
Levinas, Emmanuel, 198
Lévy, Bernard-Henri, 206
Lévy-Bruhl, Lucien, 31
Lewis, Arthur, 65
liberalism, 112, 159; making use of,
  114–17
Libération, 203

liberation movements, 63; objectives of,
  222
Liberia, 201–2
Libya, 101, 131
life expectancy, 76
Locke, John, 25, 26, 57
logical and prelogical mentalities, 31
Lomé Convention (1975), 91, 135
Londres, Albert, 59
Loti, Pierre, 38
luxury, habit of, 122
Lyautey, Louis, 44

Madagascar, 44, 76; massacres in, 55
Madani, Abassi, 193
Ben Maimon, Moses, 44
Malaysia, 129, 145, 147, 163
Manguelle, Daniel Etounga, 234
manifest destiny, 25, 27
manufacturing, migration of, 105, 146,
  149, 160
Mao Tse-tung, 61
maquiladoras, 147
market access, asymmetrical conditions
  of entry, 121
marriage, minimum age of, 203
Marseille, Jacques, 77
Marx, Karl, 46, 48, 50, 57; view of
  colonialism, 48–9
Marxism, 62, 64, 66, 112, 218
massacres, relation to genocide, 34
Massoud, Commander, 206
master's view of history, deconstruction
  of, 210
Maya Indian exhibition in Venice,
  192
Mediterranean, as *mare nostrum*, 31
memory, 130–35
memory cults, 214–17
Merck company, 148
Mérimée, Prosper, 38
Messaoudi, Khalida, 197, 219
Mexico, 15, 83, 104, 147, 150;
  bankruptcy of, 105; US investment
  in, 151
migration, 40, 43, 106, 132, 183;
  European Union harmonization of
  rules, 135; from Europe, 96;
  international, curbs on, 130–31; of
  labour, to Europe, 134 (of skilled
  labour, 136); of manufacturing, 146,
  149, 160; threat of, 81; to United
  States, 39
Mimouni, Rachid, 225
Mobutu Sese Seko, 207